BEHIND
THE SONG

EDITED BY K. M. WALTON

sourcebooks
fire

PUBLISHED BY SOURCEBOOKS FIRE, AN IMPRINT OF SOURCEBOOKS, INC.
P.O. BOX 4410, NAPERVILLE, ILLINOIS 60567-4410
(630) 961-3900
FAX: (630) 961-2168
WWW.SOURCEBOOKS.COM

LIBRARY OF CONGRESS CATALOGING-IN-PUBLICATION DATA IS ON FILE WITH THE PUBLISHER.

PRINTED AND BOUND IN THE UNITED STATES OF AMERICA.
VP 10 9 8 7 6 5 4 3 2 1

TO ALL OF HUMANITY, BECAUSE MUSIC IS OUR UNIVERSAL LANGUAGE.

TABLE OF CONTENTS

VI   **INTRODUCTION**

1   **FOREWORD**

By Ameriie

6   **SUBURBIANA (OR, THE RETURN OF SUPER FROG)**

A short story inspired by Arcade Fire's "The Suburbs"

By David Arnold

28   **MISS ATOMIC BOMB**

A short story inspired by the Killers' "Miss Atomic Bomb"

By Anthony Breznican

64   **"COLD BEVERAGE": THE SONG I WROTE THAT CHANGED MY LIFE**

A personal essay

By G. Love

82   **TIFFANY TWISTED**

A short story inspired by the Eagles' "Hotel California"

By Ellen Hopkins

104   **HOW MIRACLES BEGIN**

A personal essay inspired by James Howe's and Mark Davis's "Planting Trees"

By James Howe

126   **THE OPPOSITE OF ORDINARY**

A personal essay inspired by Leonard Bernstein's and Stephen Sondheim's "Somewhere (There's a Place for Us)"

By Beth Kephart

142 ABOUT YOU NOW

A short story inspired by
Oasis's "Wonderwall"

By Elisa Ludwig

172 YOU KNOW SOME-THING'S HAPPENING HERE (BUT YOU DON'T KNOW WHAT IT IS)

A personal essay inspired by
Bob Dylan's "Ballad of a Thin
Man"

By Jonathan Maberry

190 TIME TO SOAR

A short story inspired by Amy
Winehouse's "October Song"

*By Donn Thompson Morelli, a.k.a.
DONN T*

218 CITY GIRL

A short story inspired by
Keane's "Somewhere Only We
Know"

By E. C. Myers

256 SECOND CHANCES

A short story inspired by
2NE1's "It Hurts"

By Ellen Oh

286 ANYONE OTHER THAN ME

A short story inspired by Dave
Matthews Band's "Dancing
Nancies"

By Tiffany Schmidt

322 THE RIDE

A short story inspired by
Jimmy Eat World's "The
Middle"

By Suzanne Young

342 DOOMED?

A short story inspired by
Marcy Playground's "All the
Lights Went Out"

By K. M. Walton

364 PLAYLIST

367 ACKNOWLEDGMENTS

INTRODUCTION

Dear Reader,

Clearly, you love music as much as I do. Thank you for choosing to read *this* anthology!

I'd like to share how *Behind the Song* came to be…

When I hear a song I like I find the lyrics online for two reasons: (1) so I can sing along like nobody's watching; (2) because I love creating the song's backstory in my head as I listen, oftentimes fabricating *entire* stories. So there I was, driving and listening to Radiohead's "Fake Plastic Trees" loud enough to feel it in my skin, the last lines of the song hanging there, breaking my heart, and my mind cooked up a story—an emotionally lost teenage girl searches for acceptance and love from a guy who would never be capable of fulfilling her needs.

I hit a red light, and then it came to me: what if I gathered fellow YA authors, and maybe even musicians, and let them choose one of *their* favorite songs to interpret into a short story or write a personal essay? It could be a killer anthology.

My best ideas materialize when I'm alone in my car jamming to music.

I hope you have as much fun reading the anthology as I had editing it. What an honor it was to work with this accomplished group of contributors, including our foreword writer, Ameriie. Since we're all music lovers here, it would be cool if you checked out their websites, followed them on Twitter, read their other books, and listened to their music.

Lastly, to enhance your reading experience to the highest degree, I implore you to listen to the playlist at the end of the book. Listen, read the accompanying piece, repeat as often as you like.

Rock on. Listen loud. Always sing along.

Sincerely,

K. M. Walton

FOREWORD

BY AMERIIE

MUSIC IS THE SOUNDTRACK OF OUR LIVES.

A melody can transport us to a particular moment in our past. It can keep us stuck in the present, too, if we prefer (*No, I don't want to go out. I just want to play* Wrecking Ball *on repeat and wallow in this until I'm all cried out, OK?*). Sometimes we need a song to take us to an oft-imagined destination in our future. Sometimes the future destination is right around the corner—like, literally, the party is five minutes away and we need this pre-jam session. Sometimes it's as simple as requiring a song for much-needed gym inspo.

We often listen to a song on repeat to remain fixed on a feeling. Music is a sort of time capsule that way; it marries a moment in time to an emotion, and it's there whenever we need it. I have a theory about this. Whenever we find ourselves excited by a new artist, it's because their music speaks to us in a very specific way. Whether their sound exports us to a singular point in our past, or it speaks to a current circumstance, this new discovery imprints itself into our lives and onto our very souls.

This cannot be undone, cannot be unseen.

This will likely be our favorite piece of music from said artist because there's nothing quite like Firsts, much to the chagrin of many an artist. I'm pretty sure "You still haven't topped *Reasonable Doubt!*" drives Jay Z up a wall.

A curious thing about music is that it requires hardly anything of you. You needn't think, you needn't process, you needn't give much of your time. All you need to do is listen—and even half listening will do. Because music has a way of slipping into your subconscious. It's a straight hit to the bloodstream.

I've always thought that if humanity were to be visited by malevolent extraterrestrials, that if they'd been observing us for a while, they just might blast us to smithereens. We have, after all, been doing that to one another for eons. But if they had a chance to listen to our music, to our art, to the language of our souls... Well, let's just say we might stand a chance.

Music not only dissolves boundaries between ourselves and sound, but it also has the potential to dissolve boundaries within humanity, itself, even if, upon first impression, we might feel we have nothing in common but the song we're listening to. That's the thing about boundaries: once they disappear, they take a whole lot of preconceptions and misconceptions with them. It's the reason music from "outsiders" tends to top lists of Things You Are Not Allowed to Have. This goes for repressive governments and elders alike. Music is practically a zip file of culture, ideas, and free thought, and it's no wonder that in Nazi Germany, for instance, the last thing the Nazis wanted was the country's citizens reveling to "Negro music," as jazz and its "jungle" sound was viewed as a threat to morality and Aryan purity. They understood how music could be as dangerous to their Nazi future as physical weaponry.

And they were right. It's how music works: slinking into your subconscious and showing you something *over here, over here, what do you think about this?* without being didactic and boring. Eyes and minds tend to open when no one is looking, when the only thing caught is a vibe.

Everything is energy. Everyone and everything is vibration. The truth is, music is not only humanity's universal language, it's the universal language of the universe, itself. It's everything there is and ever was. It resonates with us because it *is* us.

Like the songs that inspired them, these stories and essays will transport you into the future and into the past, into worlds familiar and into worlds strange. You will discover ordinary people who change the world in miraculous ways, as well as ordinary people who are, themselves, miraculous forces of nature, undeterred and unfettered by stormy pasts. You will encounter epic and incredibly intimate situations, both of which are weighted equally by pain, love, and bittersweet acceptance. These stories and essays are full of firsts, full of lasts (which are usually firsts in disguise), and, like any great piece of music, you will read these and find reflected between the lines...you.

AUTHOR PHOTO
BY AMERIIE

Ameriie is a Grammy-nominated singer-songwriter, producer, and lifestyle *bon vivant*. The daughter of a Korean artist and an American military officer, she was born in Massachusetts, raised all over the world, and graduated from Georgetown University with a bachelor's in English. She began writing at the age of seven, stories of fairies and pirates and witches and phantoms. She lives mostly in her imagination, but also on Earth with her husband, her parents and sister, and about seven billion other people. When she isn't writing or creating music, she talks books, beauty, and more on her YouTube channel Books Beauty Ameriie. Visit Ameriie.com and follow her on Twitter @Ameriie.

SUBURBIANA
(OR, THE RETURN OF SUPER FROG)

A SHORT STORY INSPIRED BY
ARCADE FIRE'S "THE SUBURBS"

By David Arnold

Every time I hear this Arcade Fire song, I'm brought back to my own childhood. As a product of the suburbs, I found the imagery of a "suburban war" familiar and appealing, sure, but also begging for a narrative. It was my pleasure to oblige.

—DAVID ARNOLD

DUDE," I SAY.

"Dude," says Troy.

"*Dude.*"

"*Dude.*"

The rules of duding are simple and unwavering: you dude the other dude until that dude is completely dudeless. Troy and I are famous for it. Or at least, high-school famous. Mr. Thoman even kicked us out of English once for duding too hard. We were all *dude this* and *dude that*, and he was all, *get out of my class*, and we were all, *whaaa*? Sometimes we dude for days, like one of those chess matches where the players eat dinners and take naps in between moves, and then, just when you least expect it—*bam.*

Checkmate, dude.

We're sitting in Troy's parents' kitchen, where I've been

trying to convince him to join me in my campaign against the most horrible human to ever roam the earth: Calvin Reid Harcourt. I lean over the kitchen counter, right up in Troy's ear and whisper, "*Dude,*" to which Troy drops his head on the counter and groans, "*Dude.*"

I say it once more, this time with furious brevity, like a bullet through a silencer or the sound a bowling ball might make if you dropped it in sand. "Dude."

Troy looks up, crosses his arms. "Fine. But only if you dial down the revenge rhetoric. You're cranked to eleven, and I need you at no more than six."

"Deal. Now grab your mom's keys. It's getting late, and you know how lethargic I get."

"Sluggish, really," says Troy, grabbing the Honda keys out of a drawer. "Epic, lolling baby-head."

"Exactly. And how can a guy be expected to avenge his honor with lolling baby-head?"

"See, dude?" says Troy. "That right there, Danny. That's what I'm talking about. *Avenge your honor.* You gotta dial that shit back. No more than six, okay?"

"Right. Six. Got it."

We head out the front door together, snatching our jackets off the coat hanger as we pass. Fort Worth weather can't make up its mind. A big sun shines from a bigger sky during the afternoon, but once that sun disappears, so does any suggestion of warmth. Seasons are conditional in Fort Worth; fall is only fall at nighttime.

Troy aims the fob at his mom's Honda Pilot. The doors unlock with a *thunk* and we climb in. Troy drives. Troy always drives.

"I suppose it's futile, me asking what you hope to accomplish with this mission," he says.

"We can't let him get away with it anymore."

Troy rolls his eyes, slowly backs the SUV out of the driveway. "Always with the drama."

I don't know. Maybe other kids feel it too, the unspeakable injustices heaped upon us, one on top of the other like so many bags of fertilizer, all at the hands of some thuggish bully. If so, it's like we all agreed to stand by getting shit-bagged, grateful the bully chose us. Well, I'm done. And maybe I have a flair for the drama, like Troy said. But that doesn't mean I'm wrong. Even a broken clock is right twice a day, or some such shit.

"Step on it, Callahan," I say. *Callahan* is what I call Troy when I mean business.

Troy Callahan steps on it.

❀ ❀ ❀

Troy's parents were in Dallas for the weekend, attending their third AIMerica convention in as many years. AIMerica sold shit like pots and pans and souls. Mr. and Mrs. Callahan were dedicated AIMericans.

Exhibit A: the bumper sticker on the back of their Pilot.

Get paidriotic: Become an AIMerican

That was the beginning of the end, the minute we fully understood the level of brainwashing we were dealing with.

Exhibit B: the sign in their yard.

AIMerica: Aim for the Stars

(Go ahead, achieve the ultimate American dream)

I'd often wondered how one "aims for the stars" while attempting to convince one's longtime friends to purchase a preseasoned cast-iron fry pan in exchange for nothing more than their friendship.

A trifle. A bargain at half the price.

AIMerica did not ask much. Only that a single individual say *yes* to its product. In turn, it asked that individual to trade in three (or more) of their friends for three (or more) yesses. Then those friends only need trade in more of their friends for more yesses, and so on and so forth until no one had any friends anymore, and everyone was just saying yes to everything, everywhere, all the time.

It was the AIMerican way.

Some time ago, Troy and I decided to say yes to friendship instead of fry pans—this, in the face of a long line of lifetime warranties, and some sort of NASA-designed delectable seasoned varnish that the AIMerica brochure boasted could outlast a nuclear apocalypse.

"Our friendship could outlast a nuclear apocalypse," said Troy.

"Fuck that," I said. "Our friendship has a delectable seasoned varnish."

Troy said, "Dude," which was plenty.

I knew firsthand the modus operandi of AIMerica, having watched it destroy my parents' relationship with Mr. and Mrs. Callahan. Pre-AIMerica, our families got together every Saturday night for tacos and homemade guac. Taco Saturdays went like this: shortly after my family arrived, the parents started in on frozen margaritas and neighborhood gossip, while Troy and I played Legend of Zelda. Somewhere around frozen margarita *numero tres*, the parents got loud and their cheeks got red, which meant Troy and I could sneak our own frozen margaritas (partially melted at this point), inevitably leading to the demise of Link and his noble rescue mission. Post-guac and tacos, we gathered around the fire pit out back, stayed up late into the night roasting marshmallows and telling ghost stories, while the parents were too legit drunk to notice the kids were legit buzzed.

Taco Saturdays kicked *mucho* ass.

Until they didn't.

One Saturday—somewhere between frozen margaritas, melted marshmallows, and Troy and I playing "smoke swords" (a game where one sees how much smoke one's piss can produce on a fire in a given amount of time)—Troy's parents ushered my parents into the living room where they had this big pie chart and colorful set of brochures all set up on an official-looking tripod. The next thing I knew, my dad—who apparently understood the value of friendship over fry pans—grabbed me by the hand, and we were gone. Adios, Taco Saturdays.

From then on, Troy and I had to hide our friendship, sneak it in here and there. We were like Romeo and Juliet, only without all the kissing and wherefore-art-thous and fake-suicide-producing-actual-suicide fiascos. So nothing like them, really. More like—shit, I don't know any comparable duos.

We were a duo of dudes.

A bargain at half the price.

※ ※ ※

"Smells like shit in here," says Troy, navigating the streets of our neighborhood.

"I don't smell anything."

"How do you not smell that?"

I take a long, exaggerated sniff, hoping against hope Troy doesn't look in the back seat. It's dark and he'd have to spin a total one-eighty to see it, but still.

"Now that you mention it," I say, "it does smell a little musty. Does AIMerica sell cologne?"

As I suspected, the mere mention of AIMerica kills that line of conversation. Troy rolls through a stop sign, says, "So your plan is...what? We just walk up and knock on Calvin Reid's door? Ask if he indulged in any wayward or otherwise criminal trick-or-treating activities last night?"

"I've got a plan."

"Which is?"

I could tell him now. I could pull my plan from the shadows of the back seat and show him exactly what's going to happen. But in addition to spoiling the fun, Troy would most likely veer his parents' automobile right off the road.

"I'm going to improvise," I say. "Take a right on Dolan."

"I know where the Harcourts live," says Troy, turning right. "And you just might improvise yourself into oblivion."

"What's that supposed to mean?"

"Remember last year when a couple members of the PTO tried to organize a school trip to the gun range, which obviously got shot down because it's batshit crazy, but—"

"Pun intended?"

"What?" says Troy.

"You said *shot down*. Referring to the gun range."

"Look, whatever, point is I heard from a reliable source the idea was initiated by none other than Mr. and Mrs. Harcourt, and if they feel that strongly we should be taking up arms during school hours, I can't imagine they'll have any qualms about doing the same after dark on their own property."

"Who was it?" I ask.

"Who was who?"

"You said, 'a reliable source.' Who was it?"

"Nobody. It doesn't matter."

"Was it Todd?"

For about a month last year, Troy and I had a brief falling-out wherein he very quickly found my replacement in Todd

Blakely, a kid who deified Fox Mulder, who had every episode of *The X Files* memorized, who, above all, prized conspiratorial knowledge of government cover-ups and the inalienable (so to speak) proof of the existence of extraterrestrial life. Oh—on *earth*, I might add. Forget UFOs. Those suckers had been identified. They were among us.

"Who cares about my source?" says Troy. "We're talking about a couple of gun-toting, NRA-parading fanatics."

"Says Todd."

Troy sighs. "Doesn't mean he's wrong."

"Well, you rack up enough conspiracy theories, eventually one of them is going to pan out, I suppose."

"Danny—"

"Troy," I say. "We'll be careful. If a parent answers the door, we'll just, you know, play it cool."

"*You'll* play it cool. I'm staying in the car. This is your whacko idea."

"Did you just say whacko?"

"Ridiculous, goofy, dangerous, preposterous. It's in that family."

"Okay, well excuse me for wanting to confront my nemesis."

"*Confront your nemesis?* He stole your candy, dude. It's not like he's Doc Ock."

"First of all, Doctor Octopus was absolute *cake* compared to the Green Goblin, and second of all—shit, I forget what we were talking about."

"Nemesis confrontation."

"Right, and second of all, Calvin Reid Harcourt is worse than the Green Goblin and Doc Ock combined. He's the most nemesistic nemesis in the history of nemeses, and I fully intend on Super Frogging his ass."

Troy shakes his head. "You have serious problems. You know that, right?"

"I do, in fact."

The two of us sit in a peculiar silence as if the cushiony interior of the Honda Pilot muffles more than words, but thoughts too. Doesn't matter. We're almost there.

Looking for something to say, I pat the dashboard. "So when do the robotic parentals return?"

Troy sighs, says nothing.

"You think they figured it out yet?" I ask.

"You mean that the company they've devoted their lives to is a scam, or that they've traded away every friend they ever had all in the name of fry pans?"

"Uh, yes."

Troy doesn't answer. He doesn't have to.

❀ ❀ ❀

In 1897, four students chose Texas Christian University's mascot. This was back in the day when the school was located in Waco and called AddRan Christian University, or some such shit. Sometimes I wondered what compelled those four students to go with the horned frog as a mascot, but mostly I wondered why no one else had. Troy and I were both fairly obsessed with Super Frog, inasmuch as teenagers can be nonsexually obsessed with a thing. Neither of us said it out loud, but Super Frog had factored into both our decisions to attend TCU next year. As in-state universities go, who's going to mess with Super Frog? Bevo the Longhorn Steer? Bruiser the Baylor Bear? Rowdy the Roadrunner? My dad was a TCU baseball coach and even during losing seasons there was something in the air, something felt by players and fans alike. I like to think that thing was pride.

Or maybe it wasn't. Who could say.

Point is, our future seemed pretty freaking bright. Whole lives ahead and all that jazz. So one might wonder why we would bother seeking justice against a high school delinquent who has so little going for him that he resorts to following two relatively older trick-or-treaters (himself no spring chicken, but whatever), and then, after ninety minutes, 154 houses, and two pillowcases brimming with candy (and if you think Troy and I didn't labor over *that* mathematical equation, you may as well join the ranks of the adult Callahans and their fry-pan-loving, soul-trading ilk), sneak up behind those two trick-or-treaters, grab their pillowcases, and run.

There were five of them. Much bigger than us. But Troy and I hadn't spent all that prep time clocking maximum efficiency of seconds per house (thirty-five, to be exact, which allowed time for some modicum of politeness without encouraging actual conversation) only to watch our hard-earned loot disappear into the dark without a fight.

We ran after them like the ever-loving wind.

After a few blocks the Halloween Bandits cut left between two rows of houses, stopping short at a high wooden fence. Troy and I blocked their only way out, and even though they outnumbered and outsized us, they seemed temporarily perplexed by the current state of affairs. Each of them wore masks, so up until this moment we still didn't know who exactly we were dealing with. Eventually the taller one sighed, shrugged, and slid his hockey mask up, revealing a decidedly ugly mug.

I knew that sigh, that shrug, that mug.

"What's up, guys?" said Calvin Reid Harcourt, seemingly pleased as pudding to be having this conversation.

Now look, if history has taught us anything, it's that people with three names have it way harder than the rest of us. From the extra effort in preschool (spelling three names instead of two), all the way into adulthood (when one must choose between a variety of occupations including professional assassin, amateur skier, washed-up musician, or run-of-the-mill douchebag), toting around three names ain't no picnic. Calvin Reid Harcourt had, thus far, proven to be nothing more than a run-of-the-mill douchebag.

"Give us the candy and we'll let you go," I said.

I could almost hear Troy next to me. *Dial it down, dude.*

Calvin Reid laughed, which seemed to be just what his

minions were waiting for—some sign as to how they should adjust their own moods. They laughed accordingly, looking around at each other from behind their respective façades (mostly hockey masks, but there were two or three *Scream* costumes thrown in for good measure).

Calvin Reid wiped a lace of sweat off his upper lip. "What the hell are you guys dressed as?"

Troy and I looked at each other. What had once seemed a hilarious idea—Ewoks—now seemed exceptionally childish.

"You know what's funny?" said Calvin Reid. "We thought we were trailing a couple of middle schoolers all night." The minions laughed. "You guys are huge nerds, you know that right?"

We did, in fact, know this, but neither Troy nor myself were willing to concede that to the likes of Calvin Reid Harcourt.

So I said nothing.

Troy chose the far nobler path of clearing his throat.

Well played, dude. Well played.

Calvin Reid sort of chuckled and shook his head at us like we were hamsters doing complicated tricks. "I mean, really, it's just a couple bags of candy. What are you guys, like, in the fucking fifth grade?"

I wanted to ask what grade that made *him*, seeing as how he was stealing our candy. But I didn't. I didn't say anything. I just stood there, a furry little idiot, wondering why trouble seemed to follow me around. It's not like I asked for it. It's not like I went in search of it.

Calvin Reid raised both pillowcases chest-high. "This is ours now. Get it? It belongs to us. And there's not a damn thing you can do about it."

In my mind, I morphed into Super Frog, did a triple backflip right up into Calvin Reid's grill, spin-move, spin-move, open palm to the face, *smack!* roundhouse to the junk, *thut!* effectively incapacitating him at present, as well as diminishing any reasonable chance of future Harcourts terrorizing my neighborhood. In my head, Troy took out the minions with supreme ease, his martial-arts skills second only to my own, and together, victors at last, we feasted on the blood-candy of our slain foes.

We didn't actually move. Like, at all.

"Peace out, teddy bears," said Calvin Reid, sliding his mask back down over his face. His cronies nodded in Labrador-like approval, and as one, they walked right by us onto the street.

"We're not teddy bears!" I yelled into the dead of night. "We're freaking Ewoks!" I looked at Troy. "Dude."

"Don't dude me," he said, turning and walking the other way. "You didn't do jack-shit either."

And so it was that I found myself standing alone in an Ewok costume, in a stranger's lawn, contemplating my existence. And I began to perceive something new, something deeper than loneliness or my impending existential crisis. I felt the long, cold tentacles of vengeance wrap around my heart. It wasn't about stolen candy, not even the sobering loss of our full-sized Butterfinger bars from Mansion Row. It was about justice. Suburban justice. It was about not letting Calvin Reid *own* my ass every single time. It was about growing up. It was about channeling the bravery of Super Frog, about standing up for what was right in the face of a half dozen hockey masks (and a couple *Scream* ones for good measure). It was about the cessation of doing nothing. It was about *action*.

"What the hell are you supposed to be?"

The owner of the house (whose lawn I was standing in) had just walked out on the front porch.

"I'm an Ewok," I said.

He nodded. "Get off my lawn."

"Right. Okay."

I ran the whole way home, too excited to be upset.

I had a plan. One that involved a short trip to Texas Christian University.

☙ ☙ ☙

Troy shifts to park in the Harcourt driveway, but leaves the engine running. After my covert op to TCU last night, this makes two evenings in a row when I can basically feel my heartbeat in my toes.

The head of Troy's Ewok costume is still on the dashboard, staring me down like it owns the place.

"Danny," he whispers.

"Troy."

"You don't have to do this. They stole our candy. Big deal. We can buy more."

"It *is* a big deal, Troy."

"Why?"

"Because today, it's candy. Tomorrow, it's my girlfriend."

"Dude. You don't *have* a girlfriend."

"Dude. I might *tomorrow*."

We both chuckle, but the joke doesn't really land. I fight the urge to crack another one. I fight the urge to say *dude* and be done with it. I fight the urge to, once again, cower in the towering shadow of confrontation. We could turn around now. We could keep being sweaty little Ewoks who stand for nothing. The thing is…

"I've had it," I whisper.

"With what?" asks Troy.

I take a deep breath and look out the front windshield where the Harcourt house looms large and dim. "You ever think about why your parents joined AIMerica in the first place?"

"Almost exclusively," says Troy. "Well, that, and having sex with Stephanie Preston."

"Huh."

"Yeah."

"Well now I'm thinking about that too."

"Yeah."

I shake my head, melting away all thoughts of Stephanie Preston, then twist around and reach into the back seat,

pulling out the pièce de résistance of my revenge, the prover-
bial cherry on top.

"*Whaaaat the fuuuuu*—?" So shocked by the weight of what
he sees, Troy's vocal cords are rendered temporarily useless. In
one fluid motion, I raise the giant gray, stubby-horned fabric
in all its preposterous glory, and slide a musty-scented Super
Frog's head over my own.

Whoever wore this thing last must bathe in Old Spice.

I look left, but can barely see anything through the slit
in the mascot's mouth. I see enough, though. Troy's face is a
combination of awe, confusion, and laughter.

"*Whaaaat the fuuuuu*—" he says again, apparently still
vocally incapacitated.

"Last night"—I slip into a fit of coughs, the overwhelming
Old Spice scent getting the better of me.

"You okay?" asks Troy.

I pull it together, start over again. "Last night, I had a
vision."

Troy stares a solid foot over my eyes, into the eyes of Super
Frog.

"Hey," I say. "Down here. My eyes are in his mouth."

Troy lowers his eyes to meet my own, but only for a
moment. Eventually, they drift back up to Super Frog's eyes,
and I accept this as part of my new identity.

God, it's getting hot in here.

"We're at war, Troy. Suburban war." I clench a fist and
raise it in front of my face. Something about the anonymity

of wearing a giant frog's head makes me feel powerful, brave, and a little drunk. (Though that could actually be from the Old Spice fumes.) "Calvin Reid has had it out for us for years. And he *always* wins."

I consider the many nights of fallen Zelda, and red-cheeked parents, and buzzing on margaritas. I consider the fire pit out back, and how Troy and I waited until our parents got cold and went inside so we could duel to the death in a game of smoke swords. I think about the *mucho* ass Taco Saturdays kicked—until they didn't. And all because the Callahans continued to lie down to the Man time and time again, until they no longer knew they were lying down.

And now they deal in fry pans.

"Remember when Calvin Reid egged your house?" I ask, all-out sweating now, my words muffled by the lower lip/ upper neck of Super Frog. "We knew it was him, and we did jack-shit about it. Or how about the time he stole the entire neighborhood's bike chains during the Tour De Frankie? Not to mention the steady dose of torture and humiliation he serves up at school each and every day." Troy still stares a foot above my eyes, and this thing is really heavy, so each time I nod or make any strenuous hand gestures, Troy jerks back a little in his seat. "Calvin Reid roams our streets like a king. He answers to no one like the rest of us are just a bunch of jokers who owe him the very air we breathe. We make fun of your parents joining AIMerica, Troy, but we're no better. We've been lying down so long, we forgot what it feels like to stand up. We're losing the war, and I've had it. Tonight, all debts are paid. Tonight, my anger is righteous and justice is served. Tonight, Calvin Reid answers to *me*. Tonight, we stand up, Troy."

Cue the Honda Pilot silence.

We stare at each other for a second while I wait for Troy to break into applause, or show me chill bumps on his arm, or start sobbing uncontrollably—anything to indicate the spectacular-ness of my rousing oratory.

He glances in the back seat. "How the fuck did you get that thing in here without me knowing?"

Okay. Not what I expected.

"I know where your mom keeps the keys," I say.

He swallows, stares back up at Super Frog's eyes. "And where did you, um, acquire it?"

"The TCU locker room. It's the off-season, so I figured who's gonna miss it?"

"You broke in?"

"Dude. No. I know where Dad keeps the keys."

Troy nods a little. "You pay a lot of attention to where people keep their keys."

"Yes I do."

More silence.

"So," I say. "What did you think of my little—you know—speech?"

Troy nods. "Oh, you've lost it entirely."

I clear my throat. "Right. But I mean. You love me."

"Of course."

"And you're with me."

"Of course."

"Good." I look back at the Harcourt house. "Because I am actually a little scared."

Troy unlocks the doors. "You think *you're* scared. At least you've got Super Frog to hide behind. I'm going up there with nothing but my smoke sword in my hands."

I pull the Ewok head off the dash and toss it at him. "What about that?"

He smiles, slips it on, mumbles something I can't make out. I point to my ear, shake my head.

He says it again.

Still nothing.

"You gotta enunciate under all that fur, dude."

Troy clears his throat. "I said, *the teddy bears shall have their revenge!*"

I nod slowly.

Troy nods slowly.

A dog barks.

I look out the window. A woman is walking her dog on the sidewalk. She raises her eyebrows at me, turns abruptly, and crosses the street.

"We should probably, um, you know, do this thing."

"Right," says Troy.

I open the passenger door of the SUV, but before stepping out—before walking up to the porch, ringing the bell, and punching a very stunned Calvin Reid Harcourt in the face, thereby forever raising our flag in suburban victory—I, Super Frog, look at my best friend, an Ewok, and say the only thing there is left to say.

"Dude."

He nods. "Dude."

We get out of the car.

AUTHOR PHOTO
© DANIEL MEIGS

David Arnold lives in Lexington, Kentucky, with his (lovely) wife and (boisterous) son. He is the *New York Times* bestselling author of *Kids of Appetite* and *Mosquitoland*. One Halloween many years ago, after a long night of well-executed trick-or-treating, a few bullies in hockey masks stole David's candy. Those bullies, like Calvin Reid, were eventually brought to justice. The bag of candy was never seen again. You can learn more (about David and his books, not about candy) at davidarnoldbooks.com and follow him on Twitter @roofbeam.

MISS ATOMIC BOMB

**A SHORT STORY INSPIRED BY
THE KILLERS' "MISS ATOMIC BOMB"**

By Anthony Breznican

The Killers wrote an anthem about being blown away by heartbreak and longing, but the lyrics for "Miss Atomic Bomb" were enigmatic enough that I thought they could hold a much more sinister meaning if twisted just the right way. The key was combining them with another story—a true one—from an article I'd read about Monique Luiz, the little girl who costarred alongside a mushroom cloud in President Lyndon Johnson's infamous 1964 "Daisy" campaign ad. The ad was so notorious and frightening that she and her family kept her involvement secret for decades. I began to wonder, what if someone had uncovered this hidden truth from her past? And what if the circumstances of the world were...different? Guided by the Killers' song, one "what if" led to another, and this story was born. I guess you'd call that a chain reaction.

—ANTHONY BREZNICAN

"T EN..." THE BOY SAID AS HE BRUSHED BY CASSANDRA Roberts in the hallway.

It wasn't his voice that stopped her dead. It was the eagerness in his eyes.

"Excuse me?" the girl asked.

"Nine..." he said, softer.

For a moment, they stood face-to-face in the crush of students as lockers clattered shut and a choppy sea of hands and elbows nudged them back and forth. The boy smiled, flashing a mouth wired with silver braces. Acne flared on his cheeks like flash burns. "Eight?" he said, with a lilt at the end, like a question.

Three words. *Ten. Nine. Eight.* Each one a whisper. Each hitting her like a shock wave.

Then the boy was gone, swept away by the current of the crowd. Cassie heard Abigail Peters, her best friend, shouting for her over the heads of classmates flowing into the white light of the exit. Another friend, Mia Vaida, grabbed Cassie's hand and pulled. "We have to hurry," Mia said. "What's the matter with you?"

Cassie's eyes searched the hallway for the boy as her feet started moving. She was walking, but it felt like falling backward.

❀ ❀ ❀

They made it to the mall in record time, but it was still too late. The Republic Supply Co. had advertised a shipment of jeans going on sale that afternoon, but by the time the girls arrived, half their school was already in front of them. Even as they waited in the zigzagging line, the trio could tell there wouldn't be much left except for the odd sizes and irregulars. Cassie, who was tall and muscular for only sixteen, went to the boys' section first, since there was always more stock there. She found a remaindered pair that probably would have fit her waist, but the legs were too short. There was nothing in the store that fit Abigail's bony frame, or the stout, sturdy Mia. Literally nothing. The white metal shelves had been picked clean.

"Think you'll get any more before Christmas?" Cassie asked the clerk, a turkey-necked older man with wire-frame glasses. The man shook his head: "Not until a month or two into the new year. At the earliest." He made a clipboard appear from behind the counter, like a boring magic trick. "Have you signed up for the waitlist?"

Cassie actually *had* signed up for several waitlists, but the Republic Supply Co. only used them to let you know when a new shipment arrived. You had to be there in person to buy anything. First come, first served. She guessed the form was just a way to get people to stop nagging the clerks. "Thanks," she said, and wrote her name and contact number anyway.

The strip of shops was called The Street, but the kids all called it RetroVille, since the storefronts were built to evoke the kind of small town that had only ever existed in Hollywood back lots and the promises of politicians. This quaint little downtown was only three years old, crammed inside a modern glass and steel atrium that was meant to be psychologically pleasing to those who craved the illusion of sunshine and fresh air.

Cassandra leaned against one of the lampposts in the food court, staring through the thick glass windows as the sun sank into a purple churn of clouds rolling over a mountain range in the distance. It was late for monsoon season in the desert, but a bruised sunset always meant treacherous weather was moving in.

"Cass, check it," Abby said, nudging her friend. "Oppressive male gaze, at six o'clock." Mia, who was finishing off the last of a bottle of water the three of them were splitting, turned around to look, too.

It was the same boy from the hall, staring at them from outside the railing of the food service area. He held a plastic daisy plucked from The Street's fake-rock water fountain and wiggled it at them in a wave.

"You got a problem?" Mia called out.

The boy shook his head. His fingers plucked a petal off the daisy and let it drop at his feet. "Six," he said, just loud enough for them to hear. Then he touched a finger to his chin, pantomiming deep thought, before locking eyes with Cassie again and repeating: "Six..." He pulled off another petal.

Abby and Mia scrunched their faces, but Cassie straightened up from the lamp. "Oh crap, you know...I *forgot*," she said to her friends. "He's in Mrs. Shute's history class with us. We have a project we're doing together. Just...hang on, okay?"

Her two best friends in the world shrugged. *Whatever.* Cassie was always up to something weird. "Don't take forever," Abigail said.

"Yeah," Mia agreed. "I wanna get home before the storm hits."

Cassie walked briskly toward the boy, arms stiff at her

sides, her satchel full of books swinging from one hand like a bludgeon she might decide to use. "Can I help you?" she asked.

The boy turned his mouth down in a sad-face expression. "Five…" he said in a baby voice, lifting the daisy and plucking off another plastic petal. Cassie shoved the fake flower out of her face.

"What do you think you're doing?" she hissed.

The boy flexed another painful smile, showing off his braces and stretching his inflamed cheeks. "You *know* what I'm doing," he said. "You're Daisy."

"Uh, I don't know what you're talking abo—"

"Sure you do," he interrupted. "Everybody knows Daisy."

She couldn't speak. She had to force herself to breathe, to appear calm. "*My* name is Cassie."

The boy nodded. His eyes were half-lidded, oblivious to her lie. He wouldn't quit with the plastic flower, raising it again and saying in a baby voice: "Four…" which came out "*fwarh…*"

Cassie stole a look back at her friends. Sweat soaked her back. Her heart battered against the inside of her chest like something buried alive.

The boy smiled and touched her nose with the fake daisy. "I figured out your secret," he said. "You're the girl from that political ad. The little girl counting down the flower petals as she rips them off one by one…"

"Can you please shut up…?"

"And then the roar of the fireball behind her. That flash

of white on her face...*your* face... A mushroom cloud filling the screen..."

"I have to go..."

His rising voice stopped her. "I always wondered how they did that! Not the blast, I assume that was some green-screen special effect. But that intense white glow on your face." Cassie spun back to him. Her friends became alert and a few strangers wandering The Street turned to watch, too. "I bet you could feel the heat when you saw that light," he said. "But it's not quite the real thing."

Cassie pushed up close to him. "One more word, creep-o, and you'll be beyond sorry, I swear."

The boy extended his index finger like a magic wand and dotted a constellation in the air. She could feel it, matching the moles and freckles on her face. The ones that had always been there, even when she was a little girl. "Call me a creep again," he said, "and the world will call you *Daisy*."

"Cass, you okay?" Abby called out, still leaning against the light pole.

"Want us to call a watchman?" Mia shouted, scanning the mall for one.

Cassie shook her head, putting on a genuine-enough smile. "We're just messing around," she called back to them. "Neither of us wants to do this project."

Mia and Abby settled back against the lamppost, still staring at them.

"But I *do* want to do this," the boy said, smiling. "My

name is Michael, by the way, Michael Ulmer." He extended his hand to Cassie, who didn't take it. Michael Ulmer bit his lower lip. "Please shake my hand, Daisy."

She was trying to look anywhere but directly at him. "If I shake your hand, it'll look *weird*," she said. "I just told my friends we already know each other."

"Don't you think it's sad we don't?" he said. "I know I'm new here, but I've been in your class for two months and you never bothered to get to know me. I guess it's funny that I got to know you first. The *real* you. The one your friends over there have no idea about."

Cassie sighed through her nose. "What do you want, Mike?"

"*Michael*," he said. "And what I want is simple. I want to be friends. I want your attention... Have I got it?"

Cassie's eyes studied the floor. She wanted her friends to come rescue her. She needed *someone's* help. But—nobody could know what this boy had figured out. Cassie feared that more than anything. "I don't know what you *think* you know, but—"

"I know *everything*," Michael said, tucking the flower into his pocket. "Stop lying to me like I'm an idiot." He tipped up on his toes to look over Cassie's shoulder. Her friends had gathered their things and were walking towards them.

He leaned in close. "Since you're talking to me like I'm stupid, I'll talk to you like you're stupid," he said, the words cascading out in a hush: "*You're* the little girl from the Daisy ad, the campaign commercial that scared the living shit out of the entire United States of America and helped Chet Stillman become *President* Stillman. By a lot. By a landslide."

The words made Cassie's stomach tighten. Her eyes and head throbbed. The boy's mouth pressed against her ear. "You're the star of the most reviled piece of political propaganda ever created," he said. "And you live in a community that worships the man it destroyed."

Cassie's eyes flicked to the fake rock fountain where Michael Ulmer had stolen his plastic daisy. There was a mosaic of Stephen Dashner on the wall behind it, right between an electronic parts store and a pharmacy. The portrait stood two stories tall, and the smiling, gray-haired man it depicted had his eyes turned up to the glass ceiling of the atrium. His campaign slogan, now considered sacred text, was spelled out beneath the mosaic in green and black tile: *Promise for the future. A promise worth keeping.*

Dashner was a former Marine and father of three who had driven an M1 Abrams tank for three tours in Iraq, then later had become a lawyer, then a state senator, a governor of California, and a one-term occupant of the White House. He had been defeated in his reelection bid by Chet Stillman, a real-estate billionaire with a big mouth, deep pockets, and a shallow understanding of global geopolitics.

Shortly before the election, an Iranian-funded splinter group had detonated a dirty bomb on an American airbase in Turkey. Dashner's opponent wasn't above exploiting this incident to stoke panic and bombarded the airwaves with a thirty-second TV spot featuring a cute little girl, counting the petals of a flower before a nuclear countdown reached zero and incinerated her alive. As the child disappeared into the maw of radioactive fire, Stillman's voice intoned: "These are the stakes... To make a world in which all of God's children can live—or go into the dark." A title card read simply: Vote Stillman on Nov. 3.

And America did.

Michael Ulmer had figured out something the Roberts family kept hidden for more than twelve years: the little girl in the ad *was* Cassie. Her mother and father had taught her to hide this at all costs because the people who reviled that ad—the ones who felt manipulated by it, exploited by it, betrayed by what it led them to do—had maintained an enduring hatred for "Daisy." It didn't matter to them that she had just been a four-year-old little girl, who was so nervous on camera she repeated the word "six" in her countdown.

"What do you want from me?" Cassie asked.

Michael Ulmer's face brightened. "I want you to say goodbye to your friends so we can get to know each other better."

Cassie turned her face in profile, still unable— unwilling—to look at the boy. Her mind raced. She wanted to bolt, to run as fast and as far away as possible. But there's no place to hide from a secret you carry with you everywhere.

She walked back to her friends and Michael watched as she stood talking to them for what seemed like far too long. "Hurry up, Daisy!" the boy called out.

Abigail looked from him to Cassie and asked: "Did he just call you 'Daisy?'"

"Yeah, of course," Cassie said, shaking her head, blinking, shrugging. "Daisy...we're doing a thing on that political commercial. Extra credit."

"That ad was so gross," Mia said.

"I was glad when Mrs. Shute was done with that section," Abby added.

"Me too," Cassie said, and this was the truth.

"But it's a fascinating story, don't you think?" Michael said, interrupting the trio of girls. "We're putting together a really awesome report: 'What Happened to the *Real* Daisy.'"

"Sounds depressing," Abby said.

"And boring," Mia added.

"You'd be surprised," Michael said, rising on his toes with his hands clasped behind his back.

"Come on, let's get to it, then," Cassie said, pulling the boy's arm. "I'll see you guys tomorrow."

"Yeah, we need to go anyway," Abigail said. "The watchmen are chasing people out. Storm's almost here, and they're worried it's gonna bring in a ton of stragglers." Over by the glass walls of the atrium, security had appeared to ratchet up the metal doors on each window.

"Just don't stay up too late studying," Mia called back to Cassie. "All work and no play, babygirl. Remember what that makes."

Cassie watched her friends walk away, aching to join

them, heartsick at what this rando creep had figured out—and terrified of what he might do with the information. Then she turned back to Michael, who was grinning.

"Nice job getting rid of them," he said. "You're a really good liar."

* * *

Cassie and Michael rode silently on an electronic walkway outside the mall. She hoped that if she went along with him, she could also reason with him. But he was enjoying it all too much.

"It wasn't even an original ad, did you know that?" the boy said. "It was just a rip-off of some other political commercial they ran back in the 1960s. The whole thing: the girl, the fireball, the scary voiceover..."

"Yeah, I'm in the same history class as you," Cassie said, crossing her arms as she turned her back to him. "And can you keep your voice down? Please." There were dozens of other people on the conveyor belt ahead. Fortunately, they were transfixed by the TVs embedded every fifty feet in the corridor, broadcasting breathless reports about the storm and concerns about the high number of stragglers caught in it.

Michael Ulmer wagged a finger at her. "History class. That's when I knew," he said. "I'd been staring at you from the moment I walked into that school, Cassandra Roberts. I mean, you're gorgeous. But when Mrs. Shute showed us that frame-by-frame sequence of the ad. I just—I *knew*. Even though you're older. Even though your hair is different. Even though nobody else noticed. *I* noticed. *I* saw you."

Cassie stared down at the grinding, creaking walkway. Michael Ulmer's finger lifted her chin. "If your face wasn't so beautiful, I'd have never studied it so closely."

She pulled away from him, walking forward. "That's comforting."

"Hey, come on, now," he said, following after her. "It's a compliment."

"Compliments and threats. Two things you're full of."

"I'm not threatening you. I'm stating the obvious. People would be furious if they found out. Life would get hard for y—"

"It's already hard."

Michael Ulmer's head cocked to one side, unmoved. "Life's hard for everyone."

"What do you *want*?" she said.

The boy shrugged. "I want you to admit the truth. If only to me. And maybe, you know, showing some tenderness wouldn't hurt." She felt his hands on her shoulders, massaging. Hard. She pulled away again, which irritated him. She actually wanted to kick him in the crotch, but couldn't afford to make him angry. Not yet. Not until she found out exactly how much he knew. Or who else he might have told.

"Really, Michael, you're just flat wrong," she said. "Your imagination is g—"

The boy's hand slipped up her neck and squeezed a fistful of hair, yanking her backward. Cassie almost cried out, but held it in. No one else on the walkway noticed. A part of her was relieved about that.

"Don't lie to me again, okay?" Michael said, releasing his grip. "Next time, you'll be very sorry."

Cassie crossed her arms, hoping he couldn't see her trembling. "Fine," she said. *Fine. Stay calm.* Her eyes followed the procession of fluorescent bars across the ceiling. "I was four when we made that ad," she said. "I hardly remember anything."

But that wasn't true either. She remembered another little girl, one who looked just like her, wearing the same pink dress. Practically a twin. That little girl was crying and wouldn't stop. She had been afraid of the cameras, gliding toward her in the dark like mechanical dinosaurs. She had struggled to do the countdown, and the bright light effect frightened her even more. Crew workers were hustling that girl into the arms of her embarrassed parents as Cassie, the replacement, was guided onto the soundstage.

"I bet your mom and dad remember a lot," Michael said. "Maybe we should visit your condo and you could introduce me."

Cassie shook her head. "My mom's at work. And my dad's sick." This was partly true. Her father *was* sick, but her mother was at home, seven months pregnant. Maybe that piece of information would help. Maybe it would make Michael

Ulmer a bit more sympathetic. But she didn't want to trust him with it yet.

"I bet they'd be interested in what I could start telling people," the boy told her.

Cassie flung her arms wide. "They're not even political. They thought they were getting their daughter a modeling job. They thought it was for a damned toy commercial."

"Hm," Michael Ulmer said. "Shoulda read the fine print."

Cassie shook her head. "That flash of white on my face? They told us it was going to be the Toys 'R' Us giraffe, opening up a big vault full of dolls and bikes and action figures under a glowing Christmas tree." She huffed out a bitter laugh. "Wanna know what I remember? Being pissed there weren't any toys."

"Instead you got incinerated," Michael said, clapping his hands together. "And the rest of the country got scared into voting for a psychopath."

Cassie shook her head. "People love blaming someone else for what they do to themselves."

"Like you are now?"

"For the ten-thousandth time: I was a little kid. I had no idea what the ad was about. The election, the attacks overseas. I'd never even *heard* of Chet Stillman, and my parents... They were the *first* people disgusted by that commercial. We'd have never done it, if we'd known."

"But you did," Michael said. "Blame your mom and dad if you want. Maybe that'll get *you* some mercy. But it'll just shift more blame on them."

Cassie stared at her feet. The moving walkway ended, and the two teenagers pushed through a double-doorway that emerged onto a glass and steel gantry that extended over Covington Square, one of the community's busiest thorough-fares. This area was known as The Vista, one of the highest points open to the public. The corridor swarmed with onlook-ers watching the monsoon draw near, but Cassie had never felt more alone.

She and Michael Ulmer stared through the glass at the industrial facilities jutting from the desert in front of them, sprawling octopus limbs of armored gray boxes, clinging to the red rock of the canyon. Sentry towers and radio beacons blinked against the churning sky. In the distance, giant egg-shaped air and water purification domes faded into the wall of rain rolling toward them from the hills. Covington Square and The Street glowed beneath webbed steel-and-glass cake lids—like fallen, fading suns.

This was Joshua Tree Colony, or at least part of it. The flagship model for other survivor shelters around the world.

"On a clear day, I bet you can see so much from up here," Michael said. "Empty cities. Skyscraper skeletons. A giant toxic graveyard." He turned to her. "Funny, right?" he said. "The man *you* helped elect unleashed the very thing he scared us about in that ad. Nuclear fucking war."

"Wow. Ironic," Cassie said, rolling her eyes as she leaned back against the glass. "You know, I never thought of it that way."

✿ ✿ ✿

Most of Joshua Tree was embedded underground, a vertical fortress penetrating deep into the Mojave wasteland. This survivor city was now home to more than forty thousand people—and growing. The tidal-wave plumes of rock ash and clay erupting from the excavation exhausts on the north end of the complex were a testament to the construction underway belowground. The colonists had endured for almost a decade, although the early years had been painful, ugly, dark. The addition of surface spaces a few years ago, like The Street and Covington Square, finally provided some sunlight to the survivors, even if fresh air was still impossible. The vapors outside were about as safe for humans to inhale as the atmosphere of Venus. And the air was far from the deadliest thing beyond the colony walls.

The complex's lights drizzled away like wet paint as the toxic raindrops ran down the glass. Cassie stared at her own reflection as the boy pressed his body against her back, his hands sliding around to stroke her hips, his breath dampening her neck.

"Is it money you want?" she said. "Because we don't have any."

"You know what I want, Daisy," he said. "Don't be dumb."

His hands squeezed her thighs, and his fingers began probing the warm skin between the frayed spots in her faded, too-tight jeans. Cassie's skin crawled—but the practical side of her brain wouldn't shut off. She really *had* needed those new jeans. The ones she wore were not only disintegrating after all these years, but they were so small they pinched a red crease around her midsection that was usually still there when she woke up and squeezed back into them. New textiles were desperately hard to come by in the Republic. If this creep hadn't slowed her down in the hall after school, she might currently be in possession of a pair that were as blue and crisp as the ones he was wearing.

Cassie pushed the boy's groping hands away. "There are people around," she said.

"I don't care," he answered.

Gunfire crackled from the sentinel pillars staked high above the colony, startling them both. Cassie used it as an excuse to pull free.

Comet-trail muzzle flashes perforated the mist. A cloud of red-eyed gunship drones wafted from atop the central radio tower like it was a wasp nest hit by a slingshot. The drones plunged low over The Vista and scattered into the storm to patrol the colony's perimeter.

"Stragglers," Cassie said, pushing away from the boy. "They're already here."

❀ ❀ ❀

Down in Covington Square, hundreds of faces stood silently staring up at the drone footage being broadcast on a bank of giant TV screens.

A scattering of dark, humanoid shapes flitted in front of the cameras and disappeared into the curtains of rain. These were the stragglers—other humans who had survived the fallout and nuclear winter. If you could call it surviving. If you could call them humans.

Most survivors who weren't given sanctuary in the Republic's early shelters perished quickly after the attacks, but the stragglers had endured somehow. They stayed hidden most of the time, but swarmed the colony during storms, looking for materials, food, anything they could rip away. In clear weather, they were easy for the sentinel towers to pick off, so they usually kept their distance. But during monsoons, they always attacked in full force. The whole colony would go on alert, but as the news broadcasts kept reassuring viewers, Joshua Tree was a fortress they had never penetrated.

The flickering screens reflected in Michael's eyes. "They never show us any close-up images. Just these blurry figures. I guess it keeps our guard up, but why don't they just give us one good, long look at them?"

"Probably because it's easy to see remnants of who they used to be. Teachers, accountants, bank tellers, waitresses," Cassie said. "I've seen some up close, when I was training with the drone pilot program. It isn't...something you can forget."

"Is it true that they...that they're...?" he asked, unable to say it. Instead he held something invisible in front of his face and gnashed his teeth on it. "I heard if you kill one, the other stragglers fall on it and start eating."

"I've never seen that, exactly," Cassie said. "But I have seen three or four drag a wounded one away. And it wasn't for medical attention."

"How do you know?"

She shrugged. "Because they each ran off with a different piece."

Michael shook his head. "Animals. They deserve what they get."

"Whatever makes us feel better, right?" Cassie said. "All I can think is, if my father hadn't worked construction, building underground parking garages in the Old Days, and if my mom hadn't had that job at the Santa Monica water treatment plant, we might be outside with them."

"That's how you got picked for the colony?" Michael said. "I just assumed you were rich or something. *Hollywood* and all that."

Cassie started walking again, afraid someone in the crowd might overhear. "We got five hundred dollars for that ad. My parents donated it to Dashner's campaign when they realized what it was for." She scanned Michael's crisp new jeans again, his pristine white shirt, his perfect tennis shoes. "So, um...rich? Is that how *you* got in?"

The boy halted. "My parents both served. Dad was a lieutenant in the Seventy-Ninth Infantry Brigade, one of the first units to rise up against your boy Stillman. They rebelled before anyone. Even before the incineration of Tehran and the pre-strikes against Moscow and Riyadh and..." He swallowed, and rubbed at his eyes. "My mother was a corporal, an aircraft technician. Both of them were stationed at Edwards."

"Edwards..." Cassie said. Edwards Air Force Base was where the man they still called President Dashner had given his life, along with the rest of his cabinet and most of his military advisors and soldiers. He had survived the first wave of Stillman's attack on the base after the civil war erupted, but no one at Edwards made it past the second onslaught—the one that rained tactical warheads.

"Yeah, Edwards..." the boy said, nudging Cassie forward again. "Mom and Dad stayed behind. They were fighting. I was running. Loaded in with a caravan of other military brats headed away from the base to Santa Barbara. I saw the flashes out the back window of the bus. Been bouncing around ever since. They sent me here with about a dozen other orphans from Sequoia Colony." He tugged at his white T-shirt. "They gave us this crap when we came in. Because most of us arrived with *nothing*."

"That where you got the braces, too?"

Michael Ulmer's lips pursed shut instinctively. "Yeah," he said. "We each got a physical when we got here."

Cassie lowered her head. "My dad's got cancer. In his thyroid. Like a lot of the early builders. We've been hoping to get him in to see a doctor for a while. But it probably won't happen. You're lucky."

Michael pushed her forward through the crowd. "Yeah, lucky me," he said.

※ ※ ※

Cassie's eyes lingered on every face she passed, but she kept moving. They neared a maintenance corridor that led away from the square.

"I know what you're thinking, but don't try it," the boy said. "It's the law to report any suspected Stillman partisans. I'm actually taking a risk protecting you."

"Protecting me?" Cassie said.

"Don't kid yourself," he snapped. "This colony would banish you in a heartbeat if they found out. You know that, right?"

Cassie was quiet. "I know," she said, finally. "But if you told anyone...it wouldn't just be me who suffers. They'd send my mom and dad out, too."

Michael Ulmer yawned.

Cassie was glad she hadn't told him about her mother's pregnancy. There would be no sympathy to be found in Michael Ulmer. "You'd just let a whole family die?" she asked. "That doesn't bother you?"

"Did it bother *you* when they did that to the Koslows?"

Cassie's throat closed up. She pushed forward into the darkness of the corridor.

"You didn't speak up about *them*, did you?" Michael said, hurrying after her. "You let the Republic put a whole family on trial for being part of the Daisy ad. Their daughter was your age. You could have saved her by coming forward.

What was her name again...?" He snapped his fingers, trying to remember.

Sophia, Cassie thought. The name was never far from her mind.

She had known Sophia Koslow—or met her, at least. Sophia had been the original little girl hired for the ad. The Republic's Loyalty Commission had recovered the Koslow family's pay sheets from the agency in Los Angeles that produced the commercial for Stillman's campaign. What those documents didn't show was that an understudy, whose documents had never been discovered, had replaced Sophia. Now the Republic believed the case of the Daisy girl was closed.

"She actually looked a lot like you," Michael said. "But here you were the whole time, hiding in Joshua Tree while the Koslows and their daughter went on trial in Yosemite. I bet you were glad they didn't straight-up shoot them, like all those other Stillman loyalists. But maybe that would have been more merciful, you know? Banishing them in that old junker, watching them race shadows into the desert while the world—or what's left of it—watched them disappear... Seems kind of *cruel*, right?" He smiled, his fingers tracing Cassie's arm. "I wonder what became of her."

"I didn't make the leaders do that," Cassie said, straining hard to tolerate his touch. "I didn't make them kick out that family any more than I made them vote for a maniac who started a world freaking war. I didn't make half the country rebel against him, and I didn't make him drop warheads on his own military bases. I didn't do any of that, Michael. I was a kid. Like *you*."

"And yet it couldn't have happened without you," the boy said. "Why else would everyone still hate that little Daisy girl so much?"

Cassie shook her head. "When people can't live with their own guilt, sometimes the only escape is to destroy the innocent." They weren't her words. That's what her father said to make her stop crying as they watched the Koslows' guilty verdict come in.

"Why are you *doing* this, Michael?" she asked. "Threatening me. Us. My family...?"

Michael Ulmer clenched his fists. "I'm not threatening you. I'm looking out for myself—for what I *deserve*. I'm making sure this miserable life is a little bit better for me, which no one else is going to do. Tell me, Daisy, you ever think about the gender ratios in the Republic?"

Cassie shook her head.

"Of course not," Michael said. His voice echoed against the concrete walls. "Six guys for every girl. Across the colonies. Here in Joshua Tree, it's eight-to-one. I know my chances. Finding a girl? Being in love? Having my own family? The odds are zero for me. Would you or any of your friends choose me if you didn't *have* to?"

Cassie didn't answer. Michael grabbed her wrist, pulling her close enough to taste his breath. "That's why I'm not waiting anymore," he said. "I *want* you. Tonight. *Now*. And every night I feel like it. Or else, so help me, I'll tell the colony exactly who you are, and you and your parents can all go join the Koslows. Or whatever's left of them."

Cassie closed her eyes. There was no other choice. "Then we should find somewhere to be alone," she said. "Really alone."

"Finally," the boy sighed.

❀ ❀ ❀

Cassie led Michael to a freight elevator that descended into one of the colony's hydroponic farmscapes. They crept across a metal catwalk dangling over vast vertical fields of kale and tomatoes. The plants sprouted from white sheets of plastic that draped down into an infinite mist. Michael ran his hand along her back as they walked.

"So where exactly are you taking me?" he asked.

"Storage unit," Cassie said. "My family shares the one we're going to. It's in an older part of the colony. There aren't a lot of other places to go if you want to be alone."

"Tell me about it," Michael said. "I live in a room with six other dudes."

"And you didn't, um, tell them about me. Right?" Cassie said.

Michael bit his lip. "Not yet. Not as long as things go...nicely."

Nicely. Cassie tried not to show a reaction.

"I know I caught you by surprise, but—this is *kind of* romantic, right?" he said. "Honestly, until I figured out you were the girl in the ad, I thought I'd just be Johnny Jerkoff my whole life."

"Hey, this *is* romantic," she said.

The boy frowned. "I mean, everybody dreams about their first time. I just never thought it would be with a girl as pretty as you."

"I never thought it would be with a boy who was blackmailing me."

Cassie walked a few more steps before she realized Michael had stopped. "Or maybe that's *not* you," she said. "Maybe we could turn back n—"

Michael lunged forward and swung his fist into the side of Cassie's head. She sprawled across the metal walkway, one leg dangling over the bottomless plane of leaves. She looked up, dazed, as his twin silhouettes coalesced in her field of vision. "Don't ever say that again," he said.

Cassie crawled to her feet, her ear still ringing. Her jeans had popped their button and a new rip had appeared along the right knee. But that didn't matter much now.

Her eyes narrowed, sizing him up. Michael was roughly the same height and weight as her, and she guessed she could take him in a fair fight. Then he reached into his pocket and withdrew a knife—a ragged piece of metal with a bundle of gauze and black electrical tape wrapped around it for a handle.

"I'll use this if I have to," he said. "But I'd rather not. So *go*."

Cassie did as she was told. There was no one left to ask for help, even if she wanted to risk it.

❊ ❊ ❊

After the hydroponic fields, they climbed through a labyrinth of dark passageways before reaching a tunnel with train tracks that were overlaid with ribbons of cable. Stretching off into the darkness was an infinity of loading docks lit by dim sulfur lights.

"What am I supposed to tell my parents later?" Cassie said. "It's already so late."

"You can tell them the truth," Michael answered. "They already know who you are. And you're protecting them as much as you are yourself."

"Speaking of," she said. "Since you planned this out. Did *you* bring, uh…any other kind of protection?"

Michael's face wrinkled, then he laughed. "What? Like condoms? Don't worry about that," he said. "I'll be careful. And if not, who cares? Sooner or later we're going to have kids anyway. You and I are in this for good, Cassie. For *life*."

Cassie walked faster. They passed dozens of identical loading docks before she stopped. "Here we are," she said, and banged her fist against a metal roll-up gateway—large enough for a truck. Beside it was a smaller steel door with a single square window. "My family leases this space from the Republic with three other families from our ward. So we have the code. It's a good place to be alone when you need it. I used to come down here and read. Before we sold all the books."

She lifted the lid on a security console, revealing a chrome handle and a numeric keypad that fluttered to life with a sickly green glow when she touched it. Cassie's finger tapped out four low tones on the buttons, and something inside the door hissed, then clicked. Michael pulled up the metal latch and shoved it open into oily nothingness. Cassie reached inside and flicked on a light.

The storage room was a giant tomb with a segmented iron wall on the far side and concrete dividers separating it from the other units. It was huge, and high, and echoed with their footsteps as they walked inside. "They cram us into tiny living spaces, but these auditoriums are just sitting down here?" Michael said.

"This tunnel is one of the earliest parts of Joshua Tree. Part of a missile silo the government built decades ago. The Republic used it to haul out debris during the colony's construction—before we recycled everything. They also did decontamination in these rooms."

"People?" Michael asked.

Cassie shook her head. "People weren't rare. Metal and other building materials—that's what they were saving, mainly."

The concrete ground gritted beneath their feet. The boy and the girl were both breathing hard, but for very different reasons. "All right," he said. "Why don't you take off your clothes for me?"

Cassie pulled one arm into her sleeve, then the other and peeled her shirt off over her head. Michael stared at the girl standing before him in her tattered gray bra.

"I can't believe I'm finally going to...you know. *Do* it," he said, tugging off his own shirt and rolling it into a ball.

"No other choice now," she said.

Michael's face pinched. "It would be nice if *you* wanted it, too. Just saying."

Cassie lowered her head. She watched as he pulled off his shoes and squirmed out of his jeans. *His new jeans.* He tossed them into the dust.

Her fingers undid the zipper on her too-tight jeans with the now-missing button. She wriggled out of them, then draped them over her arm. "I'm going to turn off the light," she said.

"*No.* Leave the light on," Michael said. "I want to look at you."

She paused, then walked toward him. He cupped his hands over his nakedness as she drew near, but Cassie brushed past him to scoop up his discarded clothes. "You should be nicer to these things," she said, slapping the dirt and sand from the fabrics. "We're given so little."

She folded the clothes as she walked. "There may be a blanket in one of those boxes in the corner, if you want to lie down on something," she said. "That will make it...easier. I'll place our things over by the door."

The naked boy tiptoed across the grit-covered floor and began prying open the little cityscape of cardboard containers. "Already taking good care of the laundry," he said. "You're gonna make a fine wife, Daisy Girl, you know that?"

Her answer was the sound of the metal door slamming shut.

Michael Ulmer spun around. He was alone in the storage room.

He bolted toward the door, his fists thudding against the window just as he heard the familiar hiss and click of its lock. On the other side of the glass, Cassie stood in her underwear with her finger still touching the last numeral on the keypad.

Michael jerked on the door handle, but it wouldn't budge. Shadows of the wires embedded in the window crisscrossed his face. He began roaring as Cassie pulled on her jeans and shirt. His clothes were still in a neat pile at her feet.

"Open up, goddamn it, or I'll see you and your mother and father *butchered*," he said, spittle flecking the glass. "I'll *laugh* when they send you out into that wasteland."

"That's not going to happen," she said, raising one eyebrow.

"Yeah, I doubt they'll even *bother* to banish you. You'll be lined up against a wall and shot. The whole colony will watch. I can't wait to see your little face hit the ground. I'll *laugh*. You hear me?"

Cassie nodded. "I do hear you," she said, and smiled. "Which means you can hear me." She stepped closer to the door, almost nose to nose with the boy on the other side. "My parents and I planned for this day, the time when we might be found out. After the Republic put the Koslows on trial, we knew loyalty officers wouldn't show much mercy if they ever uncovered us. They'd blame us for what they did to that innocent young family. Just like they blamed us—*me*—for the hell on earth unleashed by the madman *they* put in charge."

Her finger traced the wires in the glass between them. "Just like you," she said. "Blaming me right now because you're locked in that room. But I didn't put you there. You did. I gave you many chances to stop this. That's more than you gave me."

The boy hammered the glass. He kicked the door. Cassie let him tire out.

"We knew, someday, somehow, someone might figure it out," she said. "We mapped escape routes. My father even managed to steal three biohazard suits from the sanitation department, in case we had to make a run for it outside. We traded all the belongings we used to keep in that storage room—the same one you're standing in right now—to get a broken-down motorcycle we've stashed in segments throughout the colony. We had a plan: if anyone ever found out—we'd run. We'd hide. We'd survive."

Michael Ulmer shook his head. "You'll never last out there. The stragglers will rip you to shreds."

Cassie snorted. "But at least we'd have a chance." Her

eyes met his. "I've come to realize that people inside here can be just as inhuman. Haven't you?"

"The air will burn your skin. You'll get sick. And if you live, by some crazy miracle, you'll turn into one of *them*... those twisted things scavenging for..."

"Maybe," she interrupted. "It's definitely a risk. But Mom and Dad researched other underground shelters, far from here. Independent tribes, separate from the Republic. Nothing as elaborate and safe as the colonies like this, but they're out there. They might welcome us."

"You won't have time," he said. "When I'm not in the dorm tomorrow, people will miss me. I'm gonna beat on this door and scream and make so much noise. Someone will hear, maybe not right away, but within hours. First they'll find me—and then we'll find *you*." His fist smacked the window again as punctuation. "Go ahead and *try* to run. The Republic has the colony sealed up tight. Nothing gets in or out."

Cassie smiled at him, sadly. "No, Michael," she said. "I guess you don't understand me. We're *prepared* to run—if we have to. And yeah, you *can't* just waltz out of the colony. Which is why we figured out where several exit points might be." She tapped the glass, pointing to the segmented metal wall. "Like this room."

Cassie walked back to the control panel and lifted the lid, tapping in a different code this time. She looked at the boy in the window. "They might miss you," she said. "But nobody is going to find you."

She turned the chrome handle and the storage room filled with swirling orange light. The segmented wall groaned and began to fold inward and rumble upward. Outside, the armored door retracted into the top of the exit port.

Michael Ulmer squealed as the cold air and rain swung tentacles of dust into the room. A cyclone of papers and photographs erupted from the cardboard boxes against the walls. Cassie watched the boy's eyes bulge as he clung to his breath. Finally his lungs heaved in the toxic air. The open sores of his acne-crusted cheeks began to sizzle.

Toxins stirred up by the monsoons made the air so much more caustic than usual. She wondered how the stragglers ever developed a tolerance for it: poisoned air and water, blighted land, freezing temperatures.

A crazy, high-pitched laugh rose from the other side of the door. "I'm going to run," said the thing that was once a teenage boy named Michael Ulmer said. His sore-blossomed face vanished and reappeared in the flashing orange warning lights. "I'm gonna run out of here and knock on the windows of Covington Square or some other place where there are people, and I'm gonna tell them! I'm going to tell them *everything*, Daisy Girl. Even if they don't let me back in! I'm going to drag you out here with me…"

"Shhh," she said. "Shhhh…" But the boy kept making noise.

Behind him, in the narrow octagonal opening of the loading bay, shapes emerged from the storm—just pencil sketches amid the waves of rain and windowblown sand.

The figures approached so slowly, so hesitantly, they hardly seemed to be moving at all.

When they saw the room held only a scrawny, naked boy, they began to move faster.

Cassie held Michael Ulmer's jeans out in front of her. They were a size too large, but that would feel so good. Relaxed fit. That's what they'd called it once upon a time. Plus, she now had a new T-shirt for her mother—big enough for her growing baby belly, too. And the shoes might fit her father. She'd have to explain the jeans to Mia and Abigail with a convincing story, of course. And she'd also have to tell them about refusing to go with that weird boy who vanished after trying to talk her into exploring dangerous, abandoned parts of the colony. But that would be okay. The little girl from the Daisy ad had gotten good at make-believe over the years. She really was a good liar.

Cassie flapped the jeans once and held them against her legs. "Thanks for these, by the way," she said. But Michael Ulmer wasn't watching her anymore. He had his back against the glass.

Cassie peeked through the window over his shoulder and saw more stick figures in the storm. Dozens of them. Most were tall and spindly, but she could make out quite a few small ones, too. The rumors were true: The stragglers were reproducing.

She guessed Michael Ulmer had about ten seconds.

"Please..." the boy whimpered. His tears and runny nose

smeared the glass. "Please let me back in. I'll never tell anyone, I promise, I promise, I'm sorry, sorrr-eeee PLEEEEASE..."

"Nine...eight...seven," Cassie Roberts said.

She closed her eyes, hugging her new jeans. She found the plastic daisy in one pocket and began pulling off the remaining petals. "Six...*six*...five...four..."

A chorus of screams from the other side of the door drowned out the rest.

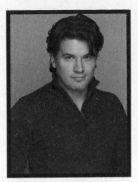

AUTHOR PHOTO
© CHRISTOPHER BOYER

Anthony Breznican was born and raised in Western Pennsylvania and graduated from the University of Pittsburgh. He has worked as a reporter for *The Arizona Republic*, Associated Press, and *USA Today*, and is currently the senior staff writer assigned to *Star Wars* and Marvel for *Entertainment Weekly*. His debut novel, *Brutal Youth*, was published in 2014. Visit anthonybreznican .com and follow him on Twitter @breznican.

"COLD BEVERAGE": THE SONG I WROTE THAT CHANGED MY LIFE

A PERSONAL ESSAY

By G. Love

"Cold Beverage" is twenty-three years old. I play it almost every night, and I will be completely honest: I love it every time. I love the music. I love the lyrics. I can't believe how much people still love to jam to it. It always blows my mind.

—G. LOVE

EARLY SUMMER 1993. I DROVE A 1963 DODGE DART. PUSH-button transmission. Distressed, but not chipped, black paint with plenty of clean chrome. Red vinyl dashboard. Red, black, and white Naugahyde seat covers. People would tell me, "Keep her oil changed and she will run forever." It had that famous American Mopar engine, the Slant 6 I think it was.

It *would* run forever.

The '63 Dart was a beater and a classic in one breath. I got her for $1,500 cash in Braintree, Massachusetts. She was my baby. I named her Miss Eloise after my great old Aunt Eloise. Eloise Klinges lived to ninety-two, and she was as wise as her years. She was stubborn, opinionated, and the boss lady for sure. I was young boy when I knew her, but her legend and legacy would surely live on in our family.

To me, the naming of people, things, and ideas has always been a knee-jerk, immediate reaction. Everything needs a name, every person needs a nickname. I'm the namer. It's just my thing, I give the names.

When I looked at the old, beautiful 1963 Dodge Dart that would be my first car there was only one name, dear old Miss Eloise.

G. Love and his dog Katie
with Miss Eloise

The night I got Miss Eloise, I took the train to Braintree, and the seller picked me up at the station. I wrote a check for $1,500 and drove her back to Jamaica Plains with no tags. I know you're not supposed to drive a car without tags, but think about it: how was I supposed to get it home?!

I got her home all right, and the first thing I did was call

Heather. Some of the guys called her "Leather Heather," I guess because she was all rock and roll. Heather was a pretty girl in the neighborhood. She dressed cool in black, and I maybe had a couple dates with her or hangs. I can't remember really. She was around. We were all trying to come up. She was into musicians, she was part of our scene, and she was a cool girl.

When I picked up Heather for a cruise, I said, "Step inside my ride for a little maiden voyage." I figured Miss Eloise would be good luck, and indeed I was off to a good start. Heather was impressed. We parked and had some fun breaking in the new ride. We made out and we scored and we were happy as can be in the 1963. We had a little rock-and-roll community and we were all in it together...

I *needed* this new ride. Things with the band were starting to happen, and I had to get my amp, guitars, PA, and microphones to the gigs. I had graduated from street musician to bar musician and things were rolling. And now, with my car, I was rolling too.

Spring came hot and heavy, and then summer heated up quick. Wouldn't you know, my brakes went out. There I was sitting in the repair shop up on Washington Street on the Brookline/Allston/Brighton border.

There was a musician friend of mine, this cat Washtub Robbie. Robbie was an older cat who had played washtub bass with blues legend Spider John Koerner and a host of others. He used to help me fix up my guitars. He was a legend of the Boston folk, blues, and roots scene, and he took me under his wing back in 1993. Whenever I saw him he always had something cool to look at, an old guitar or amp, an antique knickknack, a glass of rye. This time, though, he had a Xeroxed mag about vintage guitars and girls. Not in a sleazy way, kind of a rockabilly way.

Guitars and girls. Perfect.

As I waited for my car, I perused the mag and two words popped out like a neon sign off of the white paper: Cold Beverage. I don't even remember the sentence before it but I remember those words. You know how sometimes words hit you in a certain way? These two words got me. I remember it clear as day.

I said out loud, "I like cold beverages."

And then, while my brakes were getting fixed, I wrote a rap about how much I liked cold beverages. Since I had nothing to write on I used the magazine and wrote all around the edges of it. I wrote three verses in that service station.

Miss Eloise was eventually done, and I drove her home to my new spot on Oak View Terrace above the Irish bar, the Shamrock, in Brighton Center.

It was a five-bedroom shithole above the Shamrock, and I was lucky enough to live there—that place was a big part of my last year in Boston. I had the front room of the attic. My rapping partner, Jasper, named it the "Blues Room" on account of the low light that would come out of the high window. In the summer it would heat up real good and smell like pizza from the Greek pizza shop across the street. Their exhaust fan would blow out scents of hot dough, sauce, and cheese night and day. I wrote this song on our demo *Back in the Day* called "It's So Hot" about the feeling of that room.

There was a little five-square-foot deck on the floor below my room, and I wrote many a song out there that summer. Sitting in the pizza heat, drinking cheap lemonade, sweating, and writing lyrics. Those were the days.

Maybe that night, maybe later, I started riffing on my guitar and came up with a simple, but I guess somewhat profound, riff. Perfect in its quirkiness, perfect in its nod to the blues, and absolutely my style. I started rapping my new lyrics I'd written at the service station. It worked.

There's something about the inertia and the conception of writing a song. It always gives you a pulse. A deep and light energy. A chill up your spine and a euphoria that overtakes your senses. Almost makes you cry in a way. Even if it's a funny song. When that feeling comes, then you know you've hit gold. It's a real fleeting moment but a sincere one for sure. A little magic in the air, and you happen to be able to catch it like a firefly in a jar. I got that feeling that night when I put the music to the lyrics. Just like painting a perfect picture. Somehow it all came together in a way I couldn't have planned.

I think the best songs, and for that matter, the best things in life, come easy. I mean, you have to bust your ass to get to the time and place where they can arrive, but it's like the saying goes: put the work in and be prepared for when that golden opportunity or idea comes to you.

I was ready and it came. Just a simple little ditty that would change my life.

Later that week the band came over, and it was again one of those easy sessions. Jeffrey Clemens, a.k.a. the Houseman, my drummer, knew just what to make of it. He and my bass player, Jimi Jazz, quickly figured out the exact rhythm section groove. We worked out a break and *bang*: new song. Done and done. Just like that. Easy as could be. Another song for our rapidly expanding repertoire.

We titled the new song "Cold Beverage" and plugged it into our set at the Plough and Stars in Cambridge, Massachusetts. The praise was immediate from our growing weekly audience. As a matter of fact, our audience went viral. Our Monday-night shows went from an empty bar to a line down the block, and all of a sudden I guess I went from being a street musician to a local rock star. I mean it was literally over the course of a couple months. It was the best year of my life, and the music was deep and full of magic, promise, momentum, and energy. We were cooking.

There was a moment some weeks or months later when Washtub Robbie came up to me after the gig with a big smile and a hug and said, "Kid, I hope you like that song 'Cold Beverage'!"

I asked, "Why's that?"

"Because you're going to be playing that shit for the rest of your life!"

Washtub Robbie knew I had a hit. *I* just didn't know it yet.

Summer of 1993 sped by, filled with exciting times. Our regular shows were more packed, and we started being booked at bigger venues. We got gigs outside of Boston, and shows in Philly, NYC, and DC led to a producer and manager. We also landed an impending record contract with Epic Records.

By Christmastime we had *G. Love and Special Sauce,* our debut record, in the can, and had achieved a solid studio version of "Cold Beverage." The record dropped in the spring of 1994. The first single to release off the album was the eloquent "Blues Music"; the follow-up single was to be "Cold Beverage." We were both happy and surprised that "Blues Music," a darker, deeper, sultry song, was chosen as the single over our catchier "Baby's Got Sauce" and "Cold Beverage." Looking back, it's a good thing we dropped "Blues Music" first because it had a vibe that everyone was down with. It was heavy, and it was a statement.

"Baby's Got Sauce" and "Cold Beverage" had the same sentiments and roots, but they were catchier. For a lot of people and critics, catchy tunes can be written off. That being said, releasing "Blues Music" first gave us a certain legitimacy from which we benefited. It allowed us to *not* be a one-hit wonder. I have to thank our AR man, Michael Caplan, and his infinite wisdom for that call.

To be a single, a song must be sticky. "Cold Beverage" had much stickiness. From the intro drum fill to the first vocal shout of "YO!" To the guitar riff, bass line, energetic hip-hop drum groove, let alone the lyrics, the song was completely sticky.

Top to bottom. Sticky.

When a record company chooses a single, they might allow a video to be made. A video didn't always happen. Because our debut record was gaining steam and buzz, famous video director Mark Romanek offered to make the video for "Cold Beverage." This was a huge opportunity, and I didn't even realize at the time how lucky I was.

Most videos at the time—and this was the height of MTV's power and popularity—were lip-synched. I was not having that. I was of the mindset that everything in music had to be real. Be true. I refused to lip-synch on a video. To me, that was a sellout move. I'm a Blues Man. Blues Men don't lip-synch. The label was so hot on us they went with it. They actually brought in a mobile studio unit to record us performing live on the street while they shot the video.

The video for "Cold Beverage" came out and was immediately added to MTV's rotation. It was even on *Beavis and Butthead*, who said, "Haha this sucks." That exposure helped to blow us up. Thanks! The video played next to the big hits of Nirvana, Pearl Jam, and Beck. Here was our killer video, with a live recording, next to all of these huge-sounding produced records. Luckily, we got just enough play to put us on the map before MTV dropped the excellent video.

Who knows what would've happened if we'd used the recorded version in the video? Regardless, that brief time on MTV, with such a sticky song, garnered us thousands and thousands of fans. Looking back, it sounded too raw for prime time, and that was good. I think if it really blew up huge, it might have destroyed us and made us into a one-hit wonder. Yeah, we got exposure, but not too much. I think it was just enough.

It was clear to see this song was rapidly changing my life.

As we hit the road our audiences swelled, coast to coast. Our show got hotter and hotter. More people. More energy. The hottest part of the show? When we launched into that, "Yo! Could I get a Cold Beverage..." I mean it was fire. People couldn't get enough. Sometimes, when we were playing sultry, slow tunes, someone would yell out "Play 'Cold Beverage'!"

The shows went by. The years went by. Thousands of shows year after year, coast to coast, city to city. We continued releasing records and singles, all to varied degrees of success. Meanwhile, we had gotten into the habit of closing the show with smoking-hot versions of "Cold Beverage" resplendent with improvisational jams, freestyles, and covers mashed into it. It turned into this highlight we could depend on, and then it became a crutch.

We knew it was the high point of the show. We knew we

could use it to end the show on a highlight and bring the house down. We did. Night after night after night.

So, it became a goal of mine as a songwriter: can I write a tune that will be a bigger closer than "Cold Beverage"? Sometimes, on the very rare occasion that I *didn't* play it, I felt a certain victory: *wow, we had a killer show and we didn't even play "Cold Beverage."*

I decided to take the time to break it down and asked myself: *What was it about this song?* I tried to emulate the song structure and make new songs, but it never worked. "Cold Beverage's" composition was perfect in its uniqueness.

It was also inimitable.

The main verse riff was so simple, and yet it represented all the blues I had ever absorbed. An arpeggio on a G7 chord (in the C position) followed by a chromatic bounce on another G7 chord (in the D7) position. Both of these chords I had learned by trying to learn Robert Johnson and John Hammond songs.

The chorus shifted rhythmically off the syncopation of the verse groove to emphasize the one beat and bounced between G-C-D-G-C-D, on James Brown–style funk chords. Ninth chords.

The lyrics were simple, pure, and crucial. Yeah, the song was literally about beverages, but I stand by it. It's a poem. It's *my* poem. You can visualize the heat and visualize the drinks and feel the sensation of your thirst being quenched. And who can't sing along with the chorus? It even has one of those vocal performances where people can't understand whether I'm saying "I like Cold Beverage yeah" or "I like Cold Beverages," the former being correct.

It sure is some badass poetry.

COLD BEVERAGE

WORDS AND MUSIC BY GARRETT DUTTON / © 1994 CHICKEN PLATTERS (BMI)

Yo could I get a cold beverage
I need some leverage
It's sunny outside
Some lemonade would be nice
Or a Sprite through the drive-through
At B.K. yo I'll buy girl a drink
But girls got to pay
On the front porch I got
Some iced tea
If you like a taste of tea
Then come along with me
It's martini time
Yeah yeah feeling golden
Bring your own beverage
Just make sure it's cold

I like cold beverage yeah!

Give me frosty mug
Filled with A&W
If you got ice cream
Make it a double scoop
Milkshake at the fountain
Really good sounding
Chocolate egg cream

Yo, I'm champ cherry pounding
Caught a chill vibe
Orange juice in my ride
Wawa's to the right
They got a beverage inside
Dig me a hot coffee
Fill it up with ice
Watermelons like drink
Please fix me a large slice
Summertime is cool the heat is getting old
Yeah I'll get a beverage
Just make sure it's cold

I like cold beverage
When I'm fishing
Let's keep one thing clear
The bait's over there
The brew's right here
Two six packs and a big bag of ice

Didn't even catch a bite
But the brew tasted nice
Back to the bar
Strawberry daiquiris and a colada
I need a whole lotta them
Fruit drinks to catch me a buzz
I must tell you I'm the
Kool-Aid kid
Before you serve my drink
Please stick it in the fridge

I like cold beverage yeah!

It was as simple as could be, but it sure worked. It had catch phrases and the naming of famous drinks. Lemonade. Kool-Aid. Martini. Egg cream. Strawberry daiquiris. Sprite. A&W. Bug juice. Colada. Six-pack. Coffee. Orange juice. It had local Philadelphia references with the convenience store Wawa and the famous "Champ Cherry" soda from long-closed-down Levis Hotdogs. I still smile when I sing those Philly words. Because truly, you have to be from Philly or the Tristate area to know what the hell Wawa is, and you've got to be from Center City or South Philly (and my age) to remember Levis Hot Dogs. So that's pretty classic and a true tilt of the cap to the city that raised us.

Lyrically, "Cold Beverage" had concrete references,

which allowed listeners to visualize, which is key to connecting. People could see and actually taste this song. They could latch on to those references, visualizing them as they flew by.

I mean it was perfect.

In Lou Reed's "Take a Walk on the Wild Side" you could see the story he laid down. I believe I captured something similar in "Cold Beverage." That's what a great song does. A song should be a picture or a movie that takes the listener on a ride. I took people on a ride of refreshment. And it's no small thing, there's a reason there are happy hours, "It's five o'clock somewhere" sayings, and lemonade stands—it's as old as the cavemen. We all need a drink. From ice-cold water to lemonade and even the hard stuff. It's in our DNA, we gotta have it.

There was a radio station—Y100—in Philly that played "Cold Beverage" backed by the Beastie Boys' "Fight for Your Right" for a solid fifteen years at 5:00 p.m. on the dot every Friday afternoon.

Now it's 2016 and "Cold Beverage" is twenty-three years old. Washtub Robbie was right. I *do* play it almost every night, and I will be completely honest, I love it every time. When I start to play it I have a huge shit-eating grin on my face.

I love the music.

I love the lyrics.

I can't believe how much the people love to jam to it.

It always blows my mind. In a lot of ways, the strength of that one song, and certainly the record it's on, has been the catalyst for my long, steadfast career as a touring musician. I've continued to challenge myself on every record, to produce a song or songs that could replace "Cold Beverage" as a closer. Mostly for my own sanity and to keep pushing our live show. Indeed, we did score some great closers on the *Sugar* record, and now I usually close the set with "Nothing Quite Like Home" or "Weekend Dance."

But, I play "Cold Beverage" every night. And we always bring it. It feels better *not* to depend on it as a closer, but rather, to drop it anytime I want to bring up the crowd energy and keep the people smiling. You have to keep pushing as a musician.

Complacency is the enemy of creativity.

"Cold Beverage" definitely kept the lights on around here since it came out. I'm sure happy I got my brakes fixed that day. I'm happy Washtub Robbie gave me that old rag. I'm happy that Jim and Jeff knew just what to play. It's just one of those things. You write songs as best you can and write them for no other reason than that they just need to get written. If you do that, you'll hit gold sooner or later. And if it's real, it will make people dance until the end of time. Like my badass 1963 Dodge Dart, I think this song will run forever.

Needless to say, our crowd was a drinking crowd, and we've broken many a bar record at many a club over the years. Cheers to the greatest drinking song ever written. "Cold Beverage." I wonder what this world would've been like without that song.

Probably very thirsty.

AUTHOR PHOTO
© BRANDON FINNEY

G. Love—born Garrett Dutton—combines blues and hip-hop into what he termed "ragmop." G. Love rose from the streets of Philadelphia into the American music scene in 1994. At the beginning of his career, he fused his vocal and guitar talents with his band Special Sauce—acoustic bass player Jimi "Jazz" Prescott and drummer Jeffrey Clemens. As G. Love and Special Sauce, they released such popular singles as "Cold Beverage" and "Baby's Got Sauce." His smooth vocal delivery and unfailing dedication to touring provided a steady climb to notoriety. Visit philadelphonic .com and follow him on Twitter @glove.

TIFFANY
TWISTED

**A SHORT STORY
INSPIRED BY THE EAGLES'
"HOTEL CALIFORNIA"**

By Ellen Hopkins

Having spent a year or five in search of the Hotel California, the song has always felt representative of my youth, but its meaning has always been open to interpretation. What really drew me in was the idea of a revolving door that won't allow escape.

—ELLEN HOPKINS

THE FIRST TIME I STUMBLED INTO THE HOTEL, I WAS seventeen, a damn good guitarist and decent vocalist, looking to break into the music business and out of the mold. That night accomplished both, but not in the way I expected.

First, you need to understand the reasons I ended up there. My parents were moneyed hipsters lacking the moral fiber to commit fully to each other, preferring the experimental lifestyle of an open marriage, fueled by the substances of the day. Their parenting skills were sadly lacking, too.

"We are sojourners," explained Becky, who refused to let her children call her Mom. "Only here for a short while. So we must take every advantage of our time on this planet."

"In this universe," argued Dad, who was happy enough

with that title. "One day we'll step into another. They coexist, you know."

I think it was the mushrooms.

I don't know why they chose to have kids. Abortion was legal. My late sister, Harmony, and I were playthings with hippie names. Dolls to dress up and show off. Which worked out okay when we were little, but as we grew older, we largely looked after ourselves.

There were consequences.

For whatever reasons (parental example wasn't one), Harmony had been a dedicated student. More, she was driven to maintain a perfect GPA, with Harvard as her ultimate goal. Instead, in her senior year and just shy of eighteen, she'd fallen in love with her calculus teacher. Harmony never did anything less than full-bore, and that included romance. Unfortunately, Mr. Clare was married, and while he wasn't above having sex with a student, divorce was apparently against his religion. When he cut things off with Harmony, she totally shut down.

Whether because of brain chemistry or simply circumstance, she tumbled into a bottomless, black, cerebral hole. Lost her GPA in a single semester, and with it any hope of an Ivy League college. Two weeks before graduation, she swallowed a bottle of Becky's Percocets, climbed into the bathtub fully clothed, filled it. Sank under. She didn't bother to leave a note. Probably figured no one would read it.

Here's the thing. I'd seen it coming. Said nothing. It was Harmony's life, I believed, to stumble through or exit prematurely. Her choice. After we found her, water-bloated and bone white, I regretted that decision. She was my sister, after all, and one of the few people in the world I could talk to. But it took the Reaper's knock to make me understand that, and then it was too late.

Becky freaked out. Erected a teepee in the backyard and basically moved in there, playing Jim Morrison on an endless loop and sleeping with anyone—male or female—who'd drop by, stash in hand.

Dad fell into an alternate universe. I suppose it might have been attached to our own, because he seemed able to wander back and forth at will, mostly ignoring the activities just outside the back door.

I think it was the peyote.

As for me, I turned anger (at my parents) and guilt (about Harmony) into black drifts of music, with lyrics that said nothing but explained everything, at least if you could get to their meaning. Most people couldn't. That included my girlfriend at the time. Sarah was naturally pretty and sweet as cream, but as hard as she tried, she couldn't help my emotional turmoil. And as my music grew darker, Sarah began to pull away.

"You used to sing such beautiful songs, ballads and such. Now it's all death and destruction."

I liked Sarah a lot, and really wanted to apologize, but

what came out of my mouth was, "I'm working stuff out. If it bothers you, there's the door."

After she was gone, I went back over my most recent efforts and had to admit she was right. Death and destruction. As far as I was concerned, I was a genius, anyway. Not long, I thought, until I would be a wealthy genius, all on my talent.

As soon as I decided my path into the future, I cleaned out a decent bank account (yuppie parents gift chunks of money in lieu of actually shopping for presents they're pretty sure you won't like anyway) and bought a well-used TR6, positive the classic Triumph was the perfect car for me. Had I really considered it, I would've picked something with a back seat. Something I could sleep in.

Three weeks 'til summer break would officially start, I took an unexcused leave of absence from school, thinking I might go back for my senior year in the fall, but probably not. Genius musicians don't require diplomas to make their millions.

I knocked on the flap of the teepee, which was ridiculous as it made no noise, but somehow it felt necessary. "Hey, Becky? I'm off in search of fame and fortune. I'll send postcards."

"Lennon?" came her reply. "That you?"

"None other."

"Thought so. I'd kiss you goodbye, but I'm naked."

"Yeah, that would be weird. See you."

"Don't get arrested."

That was it. No *when will you be back?* No *how will you take care of yourself?* Just, *don't get arrested.*

I stopped by Dad's alternate universe, requested he join the one I was currently standing in so I could tell him so long.

"Where you going, son?"

"LA, I guess. When it comes to music, it's that or Nashville, and country isn't my thing." I wasn't sure how accurate that was, but it sounded like I'd done my research.

"You okay on cash?"

"If you've got some to spare, I won't say no. Oh, and maybe a little bud, too?"

Weed was all I'd tried at that point, and I figured I shouldn't show up on the music scene without some sort of substance in hand. Dad was happy enough to oblige.

"Careful," he said, as I walked out the door. "All kinds of cons in LA."

Fair warning. Too bad I didn't heed it.

Armed with five hundred dollars, one of Dad's credit cards (for emergency purposes *only*) and a half ounce of excellent Oregon weed, I hit the road, and since I had the entire summer ahead of me, decided to take a scenic mountain route. I'd seen the coast before. Southeast from Portland, the highway meandered through Bend and Klamath Falls. With stops to piss and eat and toke, that took most of the day.

I might have gone farther, but the weed was pretty good, and I found I didn't like driving wasted on a strange stretch of road in the dark. Rather than squander money on a motel room, I slept in the car, or tried to. Even with the seat pushed all the way back, it was an uncomfortable night.

The next morning, I dropped down into Susanville, California, and then on into Reno, where I added to my cash stash, playing Dora (my precious Martin guitar) in the riverside park for tips. I didn't earn much, but it felt good, like my talent did have value. And it made people smile. I hung out in the Biggest Little City for a few days, and struck up an acquaintance or two, which is easy enough to do when you're the one supplying the smoke. In trade, I got to sleep on their couches.

Eventually, though, I figured I should get back on track. The music industry waits for no man. I loaded Dora into the passenger seat of the TR6, and off we went, south on Highway 395. There were places to stop along the way, things that must be seen, according to my pre-trip planning. The weird tufa towers of Mono Lake deserved a look, as did Mammoth Mountain, though it was the wrong time of the year for anything like skiing. It was a very long day of travel.

Beyond the beauty of the mountains, and before heading west toward the congestion of LA, 395 flattened into a long stretch of desert. I'd smoked weed all afternoon, could smell the remains of a blunt in the ashtray. Buzzed, dog-tired, I was considering spending another uncomfortable night in my car when ahead in the distance I saw a shimmering light that promised the possibility of food and a toilet, if nothing else. Peeing in the desert is one thing...

As I approached the shimmering beacon, the night closed in around me, dark and disturbing. No moon. No stars. No light at all that I could discern, except the one. It lured me off the main highway, onto a rutted road, but by then it had become my only hope for a peaceful night's slumber. Or something.

If I'm absolutely honest with myself, at first sight I should have turned around, motored on out of there, and not looked back, not even in the rearview mirror. The aura hugging the place was blood red, anything but illuminating. And yet somehow still inviting.

The hotel itself appeared ageless, its architecture a strange blend of baroque and Frank Lloyd Wright. All the windows I could see were lit, and so, I soon found out, were the people behind them. The entrance was a grand revolving door, the kind you see gracing expensive properties in major metro-politan areas. Beside it was a sign that said: WELCOME TO CALIFORNIA. Considering I'd been driving in the state for hours (hadn't I?), I found that slightly unsettling.

Dora and I went inside, anyway.

The bellman, who'd been nodding off, looked up and turned sleepy eyes in our direction. "Luggage?"

"Just Dora here and my backpack."

"Need any help?"

"Lots. But not with my stuff." The joke thumped almost audibly.

"Suit yourself." He licked his lips suggestively, reminding me of a jungle cat on the prowl. "If you change your mind, my name is Harry."

His name tag said "Night Man." I didn't ask, or argue.

As I started toward the front desk, Harry said quietly. "Watch out for our proprietress. She's Tiffany-twisted."

I assumed it was her very cool name, so when the woman looked up and smiled, I greeted her that way. "Hey, Tiffany. I'm hoping you have a room for the night."

Her face hardened immediately, and she seemed to age a decade. Still, she was hot—all chiseled and blond and tan. "So happens accommodations are available." She studied me for a moment. "How old are you?"

"Twenty-one," I lied.

"Huh. Isn't everyone? Well, go ahead and fill out a registration form, please. Just be aware that once you've been entered into our system, you'll remain permanently in our database."

My writing hand paused. "What does that mean?"

"Nothing, really. You'll get special offers once in a while. We like repeat customers, and hope to entice you back. In fact, since this is your first time here, I'm prepared to offer you a discounted rate."

"That's very nice of you. How much?"

"Depends on your preferred accommodations. Would you rather be up, or is a lower floor more your style?"

"Hey, why go down when you can fly, right?"

She smiled. "My kind of man, uh..." She glanced at the register. "Lennon. Huh. Well, *coo coo cachoo.*"

The reference wasn't entirely lost on me. I mean, who doesn't know "I Am the Walrus"? Still, of all the Beatles songs she might have chosen, why that one? "What do you mean?"

"I am he as you are he as you are me and we are all together."

Okay, the chick was weird, but rather incredible to look at. A real pornographic priestess, as John Lennon himself might have said. And the way she was staring at me made me wonder if the interest in her eyes was real. This music thing had definite possibilities. "Uh. Yeah."

"How long will you be staying with us?"

"Oh, just one night. I'm on my way to LA."

"Isn't everyone?" she repeated. Then she pointed at Dora and sang the first line of an old Byrds song, though she sounded more like the Patti Smith version. "So you want to be a rock 'n' roll star."

"Well, yeah. Gonna give it a shot, anyway."

"Some of our other guests might be able to help you with that. We're incredibly connected here. And you look like you'll fit in just fine."

I had no idea what she meant by the last sentence. Still, it was interesting to know there were other musicians staying in the hotel. "That's great to hear. Hope I'll meet some of them."

"Oh you will. You definitely will. And since you don't seem to be in a real hurry, I'll go ahead and hold your room an extra night, just in case. You can cancel any time without penalty." She ran Dad's credit card. Yeah, I knew it was supposed to be only for emergencies, but I didn't want to spend a big chunk of my cash on a place to crash for the night. She handed me my key. "There you go. You may now enter the kingdom."

What the hell was she talking about? I chalked up my confusion to not enough sleep and too much weed. "A-okay, Tiffany."

That drew a scowl. "I'm Pearl. If you're interested in Tiffany, I can arrange that. Why don't you take your stuff up to your room, and then join our celebration in the ballroom on the ground floor? It's gonna be a blowout."

Party? Oh, yeah. "See you in a few."

I exited the elevator on the fourth floor to find the entire hallway lit with gas lanterns. Considering the glare of the lobby, the low light was unsettling, like stepping into another dimension, one where finding the correct room number proved something of a challenge. Especially since every door seemed be numbered 420. "What the..." I said out loud.

"Something wrong?" The voice, like the girl holding a candle, materialized out of thin air. At least, I never saw her coming.

I turned and almost bumped into the most exquisite creature I'd ever been that close to. My breath caught in my throat at her pale china-doll beauty, and it was all I could do to choke out, "I'm having a hard time finding my way."

"Let me help you."

She took my key and led me down the corridor. I followed, focused on the slight sway of her narrow hips beneath her gauzy white dress, and was suddenly gripped by desire so bold it almost dropped me to my knees. *This could be paradise, or a clear path to hell,* I thought. Not that I cared either way.

"Are you Tiffany?" I managed to ask.

She stopped in front of a door, turned, and smiled. "No. I'm Candy. How do you know Tiffany?"

"I don't. Just something I heard about."

"Be cautious, Lennon. I don't recommend Tiffany for beginners. Ditto Mercedes."

How did she know my name? And what did she mean by that? This was the most confusing place ever. But at that point I was more intrigued than scared. Candy opened the door to Room 428—turned out I couldn't see that well by lantern glow—and used her candle to light a gas lamp hanging on the wall of what appeared to be a windowless cubicle. "They don't want people to see out or what?"

"Or what. Our guests prefer privacy."

I glanced around the sparsely furnished room—one king bed, a small chest of drawers, a single nightstand with another oil lamp. No clock. No TV. No radio. "You guys definitely save money on electricity. But what about entertainment?"

Her laugh was the chime of a mission bell. "Plenty of that here, sweetheart. Are you coming down to the feast?"

"Oh, there'll be food, too? Great. I'm starving."

"You won't leave hungry, that I promise."

"Awesome. I'll freshen up. You'll be there, too, won't you?"

"I will if you want me."

I wanted to throw her straight down on the bed and

take her right there. Didn't think that would be prudent, though, so I watched her leave, hungrier than ever, and not for food.

The bathroom was little more than a closet, but at least it had running water. I used the toilet (which was what had drawn me toward the hotel, after all), washed up, and combed my hair. That proved pointless, because by the time I joined the revelers, most of the party had spilled out of the ballroom onto a breezy courtyard, where they danced to live music provided by a group who seemed able to handle all requests.

What a crowd it was. Pearl was there, and Candy, who was immediately at my side. She pointed out Mercedes, Molly, and Tiffany, who sparkled in a short, tight dress the color of pink champagne. But what struck me most were the guys, every one of whom was almost as pretty as the women. Somehow, I'd stumbled across an assembly of the beautiful folk.

"Wow," I commented to Candy. "Do you screen your customers according to their looks?"

Her melodic laugh lifted into the cool evening air. "Those are the faces they want you to see. Underneath, there's plenty of ugliness. Now, what can I get you?"

Loaded question. "You."

"Excellent choice. But not on an empty stomach."

Candy took my arm and steered me toward a huge table, loaded with platters. Most of the offerings were designed to appeal to a sweet tooth, but I managed to score some fruit, cheese, and crackers before moving on to dessert. I was nibbling on a sugar cookie when Tiffany and an older dude wandered over.

"Hey there," she cooed seductively. "I'm Tiff and this is Ron. Pearl said you're looking to break into the music biz. Ron happens to be a producer."

"Yeah," agreed Candy. "He's an icon."

I gave the guy a once-over. He was maybe forty and obviously worked out. His clothing was Armani casual, and his salt-and-pepper hair was expensively cut in perfect layers. "Good to meet you, Ron."

"You play? You sing? What?" he asked.

"Both."

"How 'bout you take a turn with the band and let me see what you've got?"

"Dora's upstairs."

"Who's Dora?" sniffed Tiffany.

"My guitar."

"Oh, good. I thought maybe you were spoken for."

"Don't worry," said Ron. "Mick over there will let you borrow his."

I broke out in a bad case of nerves. I was good, yeah. And people in that Reno park liked me, yeah. But this could jump-start my future, and if I didn't comply my career would remain on hold. "What should I play?"

"Show me some lead. Clapton, maybe?"

Honestly, most of my guitar work was acoustic, but I'd played a little electric and figured it couldn't be all that hard to sound like Clapton. Yeah, I know better now, but that night bravado made up for a lack of practice. Then Candy offered a little incentive.

"Just a taste for now."

It was the sweetest kiss I'd ever enjoyed, not that there'd been all that many previously, and those were with girls, including Sarah, as inexperienced as I. But I didn't have to know anything special that night. Candy taught me everything I needed to know. Her mouth was cool and the tip of her tongue icy-cold as it darted across my lips, chilling their overheated skin instantly.

I went numb. "Wow," was the best I could do.

"There's a whole lot more where that came from. Now let's hear you play some rocking guitar."

Mick was accommodating, and so was the rest of the band. I played a few licks to get used to the unfamiliar instrument, and then consulted with the other guys about which Clapton song, of the few I knew fairly well, would be best.

Fittingly, we chose "Spoonful."

High on Candy, bolstered by ego and fine backup, I launched that Cream song without hesitation. What I didn't know I faked, and faked it with everything I had. We played for damn near ten minutes, growing sweatier by the second. The crowd danced and a few sang along. By the time I finished, my fingertips were sore and I was tugging breath, but totally exhilarated, especially when raucous applause broke out. I'd never felt so great in my life.

Candy rushed over, gushing, "That was incredible."

Right behind her came Tiff, who took the guitar out of my hands and gave it back to Mick. "Ron would like a word with you inside, if that's okay."

"Well, sure." I was gonna go far, gonna fly. I could feel it.

That was confirmed by Ron. "Come on in. Have a cigar. I'm impressed by your talent, and you've got the look. I'll need another audition or two to sign you on the dotted line, but I don't think that will be a problem, do you?"

"I sure hope not."

"Oh, listen to him, Tiffany. We'll have to do something about that fresh-from-the-Oregon-woods demeanor. I say we show the boy an out-of-this-world time, boost his self-esteem. You up for that, Lennon?"

A better time than I'd already had? "Hell, yeah." I didn't even ask how he knew where I was from.

What followed was something a boy my age could not have made up in his most lust-fueled imagination. It was like walking straight onto the set of an unrated movie, one populated by the beautiful folk.

Girls.

Boys.

Undecideds.

Everyone in various states of undress. Everyone indulging in various substances. Everyone celebrating *la dolce vita*.

Candy.

Molly.

Pearl.

Mercedes.

Tiffany.

I tried valiantly to leave the last two alone. Too hardcore for beginners, that's what Candy said, and watching the old-timers made me believe that was true. With Tiffany, especially, anything went. It was a sex, drugs, and rock 'n' roll orgy. Mick and the band played their instruments, and then played. Ron directed, and the things he asked for opened my eyes to the underground world of the music industry.

I wasn't exactly a virgin, but like my kissing, I hadn't had a whole lot of practice. Luckily, everyone was more than willing to show me the ropes. Figuratively *and* literally. Cocaine enhanced both my courage and performance. It was heady. Surreal.

Girls touching girls.

And boys.

Boys touching boys.

And girls.

We went all night, and well into the morning. By the time I crawled into bed, still buzzed, but spent, I was grateful Pearl had booked the room for an extra night. Caught a few hours of sleep, then it was back to a whole new round of feasting, though I really wasn't all that hungry. Well, not for food.

Night two, I auditioned for Ron again. On guitar. And on the floor. Turned out that was the kind of cigar he'd offered the previous evening. I tried to say no, I'm really not gay, but he insisted on having his way. "I can make or break your career right here." I knew he was right and relented. Luckily, with the smorgasbord of powders and rocks available, I could pretend I was somewhere else, with someone else.

After that, I dove into the scene. I joined the band, signed up with Ron. Problem was, none of them had a clear plan for the future. At least the gigs we played covered our room and board, and I got to do some original songs. Two were deep-track metal—"The Irony of Suicide" and "Shallow Water Drowning." One was a ballad, and when I sang it I closed my eyes, conjuring Sarah's face because she was my "Willamette Angel."

But the hotel's lure was impossible to fight. I stayed for months, an endless cycle of flying and crashing, fed by Candy, Molly, Mercedes, and rock 'n' roll. Finally, though I'd done my best to avoid her, I even tumbled for Tiffany. That one almost broke me.

Tiff was seriously insatiable. She wouldn't let me eat. Wouldn't let me sleep. She was a demanding mistress, and what she wanted was my soul. It wasn't like no one had warned me that even the tiniest taste could very well be the end of Lennon. At first I was happy to give her pieces, a little of me here, a little more of me there. But my brain began to jumble. Sometimes she was Crystal. Always, she was ice. Didn't really matter. I wanted her more than anything. Even my attraction to Candy faded.

Before long, I, too, became Tiffany-twisted.

My skin crawled with need. My brain screamed for more. I might've died right there in Tiff's arms, except for an intervention of fate. See, what I hadn't understood in the beginning was that the party carried a hefty price tag. Eventually I spent every penny I'd brought, and every cent I earned. Then I put what I could on credit, but finally the card maxed out. I wondered if Dad was angry. It was the first time he'd even crossed my mind in a long while.

One night I was sitting cross-legged on the floor, strumming Dora. I was considering selling her, or trading her for another week's stay. After that, all I'd have left was my car, if it was even still there. Was it there? Could I find it in the parking lot? Would it start?

My car.

My guitar.

Highway 395 north.

Home. The green woods of Oregon.

Sarah. Was it too late to apologize?

Becky. Had she missed me yet?

When I got to Dad, I closed my eyes around a mad flood of tears, and I swear my sister's voice came floating up out of the ether. "It isn't so hard to die. You're close already. Just let go."

"Harmony?"

I thought of the last time I saw her, concrete stiff and waxy-skinned in her satin-lined casket. Dead. Deceased. Soon to decay. In a moment of clarity, I knew I wasn't ready to wind up earthworm food.

I jumped to my feet, swaying with my head's sudden change in altitude. I wasn't exactly sure I could drive, but I figured I'd better try. I stuffed everything into the backpack gathering dust under the bed, nestled Dora into her case, and opened the door.

As always, the hallway was dimly lit, and I stumbled on an odd lump in the carpet. When I looked up from my tripping feet, it seemed the corridor had grown longer. I ran its length, searching for the elevator, but could not find an exit. Where was I? Nothing was familiar. And then the lamplights faded to near darkness.

Somewhere, I knew, was a staircase, to be used in case of fire. I felt along the wall until, finally, I located a big metal door. Beyond, it was totally black, but my feet found steps, descending toward the passage I needed. Down. Down. Carefully down. One flight. Two. Three. Finally, by my count, I reached the ground floor.

When I opened that door, the lobby's glare hit my eyes full force, lifting little clouds of sleeplessness to float across my irises. Still, I could see the front desk was unmanned. No Pearl to greet newcomers or arrange for my departure. Night Man was on duty, however.

Close to panic, I yelled, "I need to check out!"

He glanced at me with no real interest. "Relax, dude. You can check out whenever."

"Great. Thanks. I had a good time, but I need to go home now."

I pushed into the revolving door. It kept spinning round and round, and every once in a while I'd catch blurry glimpses of home. Becky, meditating in front of her teepee. Dad, picking mushrooms in the Oregon woods. Sarah, kissing some random guy. With each revolution, I tried damn hard to come down.

Clear my head.

Find my way out.

Remember the boy I used to be.

I don't know how long I was stuck in there, but finally that damn door spit me out into the hotel lobby.

Harry looked up from his newspaper. "Welcome back. Luggage?"

"No! Don't you remember? I told you I want to check out."

"You did, Lennon, you did. And you can do that any time you like. Only problem is, you can never leave."

AUTHOR PHOTO
BY SONYA SONES

Ellen Hopkins is the award-winning author of twenty nonfiction titles, twelve *New York Times* bestselling young adult novels, and three novels for adults. She enjoys mentoring other writers, especially teen writers, and traveling in support of her work and readers. She lives near Carson City, Nevada, with her extended family, two dogs, one cat, and too many aquarium critters. Visit ellenhopkins.com and follow her on Twitter @ellenhopkinslit.

HOW MIRACLES BEGIN

A PERSONAL ESSAY INSPIRED BY JAMES HOWE'S
AND MARK DAVIS'S "PLANTING TREES"

By James Howe

Imagine the story behind a favorite song. "Anthem" by Leonard Cohen was the first that came to mind. But then there were "When I Was a Boy" and "After All" by Dar Williams. And "Easy People" by the Nields. And any number of songs by Mouths of Babes or Over the Rhine or Meg Hutchinson or Janis Ian or John Gorka or Eliza Gilkyson or Sam Baker or...well, it was going to be a problem. There were so many songwriters whose songs I love and whose lyrics speak to me. And then I thought, "Wait! Mark and I write songs. And I won't even have to imagine the story behind them. I know the story behind every song we've written." Right away I knew which song it would be, because every time we sing it I feel in my body how much it means to me and how important it is to share its words with others. This is the story behind that song. It's called "Planting Trees."

—JAMES HOWE

Each day in India
A man walks alone
For forty years he's planted trees
Where none before have grown
With sticks and seeds
He farms gray sand
Now elephants roam a forest
Born from one man's hands

His name is Jadav Payeng. He lives with his family in a small hut on the banks of the Brahmaputra River in Assam, India. I have never been to India. I have never met Jadav Payeng. But he has changed me as surely as he has changed the once barren sandbar of Majuli Island. The miracle he has created in my life is a small one compared to the miracle of a thriving forest rising from sand, but who can measure a miracle or know where it will lead? And while it may be a bit self-aggrandizing to say that writing a song is a miracle, that's how it feels to me each time I sing the words of "Planting Trees."

It was my husband Mark who told me I *had* to watch this KarmaTube video he'd just seen about a man planting trees in a desert. "After you see it, you'll know why *this* is what our next song *has* to be about!" (Italics, even more than Texan, is Mark's native language.)

So how did Mark and I come to write songs and perform together as Old Dogs New Tricks, only half-jokingly referring to ourselves as the World's Oldest Breakout Folk Duo? I will get to it. First, there is more to say about Jadav Payeng and the miracle he brought about on the banks of the Brahmaputra River, nearly eight thousand miles from the banks of the Hudson River in New York state, where Mark and I live and write.

Jadav "Molai" Payeng was only sixteen the summer of 1979, when he saw the bodies of snakes washed up from the flooding river near his home and left to die on the parched sandbar. Because there were no trees to provide cover, the snakes died of dehydration and exposure in the searing heat. In his words, Jadav "sat down and wept over their lifeless forms." And in that moment, it occurred to him that if so many snakes could die in such a way, then one day the human race itself might perish.

Something had to be done. Trees had to be planted. Jadav began with a handful of bamboo seedlings, hoping these hardy plants would take hold in the sandy soil. Thanks to his painstaking efforts, the seedlings grew into a huge bamboo thicket. And then—here's where the word "miracle" comes into play—so did the wide variety of trees Jadav began to plant despite the naysaying and derision of his elders. As we say in the song, "with sticks and seeds he farmed gray sand." The trees grew and they grew and they grew until they became a forest, each from a single seed planted, watered, pruned, and cultivated by a solitary man who walked into a desert each morning and, in time, over the course of nearly forty years, returned from a lush, green forest each night.

Jadav Payeng has earned the title "The Forest Man of India." His self-made forest of 1,360 acres is now called the "Molai Sanctuary," after his nickname of Molai. It is home to more than a hundred elephants who spend three months of their migratory year there, as well as other animals—birds and Bengal tigers, rhino and deer, and, yes, snakes—who live there year-round. He has received honors and acclaim, yet he still goes into the forest each day, still lives in the same small hut with his wife and three children, still makes his living raising cattle and selling milk. He has not been transformed by the attention he has received as much as he has trans-formed his corner of the world and, *because* of the attention he has received, has made many people think about environ-mental issues in a new and personal light.

And he has made many—myself included—think about the ways one can, in the words of Mahatma Gandhi, "be the change you wish to see in the world."

"I worry about the fate of the world, just like everyone," he has said. "I see bad things happening on my island and I do what I can to help. I'm just a simple man. There are many just like me."

It is debatable that there are many just like Jadav Molai Payeng. Many of us think about how we wish the world were different, but do little to make it happen. Most of Jadav's friends have left Majuli Island for professional careers and comfortable lives in nice homes and city apartments. Jadav remains, doing his solitary work and changing the world one tree at a time.

"The forest," he says, "is my sole life achievement. Today I am the happiest man in the world."

"Look how contented this man is with his life," Mark said as we talked about the video we'd both now seen. "Every day he leaves his small hut, walks out into the desert, and digs with a stick in the sand to plant another tree. Every day. This is what he loves doing. And he's turned a desert into a forest. How do we make this into a song?"

And where do we begin?

In thinking about our new song, the word "miracle" didn't occur to us for some time, although it seemed it would take one for us to write a song at all. We'd written only one song, and we'd done that under pressure in order to qualify for a five-day songwriting retreat being offered in the summer of 2014 by Dar Williams, our favorite singer-songwriter. And by "favorite" I mean of nearly heroic proportions.

Dar Williams, who has been writing and performing her songs for nearly thirty years, is considered one of America's finest singer-songwriters. Her fans are legion, and they are passionate. Many can cite a particular song that has changed their lives. For me, it is "When I Was a Boy," the first song of hers I had ever heard. For Mark, it's "The Christians and the Pagans." And for my daughter Zoey, it is "After All," a song she first encountered when it was taught as poetry in her high school English class. I think it is fair to say that "After All" has been a life-changer for many.

When Mark and I met in 2001, we discovered we had many things in common, with our love of music high on the list. We didn't always love the *same* music, although we did have a number of musicians in common, and Dar Williams was one of them. For years now we've listened to music together at home and in the car, and have gone to folk festivals, coffee houses, church basements, theaters, and concert halls to hear live music every chance we could. Living in the Hudson Valley north of New York City, we are blessed with abundant opportunities to see and hear our favorite musicians and discover new musicians who become favorites. More than once, we had the chance to see the legendary Pete Seeger and hear him exhort the crowd to "sing out!" because he believed that singing together was a way of making community, bridging differences, and bringing hope to the world.

We took Pete seriously. We began singing folk songs together, old favorites like "If I Had a Hammer" (a Pete Seeger song), Bob Dylan's "Blowin' in the Wind," and "When We're Gone Long Gone." We invited friends to our home for sing-alongs, or "hootenannies," as they were called back in the day. Having quite a number of friends who are talented musicians, we've had as varied a backup band as several guitars, banjo, piano, flute, a violin or two, and whatever forms of percussive instruments were at hand. To which I've recently added the cello, an instrument I studied briefly in the seventh grade and took up again—half a century later!

By the time Mark and I got married in Vermont in 2011, it only made sense that we had live music, including a square dance band, and ended the evening leading a rousing hootenanny.

But we weren't writing songs. It wasn't until a few years later, after we had started adding covers of current favorite songs to our repertoire and begun working with a voice and guitar coach, that we thought about performing. Once we thought about performing, we began to ask, "Shouldn't we be writing songs of our own?"

So there we were in the summer of 2014 at Dar Williams's

songwriting retreat, feeling a bit like a couple of frauds, with just one finished song and fragments of a first verse of a second song as all we had to show for ourselves as writers. Okay, fine, I had been writing books for children and teens for almost forty years, but I'm talking about songwriting, and that's a totally different thing. And Mark—lawyer by day, guitar-playing songster by night—had mostly written legal briefs. It took *chutzpah* to be there. Or maybe what it took was a belief in the words we were beginning to formulate as we considered the chorus for our song. If we just embraced what we loved, did each day the thing that we loved, it would give birth to…something. We just had to have faith in that process, not knowing in advance what the "something" would be. But isn't that true of all creative endeavors? You could say it's true of life.

We started with the first verse. Knowing Jadav's story and how we felt about it, it didn't take us long to figure out the words we wanted, even if it was a new kind of challenge for both of us to know how to combine those words with the music that was just taking shape in our heads. Though Mark was more the musician, we worked out the music together, just as we did the words.

It wasn't long before we decided that Jadav's story would be one of two or three stories we would use as the verses. The chorus still hadn't come together yet, but we knew that it would hold the theme of the song, the "message" that tied the stories together.

There's a man n' India
Each day for 40 years
He's walked into the ~~gray~~ desert alone
And planted a tree in the gray
                                    sand
Now a forest grows from his hand
A haven ~~o~~ that   alone
   Elephants + tigers call home.

There's a man in ~~India~~
He walks into the desert alone
Each day

Each day ~~for~~ 40 years
A man ~~his~~ walks alone
Into the desert

Each day for 40 years a man walks
Planting trees   alone

Each day for forty years
A man walks alo~~ne~~

* Each day in India
~~A man walks alone~~
~~For forty years~~ he's planted trees
where ~~none~~ before have grown

7

From

Sand
Stands
(hands)
↓
end rhyme
" from ~
his hands "

③ now
Elephants drink [from pools of blue] gray sand
~~that once~~
→   gray sand(s)   - line 2
                              _)

④ A forest born   One man's hands   - line 4
       from

---

with sticks + seeds
he farms gray sand in a forest born
~~now elephants roam~~
~~a Born~~ from one man's hands.

In trying to come up with a second verse, we considered making up a story of a gardener, but quickly realized that planting a garden was too much like planting trees. Then, perhaps because we were thinking about gardens, we remembered an amazing place we had visited the year before in Philadelphia. It was called Philadelphia's Magic Gardens, and it truly was magical. Awed by the dreamlike strangeness and beauty of the broken tile and ceramic mosaics covering every surface of the building and adjacent terrace, we wondered who could have created such a place. What we discovered led us to another story of one man's doing each day the thing that he loves and making miracles in the process.

Each day in Philadelphia
A man takes broken glass
Making art of what he finds
To heal his broken past
Now people come
To walk within his dream
And know in their hearts
The man who was redeemed

It was 1968 when artist Isaiah Zagar returned with his wife Julia from a three-year stint in the Peace Corps in Peru. Feeling lost and struggling to adjust to life back on U.S. soil, Isaiah suffered a mental breakdown that led him to a suicide attempt and commitment to a psychiatric institution where he lived for five months. It was there, polishing brass and cleaning mirrors, that he saw, in his words, "the art project that was to become my sustenance for the rest of my life."

Shortly after he left the hospital, he put aside his dream of becoming a great American painter and turned to mosaic as his medium. Using mirrors and handmade tiles, colorful glass bottles, folk art, and found objects—bicycle wheels and dishes and pots—he covered an entire building, inside and out, with mosaics that sprang not just from his imagination but from the stories of his life and family.

Doing this creative work, day in and day out, helped him get better. He continued making mosaics and more mosaics and still more mosaics. In the words of his wife Julia, it was "as though he had found his life."

Like Jadav Payeng's seeds, each piece of glass or tile or mirror was put carefully in place by one man's hands. These fragments would not grow into trees that would one day be a forest inhabited by wild creatures. But they would evolve into something wild in its own right. Untamed, primal images transformed whole sections of a city into works of art to dazzle the eye and confound and amuse the mind. And because there was so much of the artist evident in the art, the heart was touched as well. Worlds apart, forest and mosaic works of art stand as testament to what passion, imagination, and hard work can do.

Isaiah Zagar continues making his mosaics every day. He calls his murals "poems" and refers to the process of making public art that will be seen by others as "a sharing of dreams." I came across that quote long after Mark and I wrote the line, "Now people come / to walk within his dream," not knowing that this was Isaiah's way of envisioning his work as well. It made me think that all art is a shared dream. Isaiah cannot tell you why he makes his murals, only that he *must*. It is what he loves to do, day after day; it is the dream he feels compelled to share.

Dar Williams's songwriting retreat was five days long. After breakfast each morning, she gave us three writing prompts for the day. One was a visual prompt; another was verbal; the last was musical. The verbal prompt given on the day Mark and I were working on the final verse of "Planting Trees" was this:

She draws a crown on me.

We had no idea what to do with it, but we wanted to try to fit it, or a variation of it, into our song. But first we needed to know what the story of our final verse would be. It had to be about a woman, we decided, since our two real-life stories were about men. But we couldn't come up with just the right real woman's story, and then we thought about the story of many real women (and men) we know: the story of teachers, and how hard so many devoted teachers work each day, doing what they love but rarely knowing what minor—or major—miracles they may be creating in

(G)
1 Each day in Philadelpia (Am)
2 A man takes broken (B-) glass (C)
3 Making art (G) of what he finds (Am)
4 To heals his broken past (Call 9)

from
shards
1 With tiles and time (Em) ART
2 He builds a * of dream (beauty)
3 Touching peoples lives → (B-)
4 from One mans pain (G-)

heart

And the passion
in his heart

He makes a world of art

Where people Come - touched
By the beauty of his
art

* Sacred Space
church / temple
cathedral
museum

With tiles and time
And shards shame
He builds a world of beauty — drawn
from his own pain.

With tiles and time
And the passion in his heart
He builds a house of dreams — filled
With the beauty of his art.

~~(CHORUS)~~ VERSE 2

    G   Am
Each day in Indiana
    Bm   C
A woman tries to reach
 G
A child locked in ~~side~~ his head
          Am
By the limits of his speech
        Bm   Cadd9
 C
When ~~at last~~ a sentence comes
             Em
    Am
Each word the ~~boy~~ has said
                   C
   Am   Bm(⁷)
Is like a jewel in a ~~golden~~ crown
          on   G
// Placed ~~upon~~ her head

the individual lives they touch. The image of a crown being drawn—or placed—on a teacher's head became a metaphor for the deep satisfaction one must feel when being given a glimpse of the miracle that may have just occurred in a breakthrough moment with a child.

Each day in Indiana
A woman tries to reach
A child locked in his head
By the limits of his speech
When a sentence comes
Every word he says
Is like a jewel in a crown
Placed on her head

We had our final verse, but decided to make it the middle verse of the song, if for no other reason than to balance out the gender references.

I don't remember at what point the chorus came together. It was probably somewhere between writing the first and second verse, or the second and third. It was important to us to find the words to the chorus fairly early on, because they would tell us what the song was about. Dar calls this the "aha" moment, the moment in writing when suddenly a word or words make it clear to you *why* you're writing this particular song. I think of it when I write songs or stories as the moment of *connection*.

You don't have to be a Mother Teresa
You don't have to die for anyone's sins
Just embrace what you love
Do each day the thing that you love
That's how miracles begin

It took us a while to settle on pronouns, ultimately agreeing that "you" made the most direct connection with the listener. This was a song that was not only about the people we were singing about, but the people we were singing *to*. We were saying to the listener: You don't have to be Mother Teresa or Jesus to make a miracle happen. Just be yourself. Do what you love. Begin.

We completed the song after the retreat was over, but the first time we sang it—or what we had of it at that point—was to Dar Williams in a one-on-one critique session. Singing these words to someone who had meant so much to us over so many years was an extraordinary moment. Dar's intent listening and generous feedback made us feel that we, beginners that we still were (and are), really were songwriters. And she put a crown on *our* heads by saying that the word "miracle"—oddly, the word we had debated as possibly clichéd or not exactly what we meant—was the payoff of the whole song: "That's what it's all about!"

Aha!

We've written more songs since and have performed them along with covers of other people's songs that we love,

1 - Verse - Story - Man in India

2 - " " - teacher - child puts a
paper crown
on her

3 - Chorus that's
the only
crown
she needs

4 - Verse - personal story?

5 Chorus ↓

6 bridge ? include a
breakthrough

7 Chorus moment

"Each day
in Indiana..."

final "when"

- Each day
inside my
head

CHORUS   We don't
~~She didn't~~
~~You don't~~ have to be mother Teresa
      ~~We don't~~   We don't
C ~~You don't have to die for anyone's sins~~
You can just ~~embrace~~ what ~~it is~~ you love
              the thing
Do each day ~~the thing~~ that you love
That's ~~when~~ how miracles begin

        G
We don't have to be mother Teresa^D
    G
We don't have to die for anyone's sins^D
Am   C
Just embrace what you love
Am   C
Do each day the thing that you love
Am   D   G
That's how miracles begin

but it is this song that I feel most compelled to sing. It is this song that embodies for me the very thing we are writing about: doing each day the thing that we love and believing in the power of that.

When Mark and I sing "Planting Trees," I don't know the effect it will have on those who are listening. When I write my words, I don't know who will read them or what they might take from them. Perhaps you, reading these words, will think about what it is that you love, will decide that each day you need to do the thing that you love, will do something that will become a miracle for someone else. None of us knows where our passions will lead us and what miracles they might create.

Isaiah was asked why he put so many mirrors in his work. He said it is to remind each passing observer: "Yes, it's YOU. YOU'RE here. YOUR dreams matter too."

You don't have to be Isaiah Zagar. You don't have to be Jadav Payeng. You don't have to teach a child or plant a tree or make art or write a song. Just embrace what YOU love. Do each day the thing that YOU love.

That's it. Really. That's how miracles begin.

PLANTING TREES

© 2014 JAMES HOWE & MARK DAVIS / OLD DOGS NEW TRICKS

Each day in India
A man walks alone

For forty years he's planted trees
Where none before have grown
With sticks and seeds
He farms gray sand
Now elephants roam a forest
Born from one man's hands

Each day in Indiana
A woman tries to reach
A child locked in his head
By the limits of his speech
When a sentence comes
Every word he says
Is like a jewel in a crown
Placed on her head

You don't have to be a Mother Teresa
You don't have to die for anyone's sins
Just embrace what you love
Do each day the thing that you love
That's how miracles begin

Each day in Philadelphia
A man takes broken glass
Making art of what he finds
To heal his broken past
Now people come

To walk within his dream
And know in their hearts
The man who was redeemed

You don't have to be a Mother Teresa
You don't have to die for anyone's sins
Just embrace what you love
Do each day the thing that you love
That's how miracles begin

To hear "Planting Trees" and to learn more about Old Dogs New Tricks, Jadav Payeng, KarmaTube, Isaiah Zagar, Philadelphia's Magic Gardens, and Dar Williams, visit jameshowe.com.

JAMES HOWE (LEFT) AND MARK DAVIS
PHOTO © PAUL HARRIS

James Howe is the award-winning and bestselling author of more than ninety books for young readers, including the popular *Bunnicula* and *Pinky and Rex* series. He writes for a wide range of ages, from picture books to young adult fiction. His novel *The Misfits* inspired national No Name-Calling Week (nonamecallingweek.org). James lives in New York state with his husband, Mark Davis, with whom he collaborates on writing and performing music as Old Dogs New Tricks. Visit the author at jameshowe.com.

THE OPPOSITE OF ORDINARY

A PERSONAL ESSAY INSPIRED BY LEONARD BERNSTEIN'S AND STEPHEN SONDHEIM'S "SOMEWHERE (THERE'S A PLACE FOR US)"

By Beth Kephart

When the beautiful Kate Walton included me in this lovely series, there was only ever one choice. I skated as a kid, and skating shaped so much about how I see the world and how I hear language. This particular song from *West Side Story* defines my childhood. It is my origin story.

—BETH KEPHART

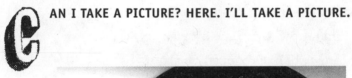 AN I TAKE A PICTURE? HERE. I'LL TAKE A PICTURE.

See? Robinson Recording Laboratories. 1015 Chestnut Street. Philadelphia, PA. 33.3 RPM. It's all right there. It's hidden in the grooves. The soundtrack to my art of yearning.

We need a platter and a spindle and a needle. We need an ice-skating rink and a temperature like snow. We need my mother and father in the ice-rink stands and me in the shimmer of a turquoise costume with a bib of white pearls, hovering over newly sharpened blades. We need the blinding glare of overhead fluorescents, rouge high on the cheeks of pretty girls, spectacles low on the noses of the judges who are dressed in down and fur, and one singular coach.

We need, I guess, a lot of things. Don't put that needle down.

We'll wait until I learn to skate on a frozen pond in Boston during a year of temporary exile from our Wilmington, Delaware, home. My father was getting a new degree from MIT. My mother and the rest of us were fighting the meringue of towering snow. One day, a diversion, we were driven to a sun-stunned pond. I strapped on skates. I soared.

I thought I soared.

I wore a thick Ace bandage on my wrist, thanks to the calamitous accident of the summer before—a snap on the chain of a swing I'd pumped high, a long flight through the air, a shattering against the ground. I wore the bulk of winter things. I noticed the twigs and the bugs and the gashes in the ice, the general direction of the accomplished, the far-off edge where no one was, and that's where I went. To the edge of no one. For the rest of that winter I, the righteous eight-year-old, claimed the no-one edge. I let skating and its rhythms fill the hollows of my bones.

It was all I needed.

When we returned to Wilmington, I haunted the public sessions of Sunday afternoons at the real rink down the road. I went around on the fringes in the counterclockwise with the crowds, and then, when the loudspeaker man interrupted the carousel music to say that it was time to change direction, I changed my direction.

I missed the no-one edge.

One day, when I was listening to the music in my bones and not that carousel sound, when I was speeding up and slowing down to express the song of me, when I was throwing myself toward myself and growing dizzy with the blur, the hometown skating queen left her perch up in the rink's balcony, where she'd been waiting for the public to go home. I'd seen her up there. Maybe we'd all seen her up there. With that celebrity gleam and those deer-sized eyes and that slick of black hair and that infinite slenderness and grace. I'd seen her up there, alone, and then I saw her stand and head toward the stairs, then disappear, and then there she was, rink level, with her white skates on, her leg warmers, her skating jacket, stepping out onto the ice. Glissading toward me. Asking (you couldn't forget it), *Did I want to learn?*

The stutter of surprise. The *Yes, I want to learn.*

She was sixteen to my ten. She took my one good hand and led me to the rink's now-emptying center. (Step aside, awe says.) She showcased the jumps she thought I might learn. She leapt from her right foot and landed on her left, the opposite of ordinary in a sport of left-to-righters. This way, this way, this way, her movements said—almost soundless, pure heraldic—and now it was my turn. Waltz jump. Toe-loop. Something in between. I did what she did, a minor version, in my thick pants and my thick coat, my arm wrapped up like a mummy.

No one but the two of us, and my heart up in my throat.

She tilted her head to one side. She showed me again what she had meant about the bend in the knee and the arrangement of shoulders and the placement of the blade on the ice. Bend. Up. Down. Glide. Arms out for balance. I tried again. She taught again. Finally she vaguely nodded. Pushed back and back and left me to it—on the edge of no one, in the opposite of ordinary.

I'm not sure we ever spoke again. I rather doubt we did. But I'd been baptized—a right-foot-to-left skater. I'd been instructed by the queen. I would forever be persuaded by her unconventional moves. I'd jump her way. Spin her way. Cut my footwork in her corners. She was different and she'd seen my difference and she'd said different was okay.

The song played even louder in my bones.

Looking back on it now, I don't know how my parents could afford the serial events of afterwards. How the public sessions became group lessons became private appointments with coaches. How the nature of my obsession and its increasing demands were perpetually managed. My parents were not rich, and each one of us was busy, but I was given this. I was acknowledged for what I was becoming. This girl who zoomed and jumped and spun on the edge and in the wrong direction. This girl with a body made of song.

My mother found a Butterick pattern and Singer-adapted it with genius, so that I might have clothes to wear to that rink of left-foot-to-right-foot skaters. She cut dresses out of flannel, put buttons on the sleeves, ran a rickrack braid in flying Vs where all the other girls wore sequins. She sat in the bleachers and watched, and my dad came, too, when he could, and they bought me real skates, and paid for the blades to be sharpened, and waited for me because I was always late, because my favorite time on the ice was when the Zamboni appeared and the rest of the skaters vanished.

Just one more jump, please.

Just one more jump. In the wrong direction. By myself.

When I was thirteen, my family moved to Pennsylvania to be nearer to my father's job, but I wouldn't leave the skating behind. With resources they never complained about expending, my parents fit me in to a brand-new rink, the Philadelphia Skating and Humane Society. The ice emitted fog in the early hours. Windows let in the early sun. The cold was trapped by a parabolic roof. There were no barricades. The ice had a smell. The coffee shop sold hot chocolate. There were photographs of the Schuylkill River, where this skating club had first been born as a search-and-rescue operation.

Skating as a search, and as a rescue.

A frozen river.

Predawn and after school, I was there. On the weekends,

in my rickrack dresses. In the locker rooms, on the ice, skating toward and away from me, leaping into chasms. More and more, I was the opposite of ordinary at a time when ordinary has its privileges, when ordinary is the ticket in, when cool is everything that I wasn't—this girl with the homemade style and the fluffy hair and the left hand wrapped like a mummy and the father who dropped her off at school after an early-morning bliss of ice and the song that only she could hear inside her bones. This girl who felt most safe on the edge of no one, and who mostly lived at that address.

You know how it is: Time goes by. We are zigged and zagged by our own limits. The double lutz is landed but the double axel eludes us. The camel spin bobbles instead of whirls. The layback makes us dizzy. We work harder, we skate fiercer, we leap higher, we circle and circle with our opposite way of doing things, and finally, we want the music we feel inside of us to be the music that transcends us, the music that emerges, with us.

For us?

I was sixteen. There was a competition looming. One day at the rink, my coach showed up with songs. Three separate pieces she'd thought to weave together as one—a competition medley. Listen, she said, and as I stood there by the machine on that quiet afternoon, as the sun floated white through the rink's square windows, "Somewhere (There's a Place for Us)" from *West Side Story* began to play. "Somewhere" sung by the instruments alone.

It was as if everything that had been thrumming within my bones since my blades first sliced a frozen Boston pond had been unstoppered. It was as if the parabolic air of the Philadelphia Skating and Humane Society was fogging up with the interior of me. "Somewhere" is a yearning song born of a *Romeo and Juliet* ache remade as the tale of two New York City gangs—and cruelly separated lovers. It's a *place for us* song. A lyric that makes displacement visible and gives hope hope. It's music that takes you right out there, to the edge of yourself, and it hurts so very much, and the hurt is the most beautiful hurt you've ever felt. The hurt is you.

It was my song now. "Somewhere."

Now put that needle down.

Now play that record cut at the Robinson Laboratories in Philadelphia that has been protected, for decades now, by an oversized plastic sleeve. Put the needle down and see me as I am, standing on my mark, an awkward sweet sixteen, my parents in the bleachers—somewhere, out there. I wear a turquoise dress and a bib of pearls and an Ace bandage tucked inside one sleeve. I wear thick, flesh-colored tights, one knee already dark from a warm-up fall. I am the song and I am about to be revealed and I am frantic with nerves, clotted, shivery, and the ice seems suddenly and altogether much too fresh and my blades are either too sharp or too dull and it is possible that I'll forget to breathe.

Put that needle down and let me breathe.

I don't remember all of it, but I remember this: I started late. The opening melody began and I stayed stuck and then, jolted, I unfroze. I was a beat behind and another beat behind, but I got myself back on track—gathering speed on a curve of backward crossovers, landing my axel, singling a double flip, scratching out a toe-pick landing. I was skating, but I was skating terrified, until, at last, the Mexican music stopped and "Somewhere" began, and the struggle was done. I became *utter,* if you can please know what I mean.

I mean: I was the Ina Bauer who sliced the rink's long diagonal. I was the height of a second axel, this one up and up and up, delayed. I was the smooth landing edge of my double lutz. I was my own cutting speed. There is a place for us, there is a place for me, and in that moment my place wasn't on the edge, but out there, under the lights, with a dress a seamstress had made especially for me and pearls in the place of rickrack. My place was there, beneath the bright fluorescents, with my mother and my father in the stands. My place was there, with my coach standing tall like she hoped I would keep standing tall. *Keep standing tall. You've got this.*

My song.

My moment.

"Somewhere."

So much yearning, and that needle in that groove. Oh. Let it play.

Until the song ends, and the program, too. Until I plow myself into a stop and curtsy to the crowd, curtsy to my parents, curtsy to my fans, wherever they are. I leave the ice and I hug my coach, I slip my skate guards on, wobble away. Later, when the scores are posted, we learn that my music had played a few over-regulation seconds too long. My "Somewhere" was excessive; deductions were required. My first place became a different place. I had, according to the rules, extended my welcome.

I would never skate competitively again. I would join the high school cross-country team and then the winter track team and then the spring track team, and when next my parents looked down upon me from the stands, I would be covered with mud and tattered by errant cleats and wearing the maroon of Radnor High. It would seem to them—and, for a while, it would seem to me—that I had left my skating self behind.

But the girl with the bones hollowed out by song is still right here. She's never stopped jumping right-to-left in a left-to-right world. She has perpetually stood on the edge of things and only rarely, and for but brief moments, and with inevitable deductions, found her way in. She has sought the opposite of ordinary in the people she has loved, the friends she has made, the stories she has told, the way she's told her stories.

She is still out there on the ice, bending her knee and leaping, and sometimes when she lands, the page she finds looking out at her is the ice itself, a frozen river, speaking. Which is what happens here, in a book called *Flow: The Life and Times of Philadelphia's Schuylkill River*. Imagining a boy and the ice in another century.

> He'll slide, and I'll hold. He'll carry on, west, and
> the boys on the east bank will begin their hollering
> back at him, "The ice won't hold," but he'll say,
> "I'm going forward." Announce it, the announce
> it loud, without turning, for it takes something to
> keep your jaunty up, and only I ever know for cer-
> tain how solid as stone and slick I am. How wide
> he might go, how far he might fall, how thorough

I am with the cold. There will be leaves trapped on my surface, colors of fall. There will be twigs and the wings of a bug. An iced-in mitten and the turned-out pages of a book and the leaking orange of a dulled-by-winter sun. His jaunty full upon him now. His walk tripping into a run, and he'll leap and land, his blades still on his shoulder, and I'll be solid. "Ice is for taking," he turn this time and call, and the others will holler again from the edge. Strap on their skates and razor in.

Imagine taking a needle to the point of blood on your palm. Imagine drawing that needle around and around, leaning in on it, forcing an edge, tearing at the creases and the lifelines, the ridges and slightest hills that forecast your happiness. Imagine the skin giving way.

That's skating.

Or sometimes, revisiting her young self with the hope of speaking to the right now of young selves, the girl with the bones hollowed out by song summons a frozen pond at night and a girl on that pond, a girl who is alone, a girl whom others have seen (and almost always treated) as merely useful, a girl who longs to be seen—at last, for once—as beautiful. Who wonders: Is anybody out there?

From the quasi-autobiographical young adult novel, *Undercover*:

It is a fabulous thing, skating at night. I can think of a song, and the song will turn itself on, and it is the only thing that matters for a while. I can lift up my arms and my soul drifts. I can bend and my knees will be percussion. I can twizzle and my hips will be a mash of the divine. Maybe I'm beautiful when I'm skating at night. Maybe I'm the queen of the stars.

That night I rode a Bauer down the center of the pond. I put a spiral on an edge, then lunged. I did a waltz jump and another waltz jump, until I had gravity in my pocket. I skated for what felt like hours, then sat for a while on the dock. Out in the woods I could hear the crunching of sticks beneath the feet of squirrels, the hooting of an owl, the wind. If there were deer between the trees, they hid in the shadows. If there were raccoons, they were one hundred percent stealth. I didn't know where the ravens had gone. I imagined them clumped up in trees.

Or sometimes the ice becomes that place where a mystery is passed, one to another. Where someone on the edge is noticed and reached toward and told a little secret. Where the past becomes the future, where frustration becomes hope.

From the Philadelphia Centennial novel, *Dangerous Neighbors*, a scene on the frozen Schuylkill of 1876, a lesson in learning to spin:

The skater is coming toward Katherine, arms outstretched. "It isn't that hard," she says, "once you get the knack of it."

She takes Katherine's hands into her hands. Her grip is strong. She strokes toward an empty place, and Katherine glides beside her. "I'm Katherine, by the way," she says.

"Oh," the skater laughs. "I'm Elizabeth. But most people call me Lizzy."

It's a good name, Katherine decides at once. She breathes and it doesn't hurt as much. She swallows, and she's still alive.

"Think of stretching your arms around a huge patch of sky," Lizzy begins. "And then of pulling the sky in hard, against your heart." Lizzy takes several quick strokes in a straight line, does something with one foot, holds out her arms. "Like this," she shouts. "Like this. You see?" Her coat kicking up, her summer skirt whirling.

It turns out not to be so very hard. Speed, power, balance, the sky pulled toward the heart—she'd never be able to explain it to another, but it works somehow, an alchemical mix that blurs Katherine's edges and gives her a fizzing, fuzzed-out feeling.

Because the writer I became, the writer I'm still becoming,

remains bound up with the music in my bones, remains instructed by the edges, remains grateful for my early instruction in the opposite of ordinary. The writer I am is forever reaching for that long-ago but not lost moment when the song inside me was also the song that others heard. When what I felt and how I was seen were the one same powerful thing.

There's a place for us.

There's a place for me.

Somewhere.

Yes. It's all I've needed.

AUTHOR PHOTO BY
WILLIAM SULIT

If **Beth Kephart** could be a song, she would be a song. Not an instrument, not a singer, but the song itself. Instead she is a writer of books, some might say too many books. Memoirs and young adult novels and middle grade novels and corporate fables and a book about teaching memoir writing, even an autobiography of a river. She's still trying to get the writing thing right. Meanwhile, she's having a lot of fun teaching what she finally does know at the University of Pennsylvania and at Juncture Workshops: junctureworkshops.com. More about Beth can be found at beth-kephart.blogspot.com.

ABOUT YOU NOW

A SHORT STORY INSPIRED BY
OASIS'S "WONDERWALL"

By Elisa Ludwig

I chose to write about "Wonderwall" by Oasis because it's a timeless pop song that, to me, really captures the essence of longing and the secret, exclusive kind of love you have when you're just learning what love is. Also in there, and (hopefully) in the story I wrote, are Big Human Experience themes like the frustration of not being able to express yourself, the fear of not knowing what your future holds, and the tender hope that there's one person out there who really gets you.

—ELISA LUDWIG

CORINNE HAPPENED TO BE THINKING ABOUT SADIE RIGHT at the moment her phone rang. This was not at all unusual. Sadie's lilting way of talking, her scratchy laugh, her random and vehement opinions had tunneled into Corinne's brain to the point where sometimes she no longer heard her own voice in her head.

"Hey Coo-Coo. Whatcha doing?"

Corinne felt her breath quicken. She looked across the kitchen to where her mom was packing up boxes of mugs, crumpled newsprint paper lying in puffs around her. "Oh, just helping get the kitchen ready. We're painting tomorrow." She'd cupped her hand over the phone, she realized, but there was no hiding who was calling.

"That's so *handy* of you," Sadie drawled. Her compliments always sounded like teasing. "House makeover?"

"We do a room every year," Corinne said. "My mom likes to keep it fresh."

As she was talking, she heard her mother sighing extra loudly. Maybe she didn't want Corinne telling Sadie about her paint obsession. Or maybe she was annoyed that Corinne was wasting time talking when she should be helping. Or maybe, probably, it was because it was Sadie on the phone.

"Dude, you should get paid for that. It's child labor."

"Believe me, I've tried," Corinne said.

"Well, if you can tear yourself away, there's a party tonight in Chestnut Hill. Galloway Prep kids...should be totally amazing in an ironic and depressing way."

"That's a good thing?" Corinne asked. Most days she was game for Sadie's plans, because her own plans usually involved watching stand-up comedy specials with her parents. Maybe this party would be better, she thought. If Sadie would be there, it might be. Besides, she didn't know how to object, not with her mom standing right there. If she'd even said the word *party* out loud, her mom would freak out.

"Oh yeah. I need you to be there with me to witness the wackiness. I'll swing by at five. We can get dressed before we head over."

Corinne would have been more worried about what she'd just agreed to if she wasn't so distracted by her mom watching her closely now. She was spinning a masking tape roll around on her finger, and she had a bursting look on her face, like she was waiting for Corinne to say something.

Corinne couldn't ignore her, not when she was looming like that. "Hey, can you, like, watch the lawn tonight?" Corinne asked.

"Oh, that was a muscle spasm. I won't hit the lights again," Sadie said.

Corinne pressed the off button on her phone. "Sadie's coming over later," she informed her mom.

"Newsflash," her mom said, getting back to work. "When *isn't* she coming over? Let's hope she doesn't bash our garage door this time. The neighbors already think we're trashy as it is."

Her mom cared way too much about public opinion. She couldn't even choose paint colors without consulting seven different celebrity magazines. "It wasn't her fault. It was dark. She couldn't see."

"Maybe she wasn't looking. And why haven't her parents offered to pay for the damage at least?"

They both knew the answer to that question. Her parents didn't know where Sadie was most of the time. Her parents probably didn't know Corinne's name, let alone that she used to have driveway lights.

Corinne's mom blew the air out of her nose now, which was an improvement over the complaining, a sign of self-control. "I suppose she's staying over?"

Corinne nodded.

"Next thing she'll want a key. But would be nice if you mixed it up once in a while. Hung out with someone a little more...wholesome." She thought people should be like breakfast cereal.

"Because my phone's ringing off the hook," Corinne shot back. Everyone in her school thought she was crazy, after the incident last year. "I don't know if you noticed, but I'm not in big demand."

Her mom looked away, finally. "You need to let go of that."

Easy for her to say. Why was it so weird that Sadie came over every week? They were best friends. They lived in different suburbs, and that was what made it special. Corinne knew they'd really chosen each other—it wasn't a friendship based on convenience or cafeteria seat arrangements.

They'd met at a summer theater program at University of the Arts in the city. It was Sadie who sought Corinne out, that one day when she followed her onto the Broad Street sidewalk where Corinne usually waited for her mom to pick her up when the session ended.

"I love your shoes," Sadie said. "I think you are going to be so awesome as CB's Sister."

Their performance of *Dog Sees God* would be the first time Corinne had ever really been on stage and she was trying not to freak out about it, because even the mere thought of standing under lights dressed up like a goth chick made her immediately start breaking out into a prickly sweat.

"Yeah?" And Corinne was actually sweating now, her

heart beating fast. She didn't trust herself around people. Not anymore. And the way Sadie was just acting like they were already friends was disconcerting.

"You just have that spark, you know?"

Corinne almost laughed in her face. The theater program had been her mother's idea; she thought it might help Corinne build confidence and channel her anxiety. Corinne hadn't been particularly excited about drama, but the idea of going to the city every day, of getting out of her little suburb where everyone knew about last year, was enough to convince her.

The girl was still standing in front of her, waiting for her to say more, and Corinne was drawing a blank. She felt like she had to acknowledge the compliments somehow, but she didn't know the right way to do that without sounding like a fake. So she just smiled.

"You're Corinne, right?"

Corinne nodded. She already knew Sadie's name, too, because there were only twenty-six kids in the program, but up until that point she hadn't really looked at her closely.

"You're playing Tricia," Corinne said. It was a smaller part, a mean girl who sleeps with her friend's boyfriend.

"Yep. She's kind of badass, don't you think?"

"Yeah, but I wouldn't want to know her in real life," Corinne said.

"No, probably not. I know plenty of girls like that. I don't take their shit."

Now with Sadie's face right in front of hers, Corinne

noticed she had a brown shag cut with a streak of pink that had to have been bleached first—Corinne knew, because she'd tried a similar thing once, with disastrous results. Sadie had intent green-gray eyes and a striped skater hoodie and a smile playing at the corner of her lips like she was about to dare Corinne to do something wild. Corinne was flattered by the attention, and a little scared of her.

The next day Sadie called Corinne over to where she was sitting in the auditorium while their teacher worked on the blocking for one of the early scenes. Then they'd started texting each other during the boring stretches in between rehearsals, Sadie sharing her random theories about the world.

Like:

S. There are only 35 people in the world. Different people, I mean.

C. Why 35?

S. I don't know. That's all I've counted.

C. What about the rest?

S. Combinations. Mixing and matching. Don't you ever notice that? Everyone is so much the same.

C. Who am I?

S. Oh, you're one of the originals, of course. As am I.

Or:

S. Love is a shared delusion. It's not a real thing.

C. That's cynical.

S. I like kissing.

C. But you don't think people really fall in love,
   like, ever?

S. I think they agree to jointly believe it. BTW, three
   o'clock is totally checking you out. And he's so hot.

Corinne looked up then and saw that John, a lanky guy with a man-bun, was scratching his butt. He wasn't hot. And he definitely wasn't checking her out. She was only slightly less invisible at drama camp, and that was thanks to Sadie.

"Made you look," Sadie mouthed, and they both cracked up.

That was five months ago. The play went okay except for the one line Corinne flubbed in the third scene, but she knew she'd never have gotten through it without feeling Sadie behind her, cheering her on. Summer ended and they were into fall and then winter, and by now it was a given, the two of them.

Corinne had friends at school still, but no one asked her to hang out on weekends. There was no one who chose her, no one who *belonged* to her, no one who seemed to get her like Sadie did. And certainly no one who seemed more interesting every time she hung out with them. Sadie was like a shiny secret charm Corinne had found by accident and carried in her pocket. Because it turned out that it wasn't Corinne that had the spark at all. It was Sadie. But Corinne would let her keep on believing it if she wanted to.

"Can you help me grab those condiment cups?" her mom asked.

Corinne, who was taller, reached up and felt around for the two little dishes she'd never once seen her parents use. Part of the painting process was purging and reorganizing. This time around, her mom was determined to fit her entire set of good china in with the regular everyday stuff.

She handed it to her mom.

"I know I look hideous right now." Her mom put the dishes down and dabbed at the sweat on her forehead. Like Corinne really cared how her mom looked. "Does Sadie know we'll be up taping and priming tomorrow by eight? Because we're getting an early start."

They always did. "It'll be okay."

Corinne took some juice out of the refrigerator and chugged it from the carton, since all the glasses were being sorted into boxes of KEEP and GIVE AWAY.

"Remind me why we're doing this again?" Her mom looked overwhelmed.

"Because you needed a fresh outlook," Corinne reminded her. "And you also said that you were going to start breaking things if you had to live with the coral another minute."

"I said that, didn't I? Thanks, *Mom*," her mother said.

"It's okay, honey," Corinne played along as she put the juice away. "Dusty Satin is going to be a life-changer."

"I hope so." Her mom really seemed to think it was as simple as that, a blue over a pink.

Corinne was crossing back toward her work area when her mom clutched her arm. "I know I've said this before. I just don't want you to get hurt. She's got issues."

Corinne took a breath and tried to squash down her annoyance, tried so hard not to snap at her mom, who was well meaning and high strung and surrounded by hours of work ahead and, other than Sadie and possibly Corinne's therapist, was the only person who seemed to believe that Corinne was not a crazy weirdo at heart. "And I've said *this* before. She's my friend, Mom. Everyone has issues. I do, too."

Of course, not everyone's issues involved going to the emergency room on a Saturday night.

"It's just the intensity of the thing that worries me."

"Worry about something else," Corinne said, pointing to a pile of containers on the countertop. "Like your Tupperware collection. You really need to get a handle on that."

At the door, Sadie made her presence known with a rapid-fire knock. She was wearing a purple skirt that matched the now-purple streak in her hair and carrying a plastic bag filled with Oreos. "Provisions," she said. "In case the party is too lame."

She took the steps two at a time until they situated themselves in Corinne's room, which after so many Saturdays like this one felt like "their" room—not that she would have ever said that in front of her mom.

Sadie started unzipping her bag and throwing piles of clothes everywhere.

"Where'd you get all that stuff?"

"Oh you know, I robbed a mall on the way over." Sadie grinned, flinging a pair of ripped jeans onto the floor, the tags still dangling from the label.

Corinne had to wonder for a moment if she was kidding. "You didn't, right?"

Sadie laughed. "No, I just brought all the stuff my mom bribed me with this month. Plus, we have to coordinate, right?"

They settled into their Saturday routine. Corinne plugged in her phone and paged through to find the right playlist. They had a whole series going, with titles for future situations in their lives. Our Next Summer Mix (for after they graduated but before they left for their respective colleges). Our Boring Weekend Mix, Our Next Door Neighbor mix (for when they got older and moved in to adjacent apartments downtown). College would have to come first, and who knew where they would even end up, but Corrine didn't want to think about that. She didn't want to think about having to live without Sadie, who was the only person she really felt safe with. So what if Corinne was a social reject at her own school? She only needed one friend, and Sadie made her feel like not fitting in made them better than everyone else.

Between them, they agreed on girl groups and Beach House and Velvet Underground and anything that came out of Sweden. Sadie especially liked nineties Britpop, bands with moptops and mopey lyrics, and she introduced Corinne to Blur and Oasis and Stone Roses. They would belt out the words until they'd funneled all their feelings into them, until there was only one meaning for the songs and it belonged to them alone.

They rarely hung out at Sadie's house. Corinne had only ever seen it from the outside. It was huge and white and modern. She told Sadie that she thought it looked like a movie set.

Sadie had just snorted. "Yeah, a dystopian hellscape. I like your house so much better, and your mom always has those good sweet potato chips."

It would've been so much easier to hang out at Sadie's without any parents watching her, but she never seemed to want that. Corinne didn't really get what was so great about her three-bedroom house with the white vinyl siding, the one that looked like all the others on the block, but she had the sense sometimes—a lot of the time, really—that Sadie liked living vicariously through her normal family who got along, and her married parents who were always home.

Of course Corinne's mom had noticed this, too.

"She's a stray kitten, isn't she?" she said once, after Sadie had spent the entire weekend with them.

"She is not," Corinne shot back quickly. "She just likes it here."

"Calm down. I'm not criticizing," her mom said, but Corinne heard the judgment in her voice. She made it sound like Sadie was some needy lonely freak, but it was so not the case. "If you keep hanging out all the time, other people will probably think you two are a couple."

She was probably kidding, but Corinne snapped because her mom's anxieties always cut through to her own. "Homophobic much?"

"You know I'm not. I just think it's kind of intense. You can't rescue her, you know. You need to think about your own health, Corinne."

"*Mom*. You're always telling me to socialize, and now I am. Please."

In Corinne's bedroom, Sadie was trying on dresses—a few of the ones she'd brought from home and some from Corinne's closet. They were the same size in pants and shoes, but tops and dresses were iffier—Corinne had bigger breasts and a little potbelly she was forever trying to hide. Sadie was leaner, probably from skateboarding and soccer, and her build was more boyish by nature.

"This one is pretty fly," Sadie said, flaring out the skirt of a bright emerald baby doll, then doing a three-quarter turn to check the back view before spinning around to the front again. "Not sure it works with these boots, though." She made a face at herself in the mirror.

Corinne tried not to think about the party, tried to get lost in the fashion show. Maybe they wouldn't even have to go. Sadie had been known to change her mind.

"What about this one?" Corinne offered her a mini shirtdress with a check pattern and buttons running all the way down the front. It was new, and she hadn't had a chance to wear it, but she knew it would probably fit Sadie better anyway. Sadie's taut stomach was exposed in the changeover, and Corinne made sure to look away.

"You don't have to do that, you know," Sadie said, and Corinne blushed.

Corinne herself picked a tank dress she'd worn all summer and layered it with a long-sleeve top underneath. She slid on a faux fur vest, some black tights and her high-tops.

"You're so creative!" Sadie said. "I would've never thought to put that together."

"Are you sure?" She wouldn't even try it if Sadie hadn't been there to encourage her.

"Totals. Only you could pull that off."

Corinne's mom knocked on the door and opened it wide enough to show her face. "Girls? We're leaving now."

Her parents were going out to LaScaza's for dinner, since the kitchen was torn up.

"Hi, Sadie," her mom said, polite and a little distant as usual. Of course this just made Sadie try harder to win her over.

"Have fun!" Sadie said with a broad smile. "They have the *best* meatballs!"

"Where are you two going?" Corinne's mom asked.

"A friend's house," Sadie said.

Her mom frowned. "A party? Do you think you should—?"

"Not a party," Corinne cut in. "We're just watching a movie at Dara's. We won't be late." She could already hear the lecture coming. Plus, because Sadie and unknown kids were involved, there would be extra degrees of discomfort. Her mom would bar her from going, probably.

Her mom lingered at the door for a moment and Corinne held her breath, waiting for the axe to fall.

But she just said, "Okay, guys. Leave me Dara's phone number and address in the kitchen before you go." Then she left.

"She's so cute," Sadie said, and it annoyed Corinne. Her mom wasn't cute at all. She was annoying, and Sadie couldn't even see how hard she was judging her, building a case against her. It was also embarrassing how overprotective her mom seemed, when Sadie could come and go as she pleased. Now she might get caught in a lie.

"She's okay," Corinne said, cuing up their SATURDAY NIGHT YAY playlist and they both settled on the bed to listen, staring up at the poster of two sloths bicycling on Corinne's ceiling. Corinne wasn't even sure why she had it ...when she'd first found it she'd thought it was funny or something, but now it seemed juvenile. She'd been meaning to get a better poster, of one of the bands they both liked.

"So the party...I'm not really sure..."

"Come on," Sadie said. "It'll be so funny. I really want you to be there. I can't go by myself!"

"It's just not my thing, parties," Corinne said.

"I know. You're shy. But you'll get over it. You'll see."

Corinne felt herself relenting. It was now or another time, but she would have to go to a party eventually. Maybe this was the best way, with Sadie.

"I felt so depressed this week," Sadie admitted quietly, as the string section opened the first few bars of "Bittersweet Symphony." "I can't wait to leave or start college or just—something."

"It's going to pass," Corinne said, but she felt inadequate trying to give advice. How could she, when she was so screwed up herself? That's why they were such a good match. At the same time, she worried that Sadie didn't have anyone else to talk to. At least she had Dr. Mittleson. What if Sadie was really alone in the world?

"You don't know how lucky you are. I mean, when I came in your mom was doing laundry."

"Laundry is not lucky. It's just chores." She would have traded Sadie's problems for her own in a heartbeat. At least Sadie's problems didn't make her an outcast.

"I think Jorge is having another affair," Sadie said. "It's so gross. He can't not screw people."

"Does your mom know?"

Sadie shook her head. "She's so clueless. If she didn't drive me crazy with her Real Housewives of Pennsylvania act I would almost feel sorry for her."

"Maybe she doesn't care."

"It doesn't matter if she cares. It's wrong!" Sadie shouted. "I care."

"Just remember: Pretty soon you won't have to deal with it."

"I know." Sadie stared up at the ceiling and whispered, "I don't know what I would do without my Coo-Coo."

"I don't know what I would do without you," Corinne said back. "I would be ridiculous and normal and boring."

"Everyone else is normal and boring," Sadie said. "I told you there were only a handful of originals. That's us."

When they lay there like this, Corinne wondered what it would be like to kiss her friend, if that would be an okay thing to do or if it would be totally weird. She couldn't really separate out if she wanted to have Sadie or if she just wanted to *be* her. They could try it, she decided. They had the kind of closeness where they could just try it, and you never knew. Not now, of course, but sometime.

There had been that other night, when Sadie came over in tears. Her stepdad had gotten drunk again, called her mother a *gold-digging bitch* and her mother had retreated into her bedroom with pills. Corinne was proud that she'd been the one Sadie confided in. But also, she'd felt that melty feeling, the confusion over who was who and what was what.

"I just don't see how she could do this," Sadie gasped through sobs. They'd lain on this bed then, and Corinne had listened and rubbed her back while she vented. "He's a horrible person, and she just wants to pretend nothing's wrong at all. I'm never gonna be like that, like either of them. Fuck alcohol, man. Fuck pills."

"It's coping mechanisms," Corinne said. "That's what my therapist says."

"Wonderwall" was playing that time, Liam Gallagher's longing voice distant but comforting.

Corinne wanted to say more. It was a good opening. She could have told Sadie more about what happened to her, why she had landed in therapy. Sadie knew about the therapy, but she didn't know about the hardest part.

"I love this song," Sadie sniffed.

"Me too," Corinne agreed, feeling the urge to confess pass. She had to be there for Sadie. She looked so small and vulnerable, it was like pieces of her were breaking off right in front of Corinne. It didn't make her any less cool—it made her seem more tragic and glamorous, if anything.

"It's kind of played out, but you have to admit it's brilliant."

They'd just listened for a while. Corinne remembered how natural it was, to just be together without talking and take in a perfect moment. How odd, when Corinne had actually been a little scared of Sadie in the beginning. Now she could almost take her for granted. She was pretty sure that Sadie felt the exact same way, that they needed each other, that they were each other's armor.

She was still holding Sadie when Sadie fell asleep. She had just lain there, not daring to move, worrying about whether she would wake Sadie up even though her hands stung with pins and needles.

Now Sadie was jumping up, springing up off the bed and swiping on lip gloss. "Come on, we gotta get there soon. Post-keg-tap, pre-puke. It's the golden window of opportunity."

Corinne struggled to shift gears. Sometimes Sadie moved

so fast it was hard to keep up with her. "Yeah. Okay." She stood up, too. "Let me find my wallet and jacket."

Corinne drove them in her beat-up Honda, with Sadie navigating from the passenger seat. She figured her mom's beloved lawn might be safer that way. "Turn at the next light. Did you know that Senator Rowell lives here?"

Corinne didn't. The houses were certainly fancy. At Corinne's school, no one lived like this. But because Sadie went to Fontwell Academy, she was tapped into a whole world of small, elite schools with names like Platt and Darnell and Plymouth Friends. Corinne hardly knew anything about them, other than what Sadie told her, and Sadie always made it sound like she hated the rich kids, she hated all the snobbery, that she only went because Jorge paid for it and her mom insisted.

"So do you know these people? Like, well?" Corinne asked.

"Oh, I've hung out with them," Sadie said vaguely. "They're fine."

Outside of the front door, Corinne's knees started to buckle. A picture of the Penn State party flickered inside her head. She saw herself on the tiled floor of a filthy bathroom, in fetal position, hyperventilating, Jen and Margit standing by her asking her over and over again if she could talk.

No, she couldn't go there. She had to block it out. It had happened once, but that didn't mean it would happen again.

But what if Sadie was the center of attention and Corinne was stuck, waiting awkwardly on the sidelines? What if she started to feel scared again, the walls closing in? What would she do?

That's ridiculous, she told herself. She's your best friend. You're in this together. She wouldn't invite you if she didn't think you'd have fun. Maybe she doesn't know about the thing, but she knows enough to know you need some protecting. And if you get sick, she'll understand.

In times of crisis you know who your real supports are, her therapist had said.

She had to prove it to herself, and her therapist, too, that she could do things like this.

On the step Corinne took Sadie's hand, too afraid to look her in the eye as she did it.

"Aw, you're sweet," Sadie said.

When the door opened, though, Sadie's fingers flexed open, dropping hers.

"Saaaaad." A guy with longish black hair opened the door. He was wearing an oxford with the sleeve buttons undone, so the shirt flapped around his arms like wings.

Sadie high-fived him. "RD! Yo yo yo."

The guy eyed up Corinne.

"This is my friend," Sadie said. "I'm allowed a plus-one, right?"

Plus-one? She was probably trying to be funny, but it struck Corinne as an odd thing to call your BFF.

"No doubt, no doubt," the guy said, nodding and sweeping his hand to the side to allow them in. Maybe this was supposed to be the ironic part? Or was it the awesome part?

She took a deep breath and followed, trying not to let her racing thoughts get the better of her. Sadie led them to the keg in what had to be a five-car garage and filled up two Solo cups. Without asking Corinne, she handed her one.

I thought you don't drink, Corinne wanted to say, but she felt like it would sound too prissy. She wasn't supposed to drink, either, because of her medication. But what else were they supposed to do at a party? Knit and trade recipes?

Still. She wished she'd had more of a plan—she'd just assumed Sadie wouldn't be drinking.

People were arranged in clumps around the living room, around the den, around some other rooms that Corinne didn't have names for. Sadie waved to some of them. One guy swooped her in for a kiss on the cheek. Another guy squeezed her waist as they moved by him. "Give it up, Dittman," she scolded him.

Sadie had never mentioned any of these people. It wasn't so surprising that Corinne didn't know everyone she knew— they went to different schools. But who was RD? Who was Dittman? Had she hooked up with either of them? She pictured Sadie coming to a party at her school, how everyone would be pretty much ignoring the two of them. Sadie was like a celebrity or something.

They passed through another long hallway, which was narrow and crowded with people that were all cramming into the kitchen. "Excuse me," Corinne said, trying to inch past two beefy dudes who hardly moved. Her heart skipped into triple time; her palms felt slick. She was way too conspicuous. She sipped at her beer, hoping it would calm her.

"Oh, there's my friend Lisa."

Corinne tried to see where she was pointing but when she looked back, Sadie had spun away from her in the gigantic house.

Shit. Don't freak out.

Another fragment of that night at Penn State floated back to her. *We can't go to the fucking emergency room, Marg. We are way too high right now. Like they're not going to see that.* And Margit: *She needs help! She seems really sick.* Then Jen, as if Corinne couldn't hear them: *Damon is here. Do you know how long I've been trying to get with him? I'm not leaving.*

No one here knew her. And that was a good thing, wasn't it? They hadn't seen her embarrass herself.

Corinne passed through one room and then another. Maybe she was supposed to talk to other people, but she was here to hang out with Sadie. Hadn't Sadie said they would laugh at everything together? By herself, it didn't seem nearly half as funny.

The guys were wearing plaid shorts even though it was winter. The girls were in crop tops and boots, caught up in jokes she didn't understand. She had nothing in common with them, and neither did Sadie. Sadie liked good music and had a tattoo of an Oscar Wilde quote on her back. She read poetry books. Why were they even here?

It had to all be some joke, she decided. Sadie would reveal

that she'd pretended to be a different type of person to get in with these people but that she really couldn't stand them. She'd only brought Corinne to the party so they could make fun of the whole scene. As she repeated the idea in her head Corinne almost felt calmer.

On her way up a staircase, she slammed into a tall skinny girl carrying three beers and two shots.

"Watch what you're doing," the girl sniped. "This is hundred-year-old scotch."

"Sorry," Corinne said.

She thought of her parents in the little neighborhood restaurant they went to every week, how they were probably eating chicken piccata and planning for the kitchen painting project, and how here she was at this party with these millionaire kids who were dragging their dirty high-tops over the oriental rugs and drinking booze that cost as much as her dad made in a month. How angry her mom would be that she was mixing her meds with beer. How she'd lied to be here, just so she could hang out with Sadie.

She didn't even *want* to be here, she admitted to herself. And now she was trapped. She had to act like she was having fun, or else she would seem even more lame and messed up than she already did.

Finally at the landing she thought she heard Sadie's voice floating above the music and unrecognizable voices. She half-expected to find her surrounded by guys, but when she went into one of the rooms, Sadie was sitting on a massive bed with a girl with long blond hair in a loose side braid. They pulled apart when the door opened, and Corinne couldn't be sure she hadn't walked in on something.

"What's up?" Corinne said, trying to keep her tone neutral even though she was rattled by the discovery of them.

"Nothing?" Sadie said, holding up a joint and releasing a cloud of smoke. "This."

"Oh," Corinne said. So maybe they had just been smoking together. "Are you Lisa?"

"I'm Jackie?" the blond girl said, confused by Corinne's confusion.

"We were just talking about this other party last summer," Sadie said. "It was so ridiculous."

"It was the most," Jackie agreed.

Corinne didn't have anything to add, so she just stood there. No one offered her a seat on the bed. Sadie had never said anything about the party they were talking about, or Jackie. Had it happened before or after theater camp?

Which made her wonder: How much about did they even really know about each other? She'd known Jen and Margit for five years. Five months was nothing. And most of that time they'd spent in coffee shops and in Corinne's room. She and Sadie had hardly stepped foot into the real world together.

But it didn't matter when you got someone, really connected. They knew the most important things, didn't they?

Not all of it. She hadn't told Sadie everything.

Holy shit. What did she take? What did you take, Corinne? Goddamn it, tell me.

"You don't have to stand there. You can go talk to other people, you know," Sadie said.

"I don't know anyone," Corinne said, feeling her throat constrict. Why was she being like this?

"Go meet them," Sadie said. "Everyone's really normal."

"Is that real fur?" Jackie asked.

"No, it's fake," Corinne said, looking down. The outfit had seemed so cool in her house, but now that she looked at it again, she could see how silly it was. "I'm gonna get another beer."

"Can you get me one?" Sadie asked.

As she turned away she definitely heard Sadie say: "Corinne's just a little possessive. She needs to learn how to chill out."

The words, the reality of them, crushed her chest, and now she really couldn't breathe. There was no foundation. The stairs were swaying beneath her feet. She tried to slow down and inhale more oxygen but thinking about breathing just made her feel more panicky. She needed to get out of here.

Was Sadie messed up already? That was the only explanation.

She made it down the stairs and started looking for a way out—a door, a window if she had to. She would get some fresh air, drink a little more beer, and then figure out her next move. She had to get it together. She thought of just getting in her car, but she couldn't run away like that. That would be silly, and even more embarrassing. How would she tell the story to Dr. Mittleson?

The speakers rang out with a few chords of plaintive guitar and Corinne heard joyful screams as she approached the kitchen.

A girl skittered in front of her. "Oh my God, I love this song!"

It was "Wonderwall." And somehow the room had become a karaoke bar. People were singing into their beer bottles. People were swaying on the marble tiled floor. People were standing on the tables and chairs. And as they shouted out all the lyrics, Corinne cringed. They were stealing all its truth from her, they were making it some cheap party song.

Then Sadie was in the kitchen, too, a dark shape in the doorway. The one person she cared about. Corinne looked up into her eyes and wanted to see apology, maybe, some hope, maybe mockery of the scene. Definitely recognition. This was *their* song.

One glance. One acknowledgment. They could laugh about it later, about these silly girls and doofy guys, and listen to a lesser-known track from *(What's the Story) Morning Glory?*

But all Corinne saw was a flash of Sadie's gray-green irises, flat and unconnecting. And then Sadie turning away to hug some other person she didn't know, the two of them singing along together.

All Corinne saw was the ways she had been wrong. What had been special between them wasn't a permanent thing.

Corinne wasn't special. It was Sadie doing something she needed to do, and now she had moved on. *Everyone is boring and normal*, she heard Sadie saying in her head.

Was that why Sadie had brought her here? To show her that?

The party, coming here, wasn't a big joke after all. This was Sadie's real life. Corinne was just some distraction, someone to comfort her when she needed help. Her boring, reliable friend.

And the song...it belonged to everybody. Nothing was hers alone. Corinne bit her lip and felt tears blooming in her eyes. She wanted to believe in so much more, about Sadie, about herself, about everything.

She grabbed Sadie's wrist. "I have to go home."

"We just got here," Sadie pleaded. "Don't tell me you're scurrying home already."

"You can stay." Though she wanted her to want to go. She wanted Sadie to choose her over this. She wanted things she couldn't name, and she knew they were too much to ask for. And now Sadie made her feel like a frightened animal. But it was true. That's what she was. Wasn't that what had happened to her before?

Why didn't you just tell us you were having a panic attack? My God, Corinne, you totally freaked us out, you ruined the whole night. It's so embarrassing—we almost got everyone in trouble. I mean, I thought you were seriously dying. Her friends had been so angry. They thought she was a drama queen.

"Hey, what's wrong?" Jackie asked Corinne as she tried to push past her into the foyer. "Are you okay?"

"Nothing," Corinne mumbled, feeling worse that the girl was actually being kind of nice, and that she was wrong yet again.

When she got home Sadie's car was still in the driveway, and her parents were home, too. She could see the blue glow of the TV in their bedroom from outside.

Her mom would say something about Sadie not coming home with her. She would say something either knowing or relieved or even worse, sympathetic—which would really wreck Corinne now. She didn't want to be lumped in with her mom, who was forty-four years old and *still* was never sure of anything.

She snuck up the stairs as quietly as she could. Then her mother's voice drifted out from their bedroom: "Have fun, girls?"

"Yeah," Corinne said, choking back all her disappointment. She silently prayed her mom wouldn't come check on her.

She didn't know when Sadie would come back for her car, but she hoped she would just take it and not knock on the door. She hoped she would just take it and go.

She quickly took off her dumb outfit and put on her pajamas and got into bed under the covers. She felt something crunch beneath her. The bag of backup Oreos. Her consolation prize. She took one out and bit into it, letting the crumbs fall on her sheets.

In the morning she would put on her old jeans and paint-stained hoodie. She would pretend everything was just fine; she wouldn't even mention Sadie, because then she might have to admit out loud what was already becoming evident in her head: two wrong people don't make a right. She wouldn't even mention it to Dr. Mittleson—what was the point?

Eventually her mother might wonder, after a few weeks, why Sadie wasn't coming around. But tomorrow she could still act like nothing happened—that was the easiest. She would get her brushes and help her parents cover up the kitchen with their fresh coat.

AUTHOR PHOTO
BY ELISA LUDWIG

Elisa Ludwig is the author of the *Pretty Crooked* trilogy and *Coin Heist*, now a Netflix Original movie starring Sasha Pieterse. When she's not writing about teens committing crimes, she's writing about teens in angsty relationships. And when she's not writing about teens in angsty relationships, she's writing about food. She lives outside Philadelphia with her family. Visit elisaludwig.com and follow her on Twitter at @elisaludwigYA.

YOU KNOW SOMETHING'S HAPPENING HERE

(BUT YOU DON'T KNOW WHAT IT IS)

A PERSONAL ESSAY INSPIRED BY
BOB DYLAN'S "BALLAD OF A THIN MAN"

By Jonathan Maberry

I picked Bob Dylan's iconic "Ballad of a Thin Man" because it was the first song that encouraged me to stop, listen, consider, and then dig deeper. And it sparked a process of introspection that allowed me to understand the forces at work in my life as a troubled kid in a dangerous world.

—JONATHAN MABERRY

KNOW I'M DIFFERENT. I'VE ALWAYS BEEN DIFFERENT.

I know it and accept it.

I didn't always accept it, though. For a long time being different was like having a disease, the kind that make you ugly, the kind where people don't want to touch you. Like that.

It took a long time to accept that I was different, and a longer time to accept that I always would be.

It was longer still before I realized that different was not the same thing as worse, bad, or wrong.

Understanding came because of a song.

I'll explain.

First, let's go stand on some common ground together.

Song lyrics are a form of poetry, and poetry by its nature is open to interpretation.

A song or poem can mean one thing to one person and something entirely different to someone else. This is well known in certain literary, scholarly, or creative circles, but is often disputed elsewhere. I know, I've been part of those arguments.

It'd be nice to say that these disputes are always friendly, that it's two friends sharing their personal insights and defending their views through reasoned argument. It would also be nice if there were actual pots of gold at the end of rainbows, but let's be real. People can't seem to agree on much these days. Just look at politics, vaccinations, race, gender equality, reproductive rights, immigration, wages, evolution, religion, and...well, pretty much everything else.

There are some people who don't even agree that the Earth is round.

I grew up in a house and in a family where shared understanding was not a given. Which is a nice way of saying I was born into a bad family. They happen. Families come in all shapes and sizes. Mine was big. I was the youngest of six kids. We lived in a three-bedroom row home in Kensington, a low-income factory neighborhood in Philadelphia. I had one older brother and four sisters. I had parents, and we had a border collie, and we all shared one bathroom. My grandmother lived two miles away. Every family in our neighborhood was just as poor as we were, and most of them had just as many kids. Some had more. I was born in 1958, and the sixties were my childhood years, the seventies were middle school and high school and college. In the early eighties, I was working jobs that put me in the path of violence and anger and conflict.

Fun times.

That's a joke, and a bad one.

I'm not sure if I was born different or *became* different. I can build a stronger case for the latter because I can actually remember a couple of moments where my internal gears shifted so dramatically that I was not the same afterward.

The first time was when I was six years old.

Young, yes. Innocent...not so much.

My father was a monster. A predator who preyed on anyone he could hurt. My sisters, our cousins. Me. We were weak, and he was of the kind who thought inflicting harm on the weak proved that he was strong. It was the bully mentality taken to an extreme. He set rules—often pointless and ridiculous—which he enforced with enthusiasm. Not because he thought the rules made sense, but because he knew we would have to break them. It gave him a veneer of justification to take us down into the cellar for consequences.

I don't need to draw you a picture.

But there were other kinds of punishment, too. For small infractions of rules he said we ought to know. As if we were telepathic.

Books were one of those things. We weren't allowed to have any unless he said so. And if we were, say, a minute late to the dinner table, or too slow getting home from school, we'd have to stand in the living room and tear up our books in front of everyone else. Page by page.

One of my sisters said that it was better than a beating.

I didn't agree. Not then, and not now.

If we played the radio too loud he'd make us break our records in half. That hurt every bit as much. There were worse physical punishments, but somehow that damaged me more. It felt like he was making us accomplices in the murder of thought and imagination.

When I was six I began spending a lot of time at my best friend's house, and two amazing things happened. First, my friend Justin and his dad were studying martial arts. Japanese jujitsu. I think Justin's dad knew what was happening at our house, so when he offered to start teaching me some martial arts, he suggested we make it a secret. We did. That would matter in a big way later. It was the first of several points at which my life pivoted, though at six I was too young to realize it.

That would change.

The other thing that happened at Justin's house was the presence of so many books and so much music. Back then people listened to records. There were no personal computers, no iPads, no iPods, no internet streaming, no CDs. None of that. People went to music stores and bought vinyl records. Singles were called 45s because the disks revolved forty-five times per minute. Albums were 33s for the same reason, but everyone called them "albums" or LPs, for "long-playing."

Justin's dad was into a lot of what my parents called

"hippie" music, but which was really a blend of British invasion, domestic pop, early psychedelic, blues, soul, funk, and folk-rock. The Beatles owned the airwaves, but they weren't the only band making everyone jump. We had the Rolling Stones, the Righteous Brothers, Curtis Mayfield, Gary Lewis and the Playboys, the Supremes, the Kinks, Leonard Cohen, Freddy and the Dreamers, Tom Jones, Herman's Hermits, the Searchers, the Zombies, Petula Clark, Gerry and the Pacemakers, James Brown, the Temptations, Sam the Sham and the Pharoahs, the Byrds, Marvin Gaye, the Beach Boys, the Four Tops, the Turtles, the Moody Blues, Sonny and Cher, the Yardbirds, the Four Seasons, Barry McGuire, Wilson Pickett, Otis Redding, Simon and Garfunkel, the Hollies, Donovan, the Animals, the McCoys, and the Who. We weren't short of new music by new talents.

But the stuff in heaviest rotation at Justin's house was the music of Bob Dylan.

I remember the first time I heard Bob Dylan sing, I thought, "Wow, he's awful."

If you've listened to Dylan, you'll understand. His genius was in songwriting, not in the quality of his vocals. His voice often sounds off-key, which I'm told it actually isn't. But it sounds that way. It sounds like nails on a blackboard, or a rusty hinge. It sounds raw, like a cawing crow trying to sing. It didn't sound anything like the smooth singers on the radio, or even the harmonies of John, Paul, George, and Ringo. But, once you get used to Dylan—and trust me, it's worth it—his singing style becomes both familiar and perfect for the words he's singing. They, too, are raw and grating, but in the most brilliant ways.

A year later, when I was seven years old, a new Dylan album—his sixth—came out, and that was another of those pivot points. The album was *Highway 61 Revisited* and it would go on to become his most highly regarded album, which is saying a lot. It was a landmark album that combined folk storytelling with electric rock. It blended some blues stylings with new sounds unique to Dylan. The songs were not love songs. They weren't the kinds of songs I'd ever heard. This was before my sisters were allowed to play their records while our father was at work. I'd never heard the phrase "protest song" before, and it would be years before the mainstream press was talking about psychedelic rock, protest rock, abstract rock, or anything like that. Maybe the newspapers in New York, New England, and the West Coast were exploring those themes, but not in blue-collar Philadelphia. Not in my neighborhood and not in my home. Those conversations wouldn't start in our neighborhood until 1967, when the draft notices began arriving and so many teens from my block got sent to Vietnam. When my brother went over there...well, that's when my sisters played a lot of Dylan and other rockers who were using music to express their anger.

I wasn't part of that conversation.

I was too young and too focused on a different kind of war. The one with my dad. The one where my father, despite his brutal treatment, was trying to make me be like him. He was a deeply racist person and ran the local chapter of the Ku Klux Klan. Yes, we had that in Philly. Actually, Pennsylvania had more KKK chapters than any other state in the whole country. My young education at home was about hating blacks, browns, yellows, and reds. It was about hating Jews. This was the midsixties, so there wasn't yet a pervasive hatred of Muslims, but if there had been, my father would have been the loudest one shouting.

When that kind of thing is all you hear, it's hard not to begin repeating certain words, certain phrases, and thinking certain thoughts.

But Bob Dylan didn't seem to share those sentiments. That confused me. His new album was named after a road that stretched from Canada all the way down to New Orleans, cutting through Duluth, where Dylan was raised. There was a lot of history attached to that road, and it wasn't all "white" history. That road was tied to black history through blues music, and Justin's dad was heavily into the blues. I'd heard a lot of that music at their house. Songs by Muddy Waters, Son House, Roosevelt Sykes, Mississippi Fred McDowell, Bessie Smith, Charley Patton, and others. Elvis Presley, who my dad thought was a "traitor to the white race" because he sang songs written by black songwriters, traveled the club route on Highway 61. And there was a cool spooky story about how a guitarist named Robert Johnson sold his soul to the devil in order to be the best bluesman in the world, and that deal was supposed to have been made at the crossroads of Route 49 and Highway 61.

I listened to *Highway 61 Revisited* more times than I can count. All told, counting all the way up to it playing now as I write this, I bet it's a thousand times. I've actually worn out vinyl copies of the album and several 45s.

There are a lot of songs on that album that matter to me in different ways, but one hit me hard at age seven and continued to stay with me ever since.

The track is "Ballad of a Thin Man."

If you listen to the lyrics, I can absolutely guarantee you won't hear the same things I did. You couldn't. We're different. Even if you grew up in the same kind of fractured household, even if you were raised by monsters, even if you had to learn young to hide your bruises from your friends and eat your pain, even if there are a thousand common threads that sew your life to mine, we're still different.

Over the years I've spoken to so many people about that song and its meaning. I've introduced people to it, read commentary on it, relistened to it as a teen, a twentysomething, a thirtysomething, a fortysomething, and a fiftysomething. I'll listen to it, I have no doubt, well into my sixties and however far beyond that I get. I have it on a dozen different playlists. Some of those playlists are songs I listen to when I want to be sad. Others are there for when I want to be happy. There are playlists for escape and playlists for arrival. There are playlists for when I want to ignite my creative fires and playlists for when I need to hush the voices in my head after a long day of writing.

That song is on more of my playlists than any other.

Mind you, there are a few that get played nearly as often. You may have heard of some of them. Or not. Stuff released before or after that year I discovered Dylan. Often they're songs that serve as inspirations for some of my writing. "Murder in the Red Barn" and "Black Wings"—both by Tom Waits—were important for me when I plotted and wrote my first novel, *Ghost Road Blues.* Laura Branigan's "Self Control" helped me dream up the Fire Zone, a magical place I've written about in plays and short fiction and which will soon be the centerpiece for my next novel, *Glimpse.* The 1982 song "Mad World," recorded by the British band Tears for Fears and then rerecorded in 2001 by Michael Andrews and Gary Jules for the *Donnie Darko* movie soundtrack. The deceptively complex and metaphorical "Hundred Kisses Deep" by Leonard Cohen, which inspired two different cycles of my short stories, the Sam Hunter werewolf–private investigator stories and the Monk Addison dark fantasy revenge dramas.

And so many others.

But I keep coming back to "Ballad of a Thin Man."

The stanzas are filled with strange imagery. At first listen—or if you look them up online—they don't appear to make any sense at all. Back in my day, we had what were called "liner notes," which were lyrics and other information printed either on the paper sleeve around the vinyl or in booklets provided with the album. I read those lyrics a thousand times. At first I thought something like, "This is stupid."

That's the kind of thought some people—kids or adults—have when encountering something they don't immediately understand. And understanding the metaphors and subtext of a Bob Dylan song is a challenge even for the sharpest and most insightful listeners.

The lyrics did not in any way speak to the complexities of my life experience. The song isn't about child abuse, gang violence, crime, poverty, or poor educational standards. The lyrics were strange and inexplicable.

But...

And here's the pivot point. That was the point in my life where I began to think beyond what I had been told. The act of deliberately trying to understand something beyond my reach made me reach farther. The desire to grasp truths that came from within—from thought and consideration—rather than accept what had been shoveled into my head was huge.

I was seven years old.

I'd already had to deal with things that were not part of any typical seven-year-old's world. I was already different, though I hadn't yet expanded my experience enough to know that what I was going through was not unique to me. It would be years before I realized that other kids got hurt like I was hurt. That realization was a different kind of pivot point. At seven, though, I thought I was a freak. One of a kind. Made from the wrong parts and put together hastily and without care. Years later, when I was more educated, more introspective, and better able to express myself, I referred to my kind of childhood as having been born in the "storm lands." I have since met many people who have emigrated from that troubled country.

At seven I was just becoming aware of how different I was, and how much I wanted to become *more* of a freak. Not less. I know, that's contrary to how it's supposed to be, but look at my reference point for "normal." Almost everyone normal around me was a monster of some kind. If that was the norm, then I wanted no part of it.

I began listening to "Ballad of a Thin Man" over and over again.

Obsessively, I suppose.

But really it was more like a focused study. I wanted to make sense of it. I suppose that on some level I felt that if I could understand that song—all on my own—then it would be proof that I had power. Any kind of power. I was still too junior at martial arts to feel powerful. Mostly I felt awkward and bruised. And no one had yet figured out that I needed glasses in order to see the blackboard in school or do much reading, so I wasn't pulling good grades.

Maybe that was part of it. The world had always been a little fuzzy to me, and the lyrics of that song, and the meanings hidden within them, were indistinct. Maybe if I could make them clear in my own head then other things might become clear, too.

The first thing I needed to do was understand who "Mr. Jones" was.

Was he me? Was the song about my own inability to understand the things around me?

Or was Mr. Jones something else? Some*one* else?

That felt closer to the mark. Once I had that thought, the door to understanding that song creaked open a half inch. My first real understanding was that Mr. Jones was a guy who didn't know who Mr. Jones was. He had no self-awareness, and I knew this without framing it in those words. I was seven, so I can't remember the exact mental vocabulary I used.

There was a line, "You put your eyes in your pocket and your nose on the ground," that was the next thing to click into place, the next thing to nudge the door of understanding open a bit more. At first I thought that it was a reference to taking off a pair of glasses and putting them, literally, in a pocket. But I knew that was wrong as soon as I thought it. My father wore glasses, and he was just as blind to things with or without them. The blindness to the world around him was part of who he was. Even at seven I was coming to suspect that; and as I grew older I know it for sure. So, no, that line wasn't about that. It was about deliberately choosing not to see. Mr. Jones *takes* his eyes off. He does this. It's not an accident, he wasn't born blind, it's his choice.

That, by the way, is the point at which I began wrestling with the question of what makes us who we are. The argument is called "nature vs. nurture," a label I didn't know then;

but I understood the concept...and I always felt the concept was wrong. It isn't always biology (nature) or environment (nuture) that shapes us. There is a component that's every bit as valid and probably more important: choice.

My father liked being a bad guy. Sure, he came from a rough childhood and was abused, but he didn't have to become abusive himself. No one has to do that. He made my childhood every bit as bad as his own, but I didn't become a predator. My father was abusive and violent because he enjoyed it. Maybe—and this is me being generous—he chose to focus on what made him happy and chose *not* to look at how unhappy it made other people. It's possible he was that self-centered. Maybe it's even likely, who knows? I wasn't in his head. But what I saw as a kid and what I understood while listening to that song was my father choosing not to look at the damage he inflicted. Or its consequences. So, in that sense, he put his eyes in his pocket.

Think about it from my perspective. A kid listening to something that was on an album. A song that was on the radio. A song that was climbing the charts. It couldn't be about *nothing*, ergo it had to be about something. And I was determined to figure out what it meant.

Why is that a pivot point? Ah. Remember the kinds of lessons I was learning from my father and his peers in our neighborhood. Intolerance and cruelty. In my father but also in the other adults—the people of power—in my neighborhood. None of them chose to see the world the way it was.

Yeah.

The song explained that to me.

Sitting and listening to it over and over again. Hearing someone else say it. Knowing that someone else understood it. Wow. That was so powerful. That one line was the lever that made me pivot. One line, a few words, that made a battered little boy think beyond his experience. To think *into* that experience. To deconstruct it and try to understand it, and by doing so gain power over it. When you understand a thing, especially a dangerous thing, it loses a degree of power over you, and at the same time you gain a degree of power over it. Not understanding something, especially if you have an active imagination, always makes something feel worse than it is.

Crazy that a lyric from a song that wasn't even about a troubled childhood helped open the door of understanding.

So, what's the result? What's the next act of that drama?

There's a saying that "you can't unlearn" something. Just as you can't unsee something.

I saw my father as a deliberate monster. Not a victim of circumstance, but as a criminal, as a man who enjoyed the power he got from doing harm. I also saw him as weaker than I'd thought because he *needed* to feel powerful. He was addicted to the power he got from hurting others. That meant that he was not as invincible and unbreakable as he seemed to a seven-year-old.

That understanding was massive. Absolutely massive.

I was seven, and in less than a year I'd be eight. Then nine, then ten. I was growing up. I knew that I would continue to grow up. I know, that seems obvious, but little kids tend to think that they are who they are at the moment. Considering who you'll be in time is a more abstract concept.

Dylan taught me to be abstract in my thinking.

At the same time, he helped me develop a kind of practicality. If I was going to get older, then I'd also get bigger. And stronger. I was already studying martial arts on the sly. There would come a point where my age and my size and those skills would align. That meant that there was going to come a point where I might be physically able to stop my father from hurting me. Or hurting my sisters.

And as I grew older, he would grow older, too. He would age past the point of his prime strength long before I came into my full power. That's the kind of race only a younger person can win.

Was the Dylan song about that kind of struggle?

Maybe. There was a lot of protest mentality in it. This was right when the Vietnam War was getting hot. The draft was starting. Nobody wanted that war, and the younger singers were writing songs about how wrong it was. The government wanted the war. They were the bigger, stronger thing that was hurting the younger, weaker thing. And that song spoke to that struggle.

So, yes, Dylan *was* speaking to me through the lyrics of that song, and through others on that album.

And I began to listen.

I listened to the other songs on the radio. Protest songs. Songs about nuclear disarmament. Songs about what we were doing to the environment. Songs about hatred and intolerance and bigotry.

All of those voices.

Speaking to me.

Calling out to me.

Telling me that I wasn't alone.

That the struggle wasn't mine. That if I was different, then that was okay. The normal world, so to speak, was the part of the world that had the power, used and misused it, and seemed to enjoy the effect.

Those of us who were different did not want to be like them. We didn't want our lives and our futures decided by either nature or nurture.

We wanted to have a say in what happened. We wanted to have a choice.

And we were determined to *have* that voice.

I was seven when I first listened to "Ballad of a Thin Man." I was fourteen when I was big enough, old enough, and tough enough to stand up to my father and stop the cycle of violence that made our house a battlefield.

All because of a song.

A song.

Yeah, man. A song.

AUTHOR PHOTO
BY SARA JO WEST

Jonathan Maberry is a *New York Times* bestselling author, five-time Bram Stoker Award winner, and comic book writer. He writes in multiple genres including suspense, thriller, horror, science fiction, fantasy, action, and steampunk, for adults and teens. His works include the Joe Ledger thrillers, *Rot & Ruin*, *Vault of Shadows*, *X-Files Origins: Devil's Advocate*, *Captain America*, and many others. He writes comics for Marvel, Dark Horse, and IDW. And he is the editor of several high-profile anthologies including *The X-Files, V-Wars, Out of Tune, Baker Street Irregular, Nights of the Living Dead,* and *Scary Out There*. Several of his works are in development for movies and TV, and has a tabletop board game out based on his novels and comics. He is a popular workshop leader, keynote speaker, and writing teacher. He lives in Del Mar, California. Visit jonathanmaberry.com and follow him on Twitter @jonathanmaberry.

TIME TO SOAR

A SHORT STORY INSPIRED BY AMY WINEHOUSE'S "OCTOBER SONG"

By Donn Thompson Morelli, a.k.a. DONN T

Birds and flight fascinate me. "October Song" was written about a bird, Amy Winehouse's pet canary, named Ava. It's a remix and rewrite of the legendary Sarah Vaughan's "Lullaby of Birdland." Another thing: October is my favorite month. It's a transitional month, it brings the chill, the time before birds in the north migrate to the south. My goal was to create a story that pulled together and amplified those themes in a poetic and compelling way.

—DONN THOMPSON MORELLI

I WAS A WHISPER OF A GIRL, LONG AND LEGGY, A PICKY eater except for what I term "fall" food. Of course, these foods weren't exclusive to fall, but they existed in my mind that way. The tenth month of the year seemed to usher in the arrival of the foods on my list of favorites, which included candy corn, butternut squash soup, sweet potatoes, more candy corn, corn on the cob, caramel apples, apple butter, and, well, candy corn. Come October, my little world was all abuzz.

At twelve years old, I was steady figuring out systems, categorizing things and counting. Counting made me feel safe. After all, potential land mines were in every field and danger was to be avoided.

I obsessed.

How many minutes could I hold my breath underwater in the bathtub? How many pogo stick jumps could I accomplish without falling off? For hours in solitude, I'd patiently carve out challenges for myself, practice in repetitive fashion until I conquered whatever task lay before me. I needed to uncover how things fit.

By twelve, I'd also come to understand that everything of major importance took place in October. It didn't. I just felt like it did, back then. That year, October's significance would boom down the corridors of time, like a too-strong note played, shifting from an unruly clanging, to a diminished buzz, to reappear as a hum. Constant, infinite. I hear it now. Octobers in Philadelphia could be arrestingly beautiful and quietly foreboding.

By twelve, I was enamored by the leaves on trees, how they surrendered to fall time with orchestrated brilliance. The change of season. Back to school and back in stride. No more summer. October was when the East Coast chill came in like clockwork. The cool air threatened. I was a breath of a girl who could never quite reconcile red, orange, yellow, and chocolate leaves falling to their end, all that dying in magnificent color. Green was how they should've left, uniform, monotone. If they were going to look richly colored and variant, they should stay forever. I've grappled with that idea from that time to this.

My birthday is in October. It's my mother Elodie Lewis's birthday and her father Daddy-Bob's. It's my first cousin

Tracey's birthday and my second cousin Jamie's. When October arrived, it was like a gong sounded. Celebrations abounded. Yet what occurred at Halloween eclipsed every one. Indeed, when I was a kid, October meant Halloween; I believed they were synonymous. So, as my twelfth birthday passed early in the month that year, like every other October prior, I felt myself become giddy. My costume, my mother's creation, had in previous years (well, four years running) been the expressed envy of the second through sixth grade classes at the Samuel B. Huey School in West Philadelphia.

Dressed in African princess garb complete with a mile-high headwrap that covered my afroed mane, the height of which seemed to eclipse my slight frame, I was elementary elegance. As icing, my mother would add a hint of blush to my cheeks, add a dusting to my lips, strap a brown baby doll to my back and place more bangles on my arms than they could hold. I was ready for a walk beside the Nile—or at the very least a stroll through the school auditorium for the Halloween promenade. My primary school costume had been prize-worthy, but this was not primary school—it was my seventh-grade year at Henry C. Lea Middle School. I was looking forward to surprising my new school and a tougher crowd with the upgraded version of what was a winning formula.

So, the countdown began. First came October 4, my birthday, then Daddy-Bob's on the fifth, the very next day. My mother Elodie's would arrive on the eighteenth, and then costume preparation and reveal at month's end. Except,

Halloween came and went that year. I don't quite remember it or Thanksgiving that year, or Christmas in the month to follow, or any holiday for several years after that October. That October, on my mother's birthday, her mother, Mother Laura, my grandmother, died. Breast cancer.

My family braved the fall and East Coast winter that year like a military troop, pushing through 'til spring. We burrowed through enemy territory with no rations and lost weapons, it felt. We pushed in head and shoulders first, through what felt like ice. We pulled ourselves over barbed wire barehanded. We bled. We survived on shallow breaths.

Laura was everybody's mother and my own father Edward's buddy. My personal cheerleader for the start of middle school: "Now, if the kids say anything bad about you or tease you in any way, you tell them *I've been where you're going!*" I had no idea what that meant at twelve. But it sounded big. So, first month in, I did that. It worked like a charm. I was too eccentric, too bright, too pint-size-revolutionary not to be teased. It was coming. I didn't fit, I never would. I would need wit. Thank God for Mother Laura; we were on a roll, one quick retort down, dozens more to learn and echo.

It was my second month of middle school when she'd returned to her home in California and died. My ace, my friend was gone. It was just October—what would I do now? I would surely never be able to come up with sayings that could thwart the attacks of wily seventh graders on my own. Mother Laura was my first encounter with loss. I remember I was in my head a lot, 'cause my heart was a dangerous place to be. There was a note that rang out that day, a howl that filled my mother's lungs released and filled the room. Like a high C of a diva to shattered glass was her scream to my heart. Grown-ups in a circle, me looking on. I was rattled. I was awake.

I've never stopped hearing that note.

This was someone else's seventeen. Another person's twenty-three. This was my twelfth year and October.

We held together until deep summer, and what felt like not enough heat to thaw the rock-hard grief the previous fall had served up, when it came again. October.

I felt guilty for wanting to celebrate without sadness. It had been a big year, one that included my having transitioned into being a young woman, blossoming, getting my period. I was thirteen. I wanted to run ahead, but my family's corporate sadness and the anniversary of my grandmother's passing pulled me to slow. My mother was sad, grieving. Whatever joy she'd experience in the months earlier bottomed to black when October returned.

She was sad for herself, sad for her dad, my Daddy-Bob. This would be his first birthday without the wife he loved. As granddad and granddaughter, Daddy-Bob and I were a refined pair. We were polite. Our birthday phone calls always included, "How's the weather?" and other meteorological and geological observations.

"Daddy-Bob, the largest ever recorded earthquake happened where?" I'd challenge.

"Uh, Chile 1960." he'd replied. He knew everything.

We were close; I was his little buddy. My frequent visits to California to see my grandparents would feature him announcing his nap time. It was his cue to me and other of his grandchildren to feel free to embark on a treasure hunt through the top drawer of his bureau, to find loose M&M's in his sock drawer while he slept or pretended to sleep.

At least I'd like to believe he was leaving a treasure to find. I never got to ask him. I don't remember a birthday call that year. He wasn't feeling well. Days later, right before the anniversary of his wife's passing, he left us. It was just too hard for Daddy-Bob to stay without his great love. A phone call from California came again that year. Three hundred sixty-one days had not passed; it felt back to back. The reverberation of my mother's murmuring, "No! I have nobody now!" when she received the news, was something it would take me many years to understand. Ten days after my birthday that year, I was aroused from the sound sleep of childhood with a jolt. This was someone else's eighteen. Another person's twenty-five. This was my thirteenth year, and October.

A year later in October, Robert Jr., my mom's oldest brother, died, just before my mom's birthday, like their mom and dad. There was a call from California, but no grownups gathering. No screams. Quiet. There simply was no more grief available. There was numb and still.

The human psyche is wondrous, the determination for perseverance powerful. At the end of emotion, the air is rather peaceful. It was only God that moved my mother, us, forward, 'cause we were planted in a place, content to be in the still forever. Life shifted beneath our feet. Was this walking or standing still? What is it that holds the heart together, what is it that tears it apart? I understood something I didn't have language for that fall, I was clear.

At fourteen, my world felt like I was wearing too-strong prescription glasses. This was someone else's twenty-one. Another person's thirty. This was my fourteenth year and October.

It would take years before October's note quieted to a whisper, before memories of fall became gentle nudges and could be met with soft smiles and warm sighs and an "Okay now, hush." There would come a day when innocent ponderings about autumn leaves changing color returned to me and when "Happy Birthday, Mommy" and "Happy Birthday, Kingston" would not betray but instead usher in a full-on celebration that might last the entire month of October. In time something immeasurable did come. A gift. The kind of gift that a friend wraps too quickly, the one where the unkempt package and badly timed delivery defy the beauty it contains. The gift for my mother lay in the road that led her to those Octobers.

The way forward was back.

She would need to revisit an experience in the past to usher in the strength and resilience to end the loud noise created. It would be the only way to heal herself and heal her family. It would be hard to tap on the shoulder and stare down the night that happened twenty years prior to the year that took her mother. She would have to go back before me and my brother, before my dad, to the time when it was just Elodie and her best friend Ava.

❀ ❀ ❀

It was impossible to believe that trash had purchased it. Garbage had built it, from the ground up. Old cans, broken toys, empty milk cartons (long before recycling would appear), crumpled candy wrappers, the smell of rotten eggs and too-aged cheese would lay the framework. Rubbish had purchased the Hill District mansion in the steel town of Pittsburgh, Pennsylvania.

The Lewises' estate stood like a great blue heron poised and stately high above the other homes in the neighborhood. Every brick and tile, every nail and floor joist, ceilings, floors and hallways every inch, and the land it stood upon, was secured outright by a brilliant and highly educated, utterly charming, and undeniably shrewd Robert Lewis, whose business happened to be garbage collection. Yes, he was a trashman by day, who seemed to wear his gray jumpsuit like superheroes in disguise do, in that Clark-Kent-into-Superman kind of way. He cleaned up well, and when he did, no sign of his workday was evident.

His elegant wife Laura was a force of nature, his Lois Lane, his *every woman* who brought home a hefty entrepreneurial salary as a cleaning woman to a wealthy Jewish family who lived in the Squirrel Hill section of the city. They were industrious; there was no shame. Bob and Elle (the name he liked to call her) were defiant. They knew something and maybe they'd tell it or maybe they wouldn't, an unusual pair.

Their road to wealth had sharp corners, was without guardrails, and lacked signage, but was sure all the same. They were an eccentric couple who lived to flaunt the story of how they came to wealth at the galas they attended, smiling inwardly when the story of their pathway to bounty was met with blank stares and bewilderment. They never bothered to answer the whys. "Oh, you work in sanitation? Why?" "You're a maid, really? Why?"

For them the answer to the myriad of questions was simply, "Why not!" It was the fifties, and for the times, they were rich. Their home was grand, six bedrooms, four baths. They were as accessible as they were elite.

The Lewises were politically connected, friends with the mayor, friends with the owner of the local speakeasy and numbers runner. They changed the landscape. Meetings happened in basements and councilmen were elected. They were the type of family who made announcements in the local newspaper. The Lewises announced graduations and weddings, their children attended cotillions and were members of Jack and Jill of America, an organization whose focus was to provide Black American youth with civic, cultural, and educational opportunities. It was the time of the 400s, the secret society of elite and well-positioned black families. Yet, of the Lewises' four children, Elodie, Naomi, Birdie, and Robert Jr., the appeal of being considered a 400 was lost on them all. All except Elodie. She wore the badge with honor.

At nineteen, Elodie stood swan-like and beautiful at five foot eleven: long legs, slender shoulders with proper curves. Her face exotic in the way that high cheekbones and doe-shaped brown eyes can be. In a word, Elodie was stunning.

At graduation from Schenley High almost two years earlier, she towered over most of her graduating class. She was unapologetic. Achieving the high honor roll and straight As happened for her with moderate study, and she seemed to excel at any discipline that required grace. Ballet and tap were her favorite, but she was merciless on a dance floor. Elodie loved to dance. If she wasn't so warm, so genuine, boys would have found her intimidating. But she was never at a loss for dance partners or friends. She could start the dance floor or clear it, and most boys wanted to dance with her just to see if they could hold their own. A tall feat: they could not. Who could?

Elodie had skills. She was the girl all the girls wanted to be, demure in an unassuming way, yet kind. Her stare and smile were captivating, her laugh bellowed. She took up space. She was an undeniable beauty, and just as school ended she'd been awarded her first modeling campaign, a billboard advertisement to be the face of VICTORY BRAND Beer Bologna. A year later, the first billboard hung high above the meat packing company's exterior. Then within weeks, the ads were all over the state. Her smiling face loomed larger than life. She imagined what people thought as they drove by en route to everywhere. She dreamed of fame and thought, "I'm going to be someone, someday."

The world seemed to open up to Elodie in the two years following graduation. She'd been approached by the Tommy Dorsey Jazz Orchestra and the Four Step Brothers to tap dance as part of their ensemble. The opportunities each felt grand and surreal. Still, the billboard ad was the highlight. The first time she saw one she was with her parents on the North side of Pittsburgh. They'd piled into the family's 1956 diamond-white Lincoln Continental Mark II to go sightseeing and to get ice cream. It was just after Sunday service at the St. Benedict Catholic Church.

They drove through neighborhood after neighborhood when her father Robert Sr. spotted it in the distance. "Oh my God, Elodie!" But she could see it too. She sat between her parents in the front seat, and as they approached she and her mother began jumping and squealing in their seats. The north side of Pittsburgh was an exclusively white neighborhood at that time, but that eighty-foot billboard starring Elodie Lewis, as she stared back with her bright eyes and flawless smile, drowned out all the background noise.

It affirmed Elodie was queen.

They all got out of the car and ran around it in different directions with excitement. When they settled down, they stood quietly looking up at the billboard there on the side of the road. It was huge, she was huge, larger than life, hanging there in midair.

The modeling jobs started to pour in, soon after her billboards appeared across the state. Life was thrilling. It was a sweltering late August afternoon by the time they returned home. She hardly remembered the ride or anything beyond the billboard as she slowly stepped across the threshold of the door.

When her middle sister Naomi greeted her and handed her the phone, the room began spinning. "Hello!" she said. It was Elodie's best friend Frieda. The legendary Sam Cooke was coming to town and Elodie was invited to be Frieda's guest. Belle, the other member of their lifelong trio, would come too. Elodie could barely contain herself. It didn't matter that it would be another two months until the show. She imagined it would be the best birthday present ever. October 17, the day before her twentieth birthday, could not come soon enough.

A buzz was in the air in the days that approached Elodie's birthday, and now it was the morning before. Elodie met the day with her usual enthusiasm. She reminded her dad that he would be her ride to Frieda's later that day as she sped through the kitchen en route to her ballet class. She looked forward to spending time with her dad, the man the rest of the family found introspective and reclusive behind closed doors. He was such a complicated man, layered, but not to Elodie. She got him, and he adored her. It would be them alone on the drive to Frieda's, catching up for two hours.

The three hours of classes seemed to whiz by. The head of the company, Mrs. Kooperschmidt, corrected her posture more than a few times. It was hard to concentrate. "Elodie, more!" she said. "Elodie, arabesque, plié, grand battement. This is quite an easy combination, my child!" she quipped.

Mrs. Anna Kooperschmidt was a petite German woman and the owner of the Ballet Conservatory, which Elodie had attended since she was a small child of seven. It was a bit of grace in the center of downtown Pittsburgh. Amid the skyscrapers and hustle and bustle of town, car horns honking and trolley cars rolling back and forth, the Ballet Conservatory sat tucked in on the second floor of a storefront. Its classical music streamed down into the street, adding elegance as a backdrop. Both the Ballet Conservatory and Fleisher's Bakery, two doors down, made a walk down Liberty Avenue a happy assault to the senses.

Yet it would've taken a lot more than the lure of cake and classical music to pacify a seven-year-old Elodie on her first day; it had been a disaster. She and most of the other girls cried through the class and the directions to run, leap, and spin. Eating graham cracker snacks and milk and squeezing her mother tightly when she arrived for pickup were the only things she enjoyed about that first class. Even so, for her mother Laura, hours-long dance classes were decidedly a more highbrow child-care experience than leaving Elodie with a sitter. Besides, there was something in Elodie that she'd hoped Mrs. Kooperschmidt could bring out.

That she did. Within weeks, Elodie was a prized student hanging on her teacher's every word. Elodie had grown from favored student to protégé in a few short years. For her teacher it was now personal, and through the years, commitment to her student Elodie grew into love, like the love for a grandchild.

Maybe it was more, given the fact that Mrs. Kooperschmidt never had children of her own. It seemed the relationships she developed with a few of the girls over the years quieted the longing in a way she could bear. Any strictness she displayed was simply a disguise for caring. They never saw her smile, but they had no doubt of her dedication to them. Her students were everything to her. It was no wonder that Elodie now taught younger students dance at the conservatory. She had a gift and patience. However, today she was neither patient nor attentive. She could feel herself going through the motions in class, catching up with herself, daydreaming. Mrs. Kooperschmidt could feel she was not there. Elodie couldn't wait for the concert.

After class Elodie grabbed her things from the changing room and hurriedly made her way downstairs and onto the street. It was sunny. It was a brisk day, unseasonably so. She whizzed past the bakery—the aroma made her smile—then came to the corner and ducked into Harrison's Pet Store. She came through the door winded. "Hi, Mr. Harrison!" she smiled, walking swiftly with purpose, her greeting polite but clearly a formality. The elderly gentleman behind the counter Mr. Harrison answered her unspoken question flatly from behind his newspaper, "She's in the back with Ava."

Elodie walked by cages and animal accessories, noticed the dogs and cats, stopped to greet a few, but was clearly on a mission. When she got to the back, she saw her oldest sister Birdie cleaning out a small cage. "Where's Ava?" Elodie smiled.

"Hello to you too!" Birdie smiled back.

"Hello, Birdie, how are you today? Where's Ava?!" Elodie giggled.

Birdie gestured to another nearby cage and Elodie walked toward it. "She's still here, nobody bought her," Birdie was pleased to report.

Elodie was simply enamored with Ava, the canary. Elodie tried to visit her at the pet store almost every day since she arrived two weeks ago. This was her canary, she thought. She just had to convince her parents of that fact. "Please don't let anyone buy her, she's mine," she said, almost trance-like.

"You know, Mr. Harrison won't allow me to do that. Besides, Mother and Daddy said we can't have any more pets." Birdie reminded.

"But Birdie, if you talk to Mother, I'll talk to Daddy; we could wear them down. Mother will listen to you." Elodie pleaded. Elodie knew that although she held a special place in her parents' heart, it was Birdie who actually got the hard things done. She was only two years older than Elodie, but she had always been like a third parent. She was the first-born girl, reliable, responsible. She could fix anything around the house; she was solid and determined. She could, in fact, convince her mother that a canary might be nice. But *would* she? Elodie had her work cut out for her, she thought.

Little did she know that on her birthday, the day she returned from her night away at Frieda's and the concert, the canary Ava would be home too, to greet her. The family had secretly agreed to give Ava to Elodie as a birthday present. It indeed had been hard work for her sister Birdie not to spill the beans that day, but even harder work later that evening for Elodie to try to bend the conversation with her father around to Ava on the car ride to Frieda's. "You know, Daddy, I stopped in to see Birdie at work today. There's a canary there, I named her Ava. She sings so pretty. I love that bird," she said pensively.

Her father smiled to himself, staring straight ahead so he would not break. "Are you sure it's a she? Male canaries are the best singers."

Confused, Elodie said, "I think it's a she. Anyway, I named her Ava," she retorted.

"Hmm, that's nice," he said as he pulled into the parking space in front of Frieda's house. She was convinced that her dad had no intention of reconsidering his position regarding Ava. The drive from Pittsburgh to Clearfield was two hours and thirteen minutes; she had *not* sealed the deal. In fact, Elodie wasn't certain that he even heard her. When she kissed him on the cheek and exited the car, she decided to let it go and focus on the fun at hand.

Her friends Frieda and Belle met her at the door with hugs and shrieks of laughter. It had been so long since they were all together. Two years. School days seemed to be a forever away. Life had taken hold. Frieda was engaged to Elliott Peaks, her high school sweetheart, who was now a Marine. She was knee-deep in wedding planning for her big day in June. Belle was a supervisor at the Hartford Insurance Company. She'd moved up the ranks quickly and was one of their youngest agents.

At first hug, it was as though the girls had never skipped a beat. They still fit. Childhood friends since they were six and seven years old respectively. Their parents and their grandparents, the 400s of Pittsburgh, were all connected in some way. Frieda's parents worked for city government; Belle's mother was a doctor and her father a lawyer.

Their chatter continued nonstop as they made the mad dash to Belle's car. She was the oldest of the girls at twenty-one and had had her driver's license for three years now. Traveling to work in Philadelphia and returning to Pittsburgh to visit family for holidays never caused her to fret. The thirty miles it would take to reach the concert was nothing compared to the 300-mile hauls she had normally driven.

They reached the Big Barn Concert Hall where the show would take place in less than a half hour. Clearfield was in Allegheny County and mostly country, so the fact that the concert would be held in a barn was fitting, Elodie thought. When they ran up to the box office window to see a "closed" sign, they were not surprised. The concert would not be for another two hours. It was early yet, and Elodie wanted a pop.

Elodie reminded the others that they'd passed a roadside store on their way to the barn. It'd started to snow, and brisker air descended. It was colder than usual for October. Elodie was glad she'd brought her coat, grabbed it, and threw it over her shoulders. It would be dark soon; the sun was setting. With time to kill, the girls barreled back into the car and trekked higher up the mountain for pop.

After leaving the Clearfield General Store, the girls lingered in the parking lot, playing music on the radio, dancing, and drinking pop. More than an hour had passed; they hadn't noticed. It was a beautiful night, pitch dark. The stars cut through the midnight sky as the car headed back down to the barn. "Wake Up Little Susie" was on the radio, and the girls moved in place in the front seat to the beat. They were finally headed to the concert. No words, just glances and smiles. This night was special and would go into the history books. That was the unspoken. The car too seemed to move like a dancer, down the mountain as the snow fell. White dust assaulted the windshield relentlessly. The wipers brushed and made new with each stroke.

The vehicle drove down and then around one curve, down then around another. Then down again and then around another. It seemed like poetry, felt like dance, movement to rhythm.

But something tripped. Skipped.

Like a needle on vinyl.

Like there should have been an "around," when there was a "straight down"—or maybe it was the opposite. Even so, when the car left the mountain into the air, that too was like ballet. Like a dream. Like *pas de chat*, "step of the cat," a leap in ballet, one of the most difficult ballet leaps to perform. The car would not land well, Elodie knew this.

With eyes closed tight, and breath held, she had one thought: "It will all be over soon."

They were out in air, flying one hundred yards, the full length of a football field. The car crashed into the one lone tree on the side of the base of the mountain and hung there, right before the depths of the river.

When Elodie woke the radio was still playing, "Wake up little Susie, we gotta go home." Confused, she attempted to assess the situation. She turned the radio off.

It was quiet and so cold and dark.

"H-how do I get out?" she panicked.

Then, in a way she would take a lifetime to articulate, she heard something. It was automatic. She had a thought. As she thought, the answer to her question arrived.

God spoke to her: "Elodie, I will make a hole in the floor of the car. Pull Belle and Frieda out."

She was talking to God.

She would later tell police and newspaper reporters and her parents what God said to her in that car.

Their car sat suspended by the tree, battered doors jammed in, no broken windows, no openings, no way out. And then before another thought, before her eyes, a pothole-sized opening was in fact there, cut perfectly.

She pushed the girls through the hole and they all landed on cold, wet, slippery ground with a thump. They'd lost their shoes, and now it was Elodie's task to get everyone up the hill to safety. With superhuman strength, she pulled one girl a few feet forward up the mountain and returned for the other girl, lifting her semiconscious body up to the place she'd landed the first girl.

The girls moaned but could offer nothing more as she dragged their full weight back and forth. One hundred yards of steep incline, seven steps at a time up, advancing, then back seven steps, to repeat. It took hours and Elodie was weary. This was too hard. She hurt. She couldn't do it. They were almost at the top when she decided to leave and go get help.

Elodie didn't want to wake the girls—she didn't have the strength—so it was quite shocking when Belle woke, groggy, grabbed her leg with a strong tug, and screamed, "You're not leaving me!" Like tumbleweeds, all three girls rolled over each other, back down the godforsaken mountain.

They were back where they'd started.

Elodie's unforgiving trek would begin again. She carried, again, what felt like dead weight. Up and down. When they reached the top, Elodie flagged a car. It was an elderly white couple, who, when they pulled in close to Elodie, debated aloud whether picking up the black girls would make them late for meeting another couple for dinner. They apologized to the girls and drove away.

This night was neither amiable nor auspicious. It was

heavy and dangerous. In the hour that followed, another car stopped. The driver, a middle-aged black man with two teen daughters himself, helped them into his car and escorted them to the hospital, only to have the girls released on questionable grounds. Mercifully, he took them to a second hospital that admitted them.

Belle and Frieda would have multiple surgeries over the next several weeks for a variety of injuries: broken collar-bones, and fractured ribs, concussions, cuts and gashes. Elodie, however, was released within days with no internal injuries, a sprained ankle, and something no one was talking about: her face. It burned a lot. The doctors had applied salve, removed her bathroom mirror from her hospital bathroom, and informed her parents that there was not much more that could be done. They'd all have to wait it out.

Elodie was not comfortable with amount of attention her accident was getting. She had to tell her story to seven separate officers and two news reporters. They all kept asking how she got out of the car. They insisted on correcting her, saying, "You fell out at the top of the mountain, right?"

Elodie would later learn that the stumbling block for the officers and reporters was that there was no way to get out of the car they had found against the tree.

There was no hole on the floor of the car.

It took the fire department to get the car doors off. No one girl, no three girls could ever have opened it. It took an entire construction crew. The windows were shattered but not broken. There was simply no way out or in. Elodie told the officer God had made a hole in the floor. After the third retelling, in private her mother admonished her sweetly, "Elodie, maybe when you tell the story you can leave out the part about God opening the car. I believe you, but these people will think you're crazy." It was on that day, Elodie decided to never tell the story in that way again.

After the accident, it would be five days before Elodie would return to her home in Pittsburgh. She received a warm welcome from family and friends, many of whom dropped by throughout the day, Mrs. Kooperschmidt included. The biggest surprise of all was Ava, the canary, the birthday present that was late getting to her. Her birthday had been four days ago, although she never remembered it coming or going that year.

She also barely noticed that the mirrors in her house were covered like in the hospital. She knew her face was injured, but she mostly felt fine. She was still on bed rest when her mother and sister Birdie came to lay in bed with her. "Don't you love Ava?" Birdie smiled. "You know we left the door wide open and she never flew out. We think she likes it in here." She laughed. Ava was allowed to fly free in the home, her cage door left wide open. The family's newest tenant was quite well adjusted.

For weeks, Elodie would spend hours talking to the bird about whatever popped into her thoughts. Sometimes Ava would sing back. It felt like a conversation to Elodie. Ava almost never did that to anyone else.

Three months since the accident. She counted.

Weekly doctor's appointments became ritual. After one appointment, her mother decided it was time for someone to say the hard thing. She recruited Elodie into the house.

Birdie discreetly grabbed a small object off the sideboard, holding it firmly at her side, hidden as they proceeded down the hall. They hoped that Ava's presence in the house would soften the blow, make the news bearable. Elodie sat on the side of her bed. Her mother started, "You know doctors don't know everything. You had a divine experience. You said God helped you in the accident. Well, the doctors say you are badly injured and that maybe you will not ever heal. They don't think they can do more for you, but I believe you will heal."

Elodie was so confused, she mostly felt fine. Her face hurt and she didn't like the treatments, but, other than that, she felt okay. Elodie questioned, "Well, what's wrong with me?"

Her sister took the mirror she was hiding behind her back and said abruptly, "You look like a monster right now. They say you got a third-degree burn and no matter what, you won't heal. The skin is too damaged. You will always have scars is what they say. Me personally, I don't believe it."

Elodie hadn't heard a word. She was transfixed by her own reflection. She hadn't been in front of a mirror in months. There was simply nothing left. No face. She was gone. She wasn't ugly, she thought.

She was alien.

Her face looked extraterrestrial. She was confused. She didn't understand when this happened. She didn't remember scraping her face in the accident. Was she in shock? By now, Belle and Frieda were home healing and back to life. Elodie had saved them, helped them. Stories had twisted and blame between parents had been tossed so rapidly that by now the girls barely spoke.

The accident was Belle's fault; her heel had gotten stuck in the gas pedal.

It was Elodie's fault; it was her suggestion to go get pop.

It was Frieda's fault; she'd planned the night and was playing the music too loudly in the car. She had been distracted.

As parents searched for answers to alleviate their respective daughters' pain, the verbal blows to each other caused irreparable damage to their lifelong friendships. It would be several years before they all would be able to put the event behind them and resume the decades-long friendships that had been the cornerstone of each of their lives.

Time seemed to just pass for Elodie. Days into weeks into months passed. And over that time, like clockwork, every Saturday morning Birdie would come to Elodie's bedroom and snap a photo. "Don't take my picture!" Elodie would reprimand.

Birdie exclaimed, "But, we have to have it for when you heal. You're going to be as good as new." Birdie's behavior was either in tune to something undefinable, like faith, or entirely insensitive and rude. Elodie was still on the fence regarding which it was.

All the while, Ava sang her through it. Ava seemed to sing through most moments. She sang through the monotony of Elodie's days. She sang through that first fall. She chirped through winter. Ava serenaded Elodie through spring. She peeped Elodie out the door to doctor visits, a thing she abhorred.

She simply dreaded the once-a-month checkups. Nothing changed, so what was the point? Seven months after the accident, she was in less pain, but hated leaving the house. It didn't matter if her mother or Birdie were escorting her. Doctors' visits were useless. Plus, she didn't want anyone to see. She'd have to pass her billboard en route to the hospital. She'd see her face before the accident smiling down at her. It felt like cruel and unusual punishment.

Still Ava sang her through it all.

Elodie's bright spot was Ava. Something in Ava's song reminded Elodie of the morning and hope. Ava seemed always happy and content. In spring, doors and windows opened on sunny days, but Ava, like Elodie, stayed put.

The day she caught a glimpse of something in the mirror that looked different, she was surprised. It was there on her cheek. The skin was smoother. It almost seemed new. Her parents noticed it too and accompanied her to the doctor who told her, it really couldn't be explained. "Her burn is third degree. In my practice I've never seen skin restore itself after a burn like this. It is impossible."

Within a year and a half, the skin on Elodie's face had returned with no traces of a scar except on a small area beneath her chin. It was an inch-sized tag, not noticeable at all. The photos Birdie took were indeed useful later, because without them there was no other evidence that something had ever occurred.

On the day Elodie received a job offer to return to modeling, Ava flew away right out the window and never returned. Elodie saw it as a sign.

It was now her turn to fly.

❊ ❊ ❊

It would take the story of Ava and all of the events around it to bring my mom Elodie through the losses that barreled through the Octobers of her adult life. She knew, if she could be with the story of Ava she might find peace. She was right. So much of life had pushed forward in the years and decades following my mom's accident.

Octobers then, now, and forever hold a place in my family's lives. Our loved ones chose to say their goodbyes in a way we would forever remember, with a kiss, near our October birthdays. How dramatic.

After the trio of Octobers that happened in *my* youth, I observed my mother Elodie go in and retrieve the truth of her past, what happened the night she actually landed at the bottom of that mountain. When she embraced the fact that she experienced something miraculous her hope returned. Like salve, she reapplied miraculous hope where needed.

God, inexplicably and undeniably, came to her, as crazy as the story sounded even to her. Despite what others thought, even contrary to the instructions of her own late mother, who was simply trying to spare her own daughter ridicule, Elodie learned to embrace her truth.

Like the pet bird in her youth, she freed herself and soared to new heights and then inspired me, her daughter Kingston, to do the same.

Melodic yet dissonant, intricate and surprising, those are some of the many notes in October's song.

AUTHOR PHOTO
BY WHITNEY THOMAS

observer. igniter. enigmatic. singer songwriter. label owner. producer. clarifier. peruser. witster. sister. muse to the mister. ma+daughter. tall drink o' water. That is innovator **DONN T**. She originally hails from Philadelphia and comes from a storied musical lineage. The quintessential independent artist and do-it-yourselfer added label owner to her list of accomplishments, when she launched Dtone Victorious in 2014. Her debut album, 2010's *Kaleidoscopic*, received international acclaim. On her follow up, 2015's *Flight of the Donn T* album, she shares co-production credit with her husband Jake Morelli, a guitarist/producer. The buzz around that album got the attention of CBS and the Grammys, who, in 2016, highlighted Donn T as an Artist of Tomorrow. Her next release will debut in 2017 and is titled *100 4 Characters*. Visit Donn-T.com and follow her on Twitter @Donn_T.

CITY
GIRL

**A SHORT STORY INSPIRED BY
KEANE'S "SOMEWHERE ONLY WE KNOW"**

By E. C. Myers

I discovered Keane's "Somewhere Only We Know" through its first U.S. music video years ago and became slightly obsessed with it. The music and images are intertwined in my mind, as the band walks through and performs in a lush forest. When I considered the song for this anthology, it suddenly clicked perfectly with a story idea I've had for a long time and helped me figure out how to write it. Strangely enough, this song's alternate U.S. music video, which I only saw for the first time recently, is an even better fit for the story.

—E. C. MYERS

ANARA TRUDGED THROUGH THE MONOTONOUS TREES, regretting the life choices that had brought her here. They were so far off the beaten path, the terrain was beating *them*—with low, whiplike branches and loose pebbles and crusty mud patches that were deeper than they looked. Deep enough to slurp down one of your favorite shoes.

Anara and Trace weren't supposed to be wandering in this wildlife sanctuary, so she had only herself to blame. She swallowed her frustration. Like the mud had swallowed her left sneaker clean off her damn foot.

Clean?

"Good point. Nothing about this expedition's clean," she muttered.

"What?" A few feet ahead of her Trace stopped and turned around.

"Nothing. Just talking to myself," she said.

"I do that too!" He hesitated. "Dad and I never stay in one place long enough for me to make friends."

"I've lived in Burlington all my life, but I still don't have friends."

Oh, really?

((Hush,)) she thought. Not that the voices in her head ever listened to her. She had to hear them—their unwanted advice, snide commentary, naughty suggestions, and the off-tune singing!—but it was all too easy for them to ignore her.

She didn't think of them as friends. More like...nosy, noisy roommates? And some were unfriendly, as if they resented the fact that they were in her mind. She had the impression they only helped her to help themselves, whoever or whatever they were. She was only part of the package.

She *was* the package.

That's what this trek was all about.

Trace pushed his long, silver bangs out of his eyes and looked at her.

"Hey. We're friends now," he said.

The blush crept down her neck and spread over her chest. Trace grinned.

Why do you trust this boy? You don't know anything about him.

((We have a lot in common...)) Anara touched the scarf

covering her bare head, missing her hair for the first time. To follow the map, they needed to see all of it at once—which included the lines on her scalp. She had thought she'd feel worse about shaving off all her hair, but it had felt right.

Appearances are deceiving.

You two are not alike, no matter how much you want to believe it.

Why won't you listen?

((I've always listened to you. But Trace is the first person to tell me what I want to know.)) Anara crossed her arms.

"—take a break?" Trace said.

"Huh?" Anara straightened and concentrated her focus on him instead of the voices. "No, I can keep going."

Trace sat heavily on a flat rock beneath a sprawling camphor tree. "*I* could use a breather, if that's okay."

Anara rubbed the back of her neck. It was sticky with sweat and bug spray, which seemed to be attracting mosquitoes rather than repelling them. Unless they were attacking out of spite.

"It's like the forest doesn't want us here." Anara sat beside Trace, scratching at a bump on the inside of her forearm. The red welt made the silvery, almost invisible map lines on her skin stand out clearly. The bump added a topographical quality to its contours, a mountain where there was none.

"It doesn't." Trace slapped at the back of his hand.

"I thought it would be different because we have the map. If this is where I—*we* came from..." She flung up a hand. A startled mosquito buzzed past her right ear. "I imagined the trees parting before us or something."

"That wouldn't be good magic."

What does he know about good magic?

Anara snorted.

"What? Why's that funny?" Trace's hurt expression showed he was really offended. So Anara wasn't alone in worrying about saying the wrong thing. Another thing they shared.

"It isn't... Just, how much magic have you seen?" she asked.

Trace gazed out into the trees. "That's the thing. You know good magic when you *don't* see it."

❄ ❄ ❄

Students had been talking all day about the strange new boy at John Dee High School, but she didn't see him herself until fourth session global studies.

Of course, she noticed his silver hair first.

So that's what it's like on the other side, she thought to herself. People always fixated on her looks when she met them—all the things that made her different from them. Bark-brown skin and ash-white hair didn't exactly blend in with the majority population of Burlington, Vermont, including her white parents and brother.

Now here she was doing that to someone else. Only in this case, she was paying attention because of their similarities. Anara had never seen anyone younger than forty with silver hair, except in a mirror. His hair was shoulder-length, frizzy, uncombed, like he couldn't control it or didn't care to try.

He slouched in his seat like he didn't want to be noticed, but he was tall, basketball-team tall. His skin was dark, like the rich loam in her mother's garden.

The voices murmured. Anara squeezed her eyes shut, feeling a migraine coming on.

((Keep it down!)) she thought.

She kept sneaking glances at him through class, often enough to see that he was noticing her too. No one could miss Anara's dark skin and pale hair, but she somehow existed in people's blind spots; usually no one really saw her unless she wanted them to. If the new boy was looking at her, she must want him to.

She started blushing.

Stay away from him.

((Why?)) she asked.

No answer.

((I'm going to talk to him. I have to,)) Anara said.

When class ended, the boy sprung up. With his long legs, he quickly covered the distance to her desk near the back of the room while the rest of the class exited.

"Hey! What's your name? How long have you been living here?" he asked.

She stared at him, dumbstruck. His eyes were amber, like hers.

This couldn't be a coincidence. They must be linked in

some way. Maybe he could give her a clue about her birth family. Maybe he was even related to her!

She recovered, tilting her chin up. And up. "I'll ask the questions. Who the hell are you?"

He grinned. "Trace Alabaster." He extended a hand.

Anara left him hanging. "I'm Anara Mackaw."

"You don't look like a Mackaw."

She frowned.

Stop talking to him. He's rude.

"Shut up," she said, realizing too late she hadn't used her "inside voice."

Trace jerked his head up in surprise. She could have fumbled the same excuse she always did when she accidentally spoke aloud, but she decided to let it lie.

She narrowed her eyes. "Then who do I look like?"

"Like me." He reached for her ponytail and then dropped his hand. "Except for your hair. Why'd you dye it?"

At the moment her hair was purple-black, but her lighter roots were showing.

People dyed their hair to stand out, to make a statement. "Just trying to fit in," she said.

"I get that."

He sat on the desk in front of hers, facing her with his feet on the chair. She almost laughed. He was so thin, his knees sticking way up, his elbows out. Slouching, head bent like a turtle's. Cute but not sexy, somewhat awkward. Charmingly so.

Yikes. She hoped they weren't related.

A word popped into Anara's head, a confusing jumble of syllables that demanded to be spoken. Many other voices rushed to silence it, but it was too late. She repeated it aloud, trying out the unusual sounds on her tongue.

"L——?" she said slowly.

Oh hells.

Trace's eyes widened. "What did you say?" He was shocked. Afraid.

"I don't know."

Much of her life was an act. Don't let people know you hear voices. Don't let on that you know things you shouldn't.

She had talked about the voices all the time when she was little, until Mother grew concerned that the stories her precocious, imaginative daughter told about hearing voices weren't so harmless.

After three meetings with a man Anara called Dr. Garlic— she still didn't recall his real name, only the way he smelled— she was convinced that the voices meant she was sick. He said he could make them go away.

But Anara would have to go away too, until she was better.

The voices told her what to say and how to behave to make them believe she was only playing a game. As long as she pretended they weren't there anymore, everything was fine; no one wanted to believe she needed help. No one would ever believe the voices were real.

Anara had grown up terrified of slipping up, being found out, and having to talk to more doctors. She never wanted her mother, or anyone else, to look at her again like she was crazy. The way Trace was looking at her now.

He stood, started to back away. Dammit! The voices had ruined things for her again. He was spooked.

She was spooked too.

She blinked back tears and jumped up from her seat. "Wait! I...I don't even know what it means."

((What does it mean? Tell me!))

"L—— is my birth name. Only my dad knows it. We never say it. Never."

Get away from him. Now. The voice was panicked.

((Why? Who is he?)) Anara thought.

The voices stilled, but her mind weighed heavily with their shock and disapproval.

Trace's forehead crinkled. "You okay? Your eyes kind of went all..." He waved his hand in front of his face. "Woogly."

"I'm fine." She took a deep breath.

"You won't believe this, but I've been looking for you," he said.

"You have." She crossed her arms. "All your life?"

"Yeah." He tilted his head quickly a couple of times to consider her from different angles, reminding her of a bird. "Not for *you* in particular, but another survivor."

Trace's eyes, so similar to hers, shone.

"Survivor? Of what?" Anara leaned away from him. "What are you talking about?"

This was too much. She had been excited when she saw

someone else who looked like her, right here in her home town, her own school. But the voices were confusing her, and now he was suggesting they were dead?

"Where are you from?" she whispered. Her heart beat faster. Blood pounded loud in her ears. She felt a spike of fear, she didn't know why. She had been searching for information about where she was born ever since she had found out she was adopted.

"A place called The City," he said.

"That's...generic." She let out a puff of air. "What, is that with a capital 'The'? Like *The New York Times*?"

"I know. That's just a rough translation. Its full name was ʃ——. It basically means 'The City of the World.' That generic name was part of its protection from discovery, but I think the founders were just arrogant."

((Is this true? Am I from The City? Are you?)) she asked.

She felt them clench up inside her, more unified in their silence than they had ever been. Against her. Against him.

"So where is it?" Anara asked. "Can you take me there?"

His face fell. "It's gone, Anara. All of it. As if it never existed."

"How? There has to be something left..."

Leave this, Anara.

"Dad and I looked for it for a long time. He hopes The City only moved and hid somewhere else. The Elders had been working on some kind of plan when we left. Big magic."

"*Magic*?" she said. "Come on."

He raised his eyebrows. "Wait. You don't believe in magic?"

"If you don't want to tell me the truth—"

"This is all true. We've been keeping an eye out for anyone else who was left behind. Our people came and went across the borders all the time, so some may not have made it back before…" Trace studied Anara. "Is that what happened to your family?"

"I'm adopted."

Trace furrowed his brow, confused. "But you're the same age as me? Sixteen?"

She nodded.

"That sounds about right."

"Where was this city?" Anara asked.

"Up north, in Quebec. It's hard to explain. Sometimes I don't even believe it myself because I don't remember it. But The City sort of *overlapped* with land in what people in the mundane world know as Anara National—" His jaw dropped. "*Anara?*"

She gripped the sides of her desk, its cool, fake wood surface slick under her sweaty palms.

"I was named for that park!" She felt dazed. Could everything he was saying be true after all? "My parents always said she'd they found me there on a camping trip. I thought they were joking. Mom comes up with the worst pranks. And my papers say I was adopted here in Burlington."

"If you were a baby, what were you doing outside The City when it disappeared? You and your parents must have been cut off from each other."

Anara bit her lip. She had been convinced she would

never fit in anywhere—or with anyone. Now she knew where she belonged, even if it didn't exist anymore or couldn't be found.

"*This* is magic," Trace said. "That the two of us randomly found each other. Pa's going to be so excited to meet you."

NO!

Anara flinched. She squeezed her eyes against a skull-splitting migraine that crashed down on her like a tidal wave. That had been more than one voice all at once.

"Anara?" Trace stretched a hand toward her.

Don't touch him!

Anara jerked away from Trace. He looked surprised. He held his hands up, away from her.

"What's wrong?" he asked.

She concentrated on breathing, blinking against the sudden, pressing pain behind her eyes. "Um. Don't tell your father about me?"

((Is that what you want? Why?))

"But we can help each other. We can look for The City together!"

"Can we keep this to ourselves for now?" *You, me, and the voices in my head.* "I need time to think about all this."

Good girl.

((We're talking about this soon. You obviously know something about him.))

"But—" he began.

"Please," she said.

"Okay." Trace offered his hand.

Anara, don't.

Why didn't the voices want them to touch?

Anara smiled. She took Trace's hand.

Fireworks.

His hand was cool, rough.

Suddenly she was tipping one way as the room went the other. Trace caught her and lowered her gently to the floor.

"You're burning up." He pressed a hand to her forehead, his face twisted with concern.

She felt a tiny flame spark just under her palm, something scratching to get out. It spread like dry paper lit with a match. Her flesh was cracking, smoldering. Every inch of skin itched and ached. She was going to throw up.

She held up her hand and turned it around wonderingly. Shimmery lines appeared, as if an artist were drawing on her skin with golden ink.

"Look…" she said.

Then Anara passed out.

❀ ❀ ❀

She was too young to remember The City, but she had vague memories of a place her parents told her the family had never visited. A sprawling cobblestone plaza. A sparkling fountain with a two-headed unicorn. A wooden cart under an oak tree, like this one, selling sticky buns for a half-coin, whatever that was. Mother said she must have seen it a cartoon or something.

"I've seen that tree before," Anara pointed at one with a diagonal gash in its trunk, like an angry old scar. "Does that mean we're on the right track?"

"I recognize it too," Trace said. "I saw it thirty minutes ago. We're walking in a damn circle. Or the trees are moving around." He kicked a rock into the underbrush.

"How does this work? If The City overlaps our world, how do we make that shift into it once we reach it?" Anara asked.

"I don't know! But The City is supposed to admit its own, no matter what." Trace looked around wildly. "We, um, need to get our bearings. Sorry."

Anara hesitated for just a moment before she pulled up her tank top to reveal her soft belly and the lines there, as delicate as strands of spider silk. She was glad they had made it far enough south on this portion of the map that this wasn't so awkward anymore. Of course, if their path continued southward...

Trace knelt before her and studied the map on her stomach. The lines were only for Anara and Trace, apparently. No one else—not the school nurse or their classmates, not even Anara's parents—could see them covering every inch of her skin.

Had these lines always been part of her, hidden like the voices? Why had they appeared when she and Trace touched? Was it him, or was it her?

What if they did more than touch?

He followed the line of the path they'd been following with his finger.

Anara giggled. "That tickles." *But don't stop*, she thought. **Sigh.**

Anara had always wondered how she could hear a sigh in her head, since the voices couldn't draw breath, but now that she believed in magic, she had to accept that anything was possible.

Magic. The map lines were enough proof that it exists. Thinking of the voices as magical took some getting used to, but it was better than imagining them as...her imagination. Or as a biochemical imbalance that needed to be corrected.

Anara was magical. She wasn't just different—she was special.

"I think we're about here," Trace said, pressing his finger to the spot where her navel should be. His touch sent a pleasurable shiver deep within, farther down. He frowned, staring at the smooth skin there. She braced herself for the question.

She didn't know what her missing navel meant, but magic was strange that way. Trace had said, "You know good magic when you *don't* see it." Somehow it must be connected to the voices in her head.

"Um," Trace said. "Your skin...?"

Anara glanced down and saw her stomach was splotched with red.

"Oh, *that*. It's a thing I do. I blush easily, for no

reason." She said it like it was no big deal, so he wouldn't make it one.

Blushing had always been a problem, never on her face but seemingly everywhere else: her chest, the backs of her arms, the back of her neck, and apparently her scalp too. It didn't take much to set it off. Embarrassment did the job as well as an innocuous comment.

When it was bad, she looked like she had a rash. Now she wondered if the blushing was the secrets inside her trying to reveal themselves, or maybe there was no more room for her to hide anything, so her emotions had to be plainly written on her skin, for all to see.

"Well, keep it up if you can. It makes it easier to see the map. I think the lines are fading," he said.

Anara held up her arms and turned them this way and that. He was right. The lines shimmered in the sunlight and disappeared from certain angles.

He stood and brushed the dirt from his knees. "But I know where we are now."

Anara pulled her shirt down. Her belly was warm. Trace led the way, and she walked alongside him, still feeling his fingertips on her.

They had followed the map from where it had first appeared, their high school, to the Esbenshade National Wildlife Refuge in upstate New York, just over the Vermont border. She was surprised that The City had moved so close to where she lived, but it had still taken them three days of walking and hitchhiking to get there, trading stories about their eerily similar experiences growing up.

((The City is somewhere in this park. It's just a matter of time before we find it. Might as well tell me what happened to it?)) she said.

Silence.

((Fine.))

"Trace, what happened to the City? Why did you and your father leave?" she asked.

"It left us," Trace said.

"Cryptic."

"I was only a few months old, but Pa says a group of—"

La la la la la la la la la la la la la la la la.

Anara winced. Trace's lips were moving but she couldn't hear what he was saying.

((Seriously?)) Anara said. ((Cut that out! I want to hear this.))

La la la la—

"So he took me and we left," Trace finished.

That was better.

"Anara?" Trace said.

"Y-yeah?"

"You had that... Sometimes you look like you're, I don't know how to describe it. Seeing inside your own head?"

Anara massaged her eyes. "Just thinking about something else."

"Anyway, Pa has never stopped searching for home," Trace said.

Anara squinted up at the canopy of trees above them. "Me neither."

"You have a family in Burlington." Trace ducked under a low branch and held it out of the way for her.

"You and your father have each other. Is that enough?" she asked. "I've just never felt...normal."

"Whatever that means."

She spread her hands. "I just don't *fit*, you know? I'm hoping that when we get to The City, I can find out why I'm... why I..." She hesitated. Could she trust him?

Trace didn't push her. He simply listened.

"I...hear voices," she blurted.

And there it was. It made her feel good to have the truth out at last. Lighter. It was a baring of her soul that was more intimate, more personal than it had been to reveal her body to Trace. It made him less of a stranger, more than a friend. An ally.

Oh, Anara.

Trace blinked. "Voices."

She braced herself for him to draw away, expecting him to turn from her, maybe even abandon this whole adventure and head back to Burlington, leaving her behind. But instead he knit his brows in confusion. "What do they say?"

Anara took a calming breath. And she told him everything.

All her life, the life she remembered anyway, the voices had told her what to believe, what to say, what to do. She stopped listening all the time as she got older, but they had defined her. They had always been there for her. But now that their secrets were coming out, she didn't know if she could trust them anymore, if she ever should have trusted them.

"What's it like having that noise in your head?" he asked.

She wiped sweat from her eyes. "Crowded. Comfortable. Irritating. Reassuring. I know you've felt isolated in the nonmagical world, even with your father around, but I've never been alone."

"That sounds nice. Unless..."

"What?"

"Are they watching you all the time? When you're in the bathroom or..." He coughed.

"Yes, even when I'm hooking up." Anara smiled when Trace blushed. "Not that it happens often."

Only once, in fact. Some guys were into the white hair thing, and Anara had been desperate to connect with someone her age, who seemed to like her. But twenty-one minutes in a closet wasn't a lasting friendship. She had become someone's anecdote, and that wasn't going to happen again no matter how lonely she was.

"Oh," Trace said.

"But it doesn't feel like someone else spying. They feel like a part of me. Most of the time I don't even notice them, they're just part of the background."

"How many are there?"

She tripped over a half-buried root. Trace grabbed her arm and helped steady her.

"More than one, I'm very sure. Could be five, could be

hundreds. They all sound the same in my head. They all sound like me."

Trace halted and held up a hand. "Did you hear that?" he whispered.

"Very funny," Anara said.

"I'm serious. Not a voice... Someone's out there."

Anara peered into the trees. She listened hard. Were those footsteps walking softly through the underbrush?

"It could be an animal," she said.

"It isn't an animal," Trace said. "We're being followed."

Anara, hide!

Anara and Trace crouched behind a thick tree as footsteps came closer, and slowed. When a man appeared across the clearing, Anara covered her mouth. He had russet skin, and his thick hair and beard were bone white. Could he be from The City?

Traitor.

((You know him?)) Anara asked.

"Pa!" Trace jumped up and ran toward his father.

The man whirled around. "There you are!" He squinted past Trace, and his eyes caught Anara's. "Come on out, girl," he said softly.

Don't, Anara.

Mr. Alabaster was wearing a long, dusty coat despite the heat. When it shifted, Anara glimpsed something strapped to his hip.

((What's that?))

A gun!

Mr. Alabaster had no reason to shoot her, and she wasn't going to get answers sitting behind a tree. She joined Trace, keeping an eye on Mr. Alabaster's hands. Just in case.

"The Daughter of The City. I'm Alton Alabaster." He bowed. "Very glad to finally meet you."

"Hello," she said.

"What's going on, Pa?" Trace asked. "Why are you following us?"

Mr. Alabaster's eyes searched her face. No...he was *reading* it.

He could see the map too.

"You've been holding out on me, son. Weren't you supposed to tell me right away if you found her?" Mr. Alabaster said.

"Sorry, Pa."

Trace was supposed to tell him when he found her? She didn't like this. She felt like an ice cube had lodged in her heart.

"The least you could do is introduce us," Mr. Alabaster said.

"You already seem to know who I am," Anara said.

"I know *what* you are, but not *who* you are." Alton scratched at his beard thoughtfully.

"Pa, this is Anara Mackaw." Trace waved his hand between them and gave her a questioning look. "Anara, my father."

Anara knew she was being rude, but the voices labeling him "traitor," the gun, him following them... It all put her on edge. She didn't trust the man, but maybe she could use him to get what she wanted.

"Let's keep moving, what do you say? I've waited sixteen years to go home, and these mosquitoes are eating me alive," Mr. Alabaster said. "You do know where we're going?"

Anara brushed past him wordlessly. She followed the trail on the back of her hand to a ring of massive trees surrounding another clearing. One had fallen a long time ago, its dead trunk pointing to the center of the meadow. The tangle of its mighty roots clawed upward, a gnarled hand grasping for the sky.

She remembered this spot. But how could that be? Anara National Park was hundreds of miles away.

This had to be a different tree, but this also was where she'd been discovered as a baby. The memories flashed crystal clear.

A voice saying, **Wake up!** Opening her eyes, seeing those exposed roots extended over her like huge, craggy fingers. She had started crying, and that's when the woman found her. Dressed in flannel, a shotgun balanced on one shoulder, a brace of pheasants clutched in one hand—gaping at the naked baby cradled in a nest of fresh, green leaves in the shadow of a dead tree. That had been the first time she saw Eveline Mackaw. Mom.

Anara sat heavily on the rotting log.

Alabaster looked around doubtfully. "Is this the place?"

"The City's close," she said.

"So what happens now?" he asked.

Anara crossed her arms. "Now you tell us what *really* happened when you left it, Mr. Alabaster."

"Anara? What do you mean?" Trace asked. "I already told you—"

Anara held up a hand. "We need to hear it from him."

"*We?*" Mr. Alabaster pushed aside his coat and rested his hand casually on the holster of his gun. He squinted at her. "You hear them?"

Despite the hot sun and humidity, Anara's blood ran cold. He couldn't be referring to the voices.

Careful, Anara.

((Shhh!))

"Tell me a story, Alton," Anara said.

Mr. Alabaster kicked at the dirt with a heavy boot. "I didn't think they'd go through with it, until The City disappeared. The plan seemed so drastic..." He looked at Anara sadly. "So cruel."

"You didn't leave The City." Anara guessed. "You were kicked out. For betraying it. 'Traitor,' they called you."

Mr. Alabaster scowled. Then his face softened. "I'm sorry, son. I wasn't entirely truthful with you." He glanced at Anara meaningfully. "But I wasn't the only one bending the facts."

"I haven't lied to Trace," Anara said.

"Maybe not, but how long have you been hearing those voices in your head? How long have you been speaking for them?"

"Traitor," Anara repeated.

"That's what they named me, and that's what I am," Mr. Alabaster shoved his hands into his pockets and bunched up his shoulders.

"Pa!" Trace said.

Impulsively, Anara stood and took Trace's hand. It seemed like both of them were about to hear something difficult, but at least they could face it together. He squeezed her hand tight and set his jaw with determination.

"Okay." Mr. Alabaster was silent for a long time. "Okay. Here's how it was. How it *really* was. I encountered a group of people on one of my trade expeditions. They were refugees from a city called Evervale, that had used up all its magic and entered the nonmagical world, and mostly died. Her people had scattered everywhere, but these forty people had settled in Quebec, to search for The City. Hoping it would take them in, let them live with magic again.

"They needed magic bad. Several of them were sick. Dying. They told me their story and begged me to bring them to The City. I told them the Elders would never let them enter, never let them share its magic."

Don't listen to him. He's spinning tales. You can't open The City to him.

Or his son.

Anara shook her head, like she was clearing water from her ears.

"Anara?" Trace whispered.

"Go on, Alton," she said through clenched teeth. The voices were murmuring now, she could barely hear him over their chatter.

"They were desperate, and they said they would reward me just for asking the question. They paid me half up front—a lot of money. What harm was there in asking? But I didn't realize they had followed me back, tracking the coins I brought with me.

"By the time I realized what I had done, they were camped outside The City. They had stolen magic before, enough that they could open a way in, given enough time. So we were under siege."

The fool!

"They tricked you," Trace said.

"Not exactly. I had my own plans." Alabaster unholstered his gun. Tapped it nervously against his knee.

Anara eyed it worriedly. Trace's hand tensed in hers. He had seen it too.

Run!

Don't let him hurt you!

((Not yet. I have to hear this.))

Go. We'll tell you the rest, but you have to go now!

Anara tugged at Trace's hand, took a half step back. She stared at him. *Be ready*, she thought, willing him to hear her. He seemed to understand.

Alabaster was scheming to overthrow the Elders, a voice said.

Anara swallowed. "You wanted to lead a coup? You were going to use the survivors from Evervale to claim The City's magic for yourself."

"Not for me! For everyone! I'd been pushing for us to open our borders for years, reveal The City to the nonmagical world. We should have been sharing our power with normal people, using it to heal the sick and dying, that kind of thing. It was only humane. But the Elders wanted to keep it all for themselves.

"They rejected my proposal to bring in the outsiders—people who needed them. And when they realized Evervale had found The City and already was working to counter its protective spells, they decided to *move* it."

Anara's mouth went dry. "How did they do it?"

He looked at her, his face a mixture of anger and...pity. "Through you."

"I don't follow," she said.

"Anara, *you* are The City. The living embodiment of all it was and all we were," Mr. Alabaster said. "Its magical essence distilled, containing multitudes. No one would look for a city inside a girl, and if they did, you'd be difficult to track down, and even more difficult to capture." He pointed the gun at her. "Or kill."

Go!

Go, go, go.

"You made me?" She spoke her question aloud to the voices. "All of you are real people? IN MY HEAD? And the magic..."

It's inside you. You are ∫a——.

She repeated it aloud. "∫a——?"

"Your true name means both 'girl of The City' and 'secret keeper.' But most people called you the repository." Mr. Alabaster looked pained. "That's what they thought of you. You weren't a person. You were meant to be a tool."

"But who was I before?" she asked. "Before they did this to me?"

"Anara…girl, I'm sorry, but you didn't exist. You weren't—"

"Born." Anara pressed a hand to her stomach, feeling its unscarred skin.

"Not born naturally, no." The hand holding the gun was shaking. "It wasn't right. Our magic wasn't meant to do that…create a new life to be used and thrown away. I told them so. I was the lone dissenter."

"They banished you," Anara said.

"Yes. Ironically, not because of my plans, which were still secret. But because in order for the spell to work, everyone had to agree with it. So I left and took Trace with me." He glanced at Trace. "The rest of it's true. We stayed with the Evervale refugees for a time, looking for you. The City."

"My parents had already found me and took me away," Anara said.

He scratched a nasty-looking mosquito bite on his chin. "I've been researching and tracking every adoption from around the time The City disappeared. A tip finally led me to Burlington. I found your family yesterday, but you had already gone off with my son." Alabaster slapped at another mosquito on his arm. "And here we are."

"*You* led Evervale to The City? It was all your fault?" Trace asked.

"The Elders brought it on themselves!" Alabaster said. He waved the gun in the air, shooing away the mosquitoes buzzing around his head. "Think about this. Your girlfriend wouldn't exist if not for me, boy. And if I hadn't brought you away from The City, you'd be trapped in her head along with everyone else. Oh yes, they're safe in there, but that isn't really living, is it?"

"What about Ma?" Trace asked. "We left her. You promised we were going to get her back!" Trace clenched his fists and took a step toward his father. He drew short when the gun jerked in his direction.

Alabaster wouldn't shoot his own son, would he?

"Of course Kaye wouldn't listen to reason. She's the one who came up with the idea to make Anara." Mr. Alabaster stood up, slapping at the side of his face.

"Ma did?" Trace asked.

"She's an Elder!" Alabaster said.

Trace was dumbstruck.

"Alton. What's the gun for?" Anara asked.

He looked at his hand as if he'd forgotten he was holding a gun. "I don't have any magic, so consider this a rudimentary reversal spell. I'm not too confident that killing you would let them all out, but hopefully it won't come to that. When The

City returns, things are going to be different, got that?" He stared hard at Anara. "Kaye? You hear me?"

"You're insane," Anara said.

"Says the girl who hears voices." Mr. Alabaster laughed. "Or I could take you back to the Evervale refugees, what's left of them. They'd figure out how to release The City, or put its magic to better use."

"You disagreed with the Elders because they didn't think of me as a person," Anara said. "So why would you kill me?"

((What happens to The City if I die?)) Anara asked.

The City dies with you.

"Because *they* control you," Mr. Alabaster said.

"They don't. I make my own choices," Anara said.

"Are you so sure of that?" he asked.

"Don't do this, Pa," Trace said.

"You shouldn't get too attached to Anara. She was made to die. What do you reckon happens if she brings The City back? Everything goes back to the way it was. Poof! No more Anara. You're losing her either way."

Trace's mouth fell open.

((True? Bringing you all back means I cease to exist?)) Anara asked.

I'm sorry.

The air buzzed around Anara. It took her a moment to realize it wasn't in her head. A black cloud of mosquitoes swarmed around Mr. Alabaster. This was their chance.

"Trace!" Anara ran. A moment later, she heard Trace's

feet pounding the dirt behind her. She heard a gunshot. A second one.

Trace grunted, stumbled, kept going.

She really missed her sneaker now.

((Was that your doing?))

The place is near.

((What place? If *I'm* The City—))

Anara was The City. All this time, it had been inside her. And she had never felt like she belonged anywhere because she *didn't*. There was no place for her in The City, and if she restored it, there'd be no her at all.

((I'm The City, so what's the map for?))

When the time was right, the spell was supposed to find a suitable location for The City to appear. We intended to guide you then.

((When?))

When you were older. When the danger was past. But we didn't count on you encountering Trace. The City always shows itself to its own.

As they ran, Anara updated Trace on what the voices told her.

"There has to be some other way." Trace gasped. "Something we can do to save you."

"It's more important that we save The City. I don't trust that your father isn't still working with Evervale," she said.

"He may not have gone through with his scheme."

"We have to get away, bring The City back, and keep him from finding it."

"But—"

"It's my decision," Anara said. "I was made for this, but it's my decision."

She checked the map on the back of her hand and led Trace deeper into the forest. The trees *were* moving, but now they were helping them. They seemed to slide away as she approached, and a quick glance over her shoulder showed the path closing behind them, blocking off pursuit.

Now *that* was good magic.

Trace cried out and fell. Anara rushed to help him. His left side was soaked with blood.

"Oh no. He shot you? Why didn't you—"

"Forget it, I'm all right. Just need to rest…" He drew in several short, quick breaths. "Anara, I'm so sorry…about my father. I didn't know. He lied to me about getting kidnapped by Evervale and The City leaving us behind. He's been using me."

"Join the club," she said. "I'm bringing The City back. But we have to find where it belongs first."

Trace shook his head and then winced. "No. We can't do this. I don't want it anymore."

"But your mother…she's waiting for you."

"I'm not choosing between you." He groaned.

"I might not disappear. The voices don't know what will happen to me," she lied. "But even if this is the end of everything for me, it'll be worth it. You'll have your mother back and your home. And you'll find another way to keep it safe from Evervale."

She checked her hands and arms. "I can't see where the map is taking us anymore. You have to."

She pulled off her tank top.

"Anara..." Trace stared at her exposed skin.

"You have to see the whole map at once."

"The lines shifted. I can barely see them anymore," he said.

The sun was setting. As it dipped below the treetops, the forest fell into early twilight.

The map was no longer continuous; the area on her forearm continued on the bottom of her foot, the section on her left breast was completed on some part of her that she couldn't see. She unfastened her bra, took off more clothes. All her clothes.

Trace looked around frantically to figure out where they were. It would have been impossible to follow every line and fit it all together mentally without Trace. Studying it with him, exploring this new aspect of her body, had been the most intimate thing she'd ever experienced. She was sharing a magical, hidden part of herself that no one else had ever seen before.

"I think I've got it," he said. "There's a river ahead."

"I sort of remember a river..."

"You do?"

"I've dreamed about it. In a place I'd never been before, I thought. It passes under the pavilion? Next to a big building with a clock."

"The City must be drawn to geography that's similar to

its old location." Trace ran his finger along the inside of her thigh. "The river's here."

She shivered.

"And if we follow it up…" He stopped. She waited. He brushed his thumb across her hip and then up her spine. "The City should be right here. Not far. Maybe one-point-five kilometers northwest."

He struggled to stand, but she didn't let go of his hand.

"What?" he asked.

Anara studied his face. The last of the sunlight filtered through the leaves and dappled his skin.

"I'd really like to kiss you." Trace leaned close.

She pressed a hand to his chest. "Me too. But not yet."

She picked her scattered clothes from the open field like flowers. "We're very close. Can you make it?"

"Let's go."

"Lead the way, Trace."

The hitch in his step was barely noticeable.

Soon they came across a large, flat stretch of land that had a sparse distribution of very young trees and not much plant life. And there was the river.

Anara pulled off her remaining shoe and slipped off her socks. She sat on the bank of the river and dug her toes into the soft, cool earth. She breathed in.

There were more voices now, talking over each other. She couldn't hear herself think anymore, or separate her thoughts from theirs. Had they ever been separate?

She followed the lines on her left calf until she couldn't see them. Their time was almost up, but they didn't need the map anymore. A gnarled oak tree—massive, old—loomed before them.

This is where it ended.

This is where it began.

"This is the place," she said.

Trace held her hand. "Are you sure?"

She interlaced her fingers in his and pressed their foreheads together.

"Goodbye," she whispered.

"Goodbye, Anara."

She closed her eyes. They kissed.

His lips were warm and rough and tasted like summer. She felt light enough to float away as her final burden was lifted.

She wanted to live.

((Wake up!)) she said.

❀ ❀ ❀

Anara opened her eyes. A gray-haired woman in a gauzy green blouse, black pants, and a red sash around her waist looked down at her with concern.

"Are you okay?" the woman asked.

"Yeah?" Trace said. She heard Trace's groggy voice through her ears and in her head at the same time.

Where was he? Anara tried to turn her head, but she couldn't move.

"I've healed your wound," the woman said.

Wound? What wound?

The bullet in Trace's left side.

The woman reached down to help Anara up. Anara took her hands, but she couldn't feel them. She couldn't feel anything. She was completely detached from the movement as she was pulled to her feet.

Anara didn't recognize her hands. In fact...

They weren't hers. They were Trace's hands.

She was in Trace's body, seeing through his eyes.

She was in Trace's body!

The woman hesitated and then embraced Trace.

"Ma?" he asked.

"Yes." She was crying. This woman was Kaye Alabaster, Trace's mother. "You're so beautiful, my love."

"What's going on? What happened?" Trace asked. "Anara! Where is she?" He looked around and swayed dizzily.

"Easy. Now that The City is restored, I'm afraid Anara is gone." She shook her head. "I'm sorry, L——."

"Dammit." He closed his eyes. "Why did you do this?" he whispered.

When he opened them, he asked, "And Pa?"

Kaye glanced behind her at a group of silver-haired people clustered in the center of a square. "He was banished. He hurt you, and now we know about his plans to seize control of The

City and her magic. He is no longer one of us. He's outside right now, looking for us, but he won't be able to enter our borders ever again."

Beyond the square, hundreds of people were gathering, crowding the streets. Silent.

"L——, thank you," Kaye said.

"Don't thank me. This was all Anara's doing. And call me Trace."

"Trace it is," she said.

Anara listened quietly as the reunited family talked. They joined the other council Elders, who were discussing how to prepare if the Evervale refugees returned. Alton Alabaster, now considered as much an outsider as any nonmagical person, would forget The City's new location once he left the area—if he made it out. It seemed the forest didn't want him to leave.

As the night wore on, when Trace was in his childhood home and began to drift off to sleep, Anara spoke.

Trace? she said. **Don't freak out.**

Trace jolted upright. "Anara?" He looked around. "Where are you?"

I'm here. Um, in your head. Don't tell anyone. *Please.*

"That's impossible," he said.

Use your inside voice, will you? You'll wake your mother up.

"Huh? Like…(((this?))"

You've got it! Oh, Trace. The City. We brought it back.

((You did. But what are you now?))

I don't know. But I don't want to tell the Elders until we know more.

((Why not? Maybe they can help.))

I don't trust the Elders, including your mom. Sorry.

((That's fair, considering what they did.))

Trace, your father wasn't completely wrong. They should share the magic.

Maybe they should even open the border one day. If they could all get along in one girl's head for sixteen years, they could make room for more people, more voices to make The City richer.

((I agree. I'll work on changing Ma's mind. But mainly because we'll need magic to get you a new body.))

Boys, Anara said.

((I didn't mean—))

I know. I don't want to get my hopes up, but I would really like that. But in the meantime, can I ask you another big favor?

((Anything.))

When it's safe, can we visit my family? They'll be worried about me. Though finding out their daughter is now a voice in her boyfriend's head might make them *more* worried. But it's better than being dead.

((Of course. As soon as we can. It doesn't seem fair that I've gotten my mother back, my home back, and you've lost everything.))

Not everything, she said.

((Whoa. Is that you?)) Trace asked.

What?

((I'm blushing. Like, a lot. All over.))

Ugh! I guess there are some other side effects. Sorry.

((Anara, you aren't a *side effect*. I like it. Reminds me of you. What were you thinking about?))

Anara sighed. She didn't know how she managed that, without any breath, but this was magic.

I was thinking...I finally feel like I'm exactly where I'm supposed to be.

AUTHOR PHOTO
BY MONIKA WEBB

E(ugene). C. Myers is the author of the Andre Norton Award–winning *Fair Coin* and *Quantum Coin*, young adult science fiction novels published by Pyr, and *The Silence of Six* and *Against All Silence,* young adult cyber thrillers from Adaptive Books. He was assembled in the U.S. from Korean and German parts and raised by a single mother and a public library in Yonkers, New York, where he survived an improbable number of life-threatening experiences— most miraculously, high school—with ample scars as proof. Visit ecmyers.net and follow him on Twitter @ecmyers.

SECOND CHANGES

A SHORT STORY INSPIRED BY
2NE1'S "IT HURTS"

By Ellen Oh

This is one of my favorite K-pop songs by one of my favorite K-pop groups. It's a slow ballad but with a unique sound. Slightly bluesy, definitely soulful. And the lyrics, about the pain that comes from love lost, seemed the perfect song for my little story about a girl who loses her sister only to realize how much she really loved her.

—ELLEN OH

T HE LAST TIME I SAW MY SISTER ALIVE WAS THE MORNING of her accident.

❧ ❧ ❧

Early Saturday and I enjoy my usual sleep of the dead when Hannah walks in to our room and jumps on me.

"Hey, wake up! I've made you breakfast."

I threw my pillow at her. There should be a law that forces all members of a family to either be morning people or late-nighters. It's frustrating as hell when one person doesn't fit in to everyone else's schedule. And when it comes to not fitting in, I'm always the odd one.

"Come on, you have to eat before it gets cold," she says, stripping me of my blankets.

"ARGH! This is my side of the room! Stay on your side!"

I grab for my comforter, but Hannah blocks me and starts tickling my feet.

"Stop it!" I shriek. I hate being tickled more than anything in the world. It makes me want to pee and barf at the same time. I try to kick my legs, but Hannah's too strong. Desperate, I throw myself out of bed, slamming onto the floor hard.

"You stupid jerk, look what you made me do!"

Hannah laughs. "Now you're up, come eat before I tickle you again."

Fuming, I push myself up. Hannah's corner of the room is always neat and organized while my side looks as if a wild animal had stampeded through it. People always comment on how our room perfectly matches our personalities. A discordant mess of magazine pictures and my own drawings that cover every inch of wall space on the right, while the left looks like an advertisement for *Seventeen* magazine's teenage fantasy bedroom with packed bookshelves and a neatly made bed.

Just then, I spy the big alarm clock sitting on Hannah's desk. It's 6:45 a.m. She woke me up before seven on a Saturday. Furious, I stomp over to where Hannah's books are piled neatly on her desk and knock them all to the ground before heading to the kitchen. The smell of pancakes and fried Spam begins to penetrate into the sleep fog surrounding my brain.

Usually our mom leaves rice and soup for breakfast, a typical Korean meal, which is all right. But pancakes are my favorite.

"Why the hell did you wake me up so early?" I yell at her. "Did Mom and Dad force you to get up when they left?" Our parents leave at five every morning to go down to the market store they own in the Bronx.

Hannah glances at me and shrugs. "I felt like cooking. You should eat it hot."

I'm still mad, but my mouth is watering as I sit down and fill my plate with food. I pour maple syrup generously over my pancakes, uncaring that my Spam gets covered too. Hannah is washing dishes at the sink and singing some new K-pop song that I've never heard of. Ever since middle school, she's been heavy into K-pop and follows the Korean billboard chart online for all the top music videos. It's how her Korean got so good. That and watching K-dramas every week with our mom and aunts. Everyone always says Hannah is pretty enough and talented enough to be a K-pop idol. Not that our mother would ever let that happen. Not her golden child. No, she won't accept anything less than a medical degree for her firstborn.

Hannah pours herself a cup of coffee and a glass of milk for me and sits down at the table. There's a little smile on her face, like she has a secret she's dying to share. She's been unusually happy these days. I wonder what's up with her.

"Aren't you eating?" I ask as I shovel an entire pancake into my mouth.

She shakes her head. "I ate a couple of test pancakes first," she says. "And you know I can't eat once I smell the Spam." Hannah shudders.

I grin as I grab two slices of Spam covered in maple syrup and shove them both into my mouth. It's a mean thing to do, given the fact that Hannah hates Spam and only makes it for me because I love it. But at that moment, all I think about is how early it is. Taking another pancake, I rip it in half and make a pancake/Spam sandwich.

Hannah grimaces and finishes her coffee.

"I washed the pans, so all you have to do is clean up your dishes," she says. "Please don't leave them in the sink all day. You know how much Mom hates that."

I shrug. It isn't like I set out to forget. I always tell myself to do them before my parents come home from the store, but I never remember. I tend to get lost when I'm working on an art project.

"Where you going?" I ask, finally taking note of her clothing.

"To the library," she says. She's packed up her messenger bag and her backpack. I'd bet a million dollars and all my art supplies that they aren't all filled with books.

I snort. "Right," I say, taking note of her curve-hugging black V-neck top and jeans. It's a lot trendier than I'm used to seeing her wear.

"New boyfriend?"

Hannah glares at me. "Not everything is about boys."

I roll my eyes, not wanting to hear a lecture. Just because she's five years older than me, my parents constantly ask

Hannah to give me advice even though I don't want it. I don't need advice from the perfect child because I'm never going to be a perfect child no matter what my parents think.

"Whatever, just wondering why you're all dressed up for the library," I say.

Hannah sighs and picks up her bags. A little bit of black leather peeks out from the corner of her bag.

"So where are you really going?" I ask.

"I told you, the library." She slides on her flats and grabs her bags.

"So you need your fancy black boots just to go to the library?"

Her cheeks flush. I knew it.

"Well, well, well, Mommy's perfect child is lying to her and sneaking around with some boy," I say, smirking at her.

"I told you, not everything is about romance or dating," she says seriously.

"Well if it isn't a boy, then tell me where you're going," I demand. Not that I really care, I just like bugging her.

"Hopefully I'll be able to tell you about it soon," she says, that same small smile playing on her lips.

"Tell me now."

"It's not any of your business," she says.

"Then I'm going to tell Mom you aren't at the library," I say.

Hannah opens the door and turns to stare at me. "Then I'll have to tell her about the art supplies you stole."

I blanch and then feel the blood rushing into my face. "You nosy jerk! How dare you snoop through my stuff!"

"I was trying to find my charger, which you're always taking," she says. "I thought it fell under your bed, but instead I find the box of missing art supplies Mom and Dad have been worrying about. You shouldn't have done it. They think one of the workers took it."

"Leave me alone!"

"Well then, if you mind your business, I'll mind mine."

"I hate sharing a room with you," I shout. "I wish you'd go away!"

"Me too," she responds. "I wish we could afford to let me stay in the dorms, but then you'd have all of Mom's attention on you all the time. No reprieve. You should be careful what you wish for."

"I don't care, anything would be better than seeing your stupid face every day!"

Hannah sighs. I can see she is really trying not to be mad. "Look, I know it's hard, but you should tell Mom and Dad you want to be an artist, not a lawyer. You're really talented."

"Like it matters what I want," I respond.

"It does matter, because you need to do what makes you happy, not what makes them happy."

"Says the girl who is going to be a doctor because Mom is forcing you to," I sneer.

"Which is why I'm telling you this now," Hannah says.

"Don't let them push you into being something you're not. Don't be like me."

"I don't want to be like you! I hate you!"

❀ ❀ ❀

That's the last thing I said to her.

❀ ❀ ❀

The police come before dinnertime. Saturday nights my parents let the store manager close up so that they can have dinner with the family. They usually get home by six to find that Hannah has made the rice, but there is no Hannah and no cooked rice.

My mom is distracted cooking dinner. She keeps calling Hannah's cell phone, but it just rings and goes to voice mail.

"Something is wrong," she mutters over and over again.

When the doorbell rings, I stand waiting in the hallway. My father finally answers the door. I'll never forget the look of horror on my mother's face as she catches sight of the officers.

"Hannah," she says. "Something happened to my Hannah."

I hear one of them say "I'm sorry, there's been an accident" and then my mom just collapses onto the floor sobbing. My dad can't even console her, it's all he can do to stand holding on to the door. They're too grief stricken to invite the officers inside. I'm the one who asks them in to our living room and pulls up chairs for them to sit on. I'm the one who helps my mom up and seats her on the sofa. I'm the one who asks them what happened.

She was crossing Sixth Avenue on Bleecker when an SUV ran the red light and barreled into the crosswalk filled with pedestrians. A big black Cadillac Escalade, one of the biggest and heaviest SUVs there is. The woman had been too busy talking on the phone to see the red light and all the people in the crosswalk. Hannah had her headphones on and was apparently looking the other way. Eyewitnesses said the SUV knocked her off her feet and then rolled over her. They said the only reason the woman stopped was because people had swarmed her car, banging on her windows. It was as if the woman had no idea she'd hit a person. My sister was just a nuisance speed bump on the way to her Pilates class.

"Was she sorry?" my mom asks. "Was she sorry she killed my beautiful girl?"

"I don't know," the policewoman says. She looks sad.

"What time was the accident?" my Mom asks. "What time did she die?"

"It happened at 4:30," the policeman answers. "She died thirty minutes later at the hospital. It took a while to find your information."

"Yes, that makes sense," my mom whispers. "That was when I felt an icicle stab me in my chest. That must have been Hannah's suffering."

At the hospital we learn that Hannah didn't go easily. That she suffered tremendous pain before she died. Bleeding to death from having all her internal organs crushed and nearly every bone in her body shattered.

They hand over Hannah's bag, and I take it because my parents can't even stand up straight. When they go to see Hannah's body, they lose all their control, crying hysterically and yelling things out in Korean. I am the only one to notice that my sister is still beautiful, even bruised and faded by death.

❁ ❁ ❁

It was my sister who named me. When I was born, Hannah was five years old and she decided that she wanted a sister named Brooklyn. Ironic, since we live in Queens. That summer my parents had taken her to Coney Island for the first time and Hannah had declared that she loved Brooklyn. My parents indulged her and let her choose my name. A five-year-old. She always joked that I should be grateful my parents didn't take her to Niagara Falls instead. The funny thing is she never called me Brooklyn. She always called me BK. I don't know why, but I tend to like it better than my real name.

I always resented my sister for having so much control over my life when I had none. And yet, my sister loved me. I resented that also. I resented her so much that I don't think I ever once told her that I loved her.

I'm sitting on the floor of our room just staring at her bed. My parents are in the living room with my aunts and uncles planning the funeral. I refuse to be with them. Suddenly I hear a ringtone. It's from a K-pop song I hate. For a second I almost yell at Hannah to turn it off. And then I remember.

I grab Hannah's bag and reach for her phone. I don't recognize the number. It must be someone who doesn't know what happened to Hannah. I'm frozen. The phone stops ringing. I stare at it in relief. I can see the battery life on the old flip phone. One and a half bars left even after Hannah... Well, the only good thing about not having a smartphone is the battery life.

The phone starts ringing again. It's the same number. I open the phone before I can change my mind.

"Hello?"

"Good morning Hannah! This is Tracy from XM Entertainment calling to reschedule your callback."

"Callback?" I ask in confusion.

"Yes, I don't think anyone explained why all the callbacks were canceled on Saturday. There was an incident outside the building and several people got hurt. So the building management made us shut down at five. That's why we had to send everyone home."

"Reschedule for what?"

"The callback for the *Who Wants to Be a K-Pop Idol?* competition," Tracy's voice is wary. "Am I talking to Hannah Lee?"

I start to cry. This was where she'd been heading to that day. This was her secret that she'd been so happy about.

"I'm not Hannah," I whisper. "I'm her sister."

"Oh, okay," Tracy sounds surprised and a bit uncertain. "Is Hannah there?"

"She was in an accident," I whisper.

"I'm so sorry, is she okay?"

My nose feels swollen in pain and I feel terrible pressure in the back of my eyes. I'm shaking hard. All my tears that had been pent up for the last two days can no longer be held in.

"She didn't make it," I gasp out just as the tears overwhelm me. I'm sobbing, my pain so deep that I don't know if I'll ever stop crying. I close the phone and lay on the floor, my hand gripping Hannah's cell phone.

When I finally stop crying, I realize that Hannah wasn't as perfect as our parents thought she was. She tried out for a K-pop singing competition. She hid it from all of us. And I know why. My parents would never have let her go. They would never have allowed her to deviate from their chosen path for her future.

And now I'm all they have left. The dysfunctional child. The one who is nothing but a bitter disappointment to them. I know what they're thinking. They lost the wrong daughter.

I think about my last words to her and my stomach clenches so hard I want to puke. I miss her so much it hurts. I go into Hannah's bag again wanting to feel her presence. I see her little notepad and pen, her Chap Stick, her iPod. Things she always kept with her. Then I spot a small pink bag that I recognize. It's a little French bakery in the West Village that makes my favorite macarons. I open the bag and there's a box with four green cookies. Pistachio, my favorite. I look at the pink bag and notice the address for the first time. Bleecker Street.

I can't breathe.

I take Hannah's iPod out and hit play. The first song is my sister's favorite 2NE1 song, "It Hurts."

I pound my head on the wall, welcoming the physical pain, because the emotional one is too great for me to handle.

"I'm so sorry Hannah, I'm so sorry I never told you that I love you. Please God, I wish I could see her again just once more so I can tell her that I've always loved her."

🌸 🌸 🌸

"Hey, wake up! I've made you breakfast."

I open my eyes and see Hannah jumping on my bed. My chest tightens. This dream is too real.

"Come on, you have to eat before it gets cold," she says, stripping me of my blankets.

I sit straight up and stare at my sister. What kind of dream is this? How torturous can my mind get? I can't take this pain. I grab for my comforter, wanting to ignore it, but Hannah blocks me and tickles my feet.

"Stop it!" I shriek. I know what happens next. I immediately throw myself out of bed, slamming onto the floor hard.

I'm lying there stunned, as I stare up at my sister's smiling face. I've missed her so much. Are dreams supposed to hurt this bad?

Hannah laughs. "Now you're up, come eat before I tickle you again."

She walks out of the door and I slap myself on the face hard. My eyes are tearing and yet I can still hear my sister's voice, singing from the kitchen. I rise unsteadily to my feet and glance over at the clock. It's 6:45 a.m. This is the morning of her accident. What is happening? How can this be? Is this reality and what happened before the dream? Could it be true? Could my prayers have been answered? I don't know what to think.

Hannah is washing dishes at the sink and singing that K-pop song I'd heard only once before. I sit down on my chair desperately trying not to cry. I'm not even hungry. I just sit staring at my sister.

Hannah pours herself a cup of coffee and a glass of milk for me and joins me at the table. She has that little smile on her face that I remembered bugging her about. Everything feels so real.

"Aren't you eating?" she asks. "I made your favorite." She pushes the plate of Spam toward me.

Ignoring the plate, I reach over and grab Hannah's hand.

"Are you really here?" I choke out. The tears start flowing. Please God, don't let this dream end.

Hannah is looking at me in surprise and alarm. "What's gotten into you?"

She comes over to check my forehead and I take the opportunity to hug her hard. I can smell her light lemony scent. She feels solid and real. I don't want to ever let go. I have so much to tell her. I open my mouth but I choke up and the words get stuck in my throat.

"There's something definitely wrong with you," Hannah said. "Are you hurt? Do you feel sick?"

I feel as if I've been hit by a train at full speed. My body's a broken mess and my brain is rattling in my head. I sway in my seat.

"Okay, you need to get back into bed," Hannah says. "I have to go out but I'll let Mom and Dad know you're sick."

"No!"

Hannah goes still.

"You can't go. I'm sick," I blurt out in a desperate attempt to make her stay. "My stomach's really bad. I'm going to throw up."

I run to the bathroom and pretend to throw up. I really go for it and retch so hard. I feel myself gag and then I'm actually fighting to keep from vomiting. The battle must sound bad because my sister is by my side, rubbing my back.

"You need rest," she says.

I climb into bed and grab her hand.

"Stay with me."

I can see the conflict on her face. But she nods. "Go to sleep, I'll watch over you."

Something about trying not to vomit and the shock of the

morning makes me exhausted. I don't want to fall asleep, I want to be with my sister. I can't help thinking this is a dream, but it feels so real. How can it be real? How can I be sleepy in a dream? My mind is reeling and I'm dizzy and nauseated. I fight hard against closing my eyes and keep a tight hold on her hand. I need to talk to her. I need for her to know how much she means to me.

"Hannah…"

"Just sleep, Brooklyn."

"No, I can't." But my eyes are too heavy.

I wake up and the clock reads 10:30. I call out to Hannah but there's no one home. I jump up in a panic. She's not in the house. There's a note on the kitchen table.

BK—I'm sorry but I had to go out. I'll be home as soon as I can. Just take it easy and rest.—H

I'm such an idiot! How could I have fallen asleep? How could I have lost her again? No! I won't. I can't. I still haven't told her how much I love her.

I pick up my cell phone to call her, but she doesn't answer. My voice mail message is blinking.

"Hey BK, I'm so sorry I had to leave you but I had a really important appointment today. I'll make it up to you and bring you back a sweet surprise. Just stay in bed and feel better, okay?"

I run to the computer and start googling K-pop auditions and finally find a Soompi forum that talks about the auditions for some big reality television series called *Who Wants to Be a K-Pop Idol?* being held today near NYU. I jot down the information and start getting ready. I feel gross but I don't have time to shower. I braid my hair, grab my thin black jacket, and run out the door.

It's late morning on a Saturday and the 7 train is crowded. Forty minutes to Times Square and then transfer to pretty much any train that'll take me to West Fourth Street. I hate the subway. Yeah, convenience is awesome and all that. But the smell and the heat in the summertime is too gross. And I can't stand watching the rats pick through the garbage on the tracks. Gross.

At Times Square, I jump on a downtown F train and immediately have to put on my jacket. The conductor's got the AC on subzero temperatures. The only good thing about it being so cold is that I can't smell the homeless guy sleeping at the back of the car. I'm too nervous to sit, so I stand by the door and stare out the window, watching the pipes snake up and down the walls and tunnels that appear and disappear before the next station stop. Only a few stops more, but then the train stops at Fourteenth Street for what feels like forever. I'm debating jumping off and running the rest of the way when the doors finally close.

West Fourth Street station. Finally I'm off, whipping my jacket off as I hit the humid steam bath that assaults me. I race up the tunnel and out into the hot ninety-plus-degree temperature.

It takes me a moment to figure out where I am. I've only come into the Village once before, when my parents took

Hannah on a college visit to NYU. I have to keep asking people for help. I know I've reached the right place when I see the long line of contestants spreading all the way down the block. I'm walking past the line slowly and nearing the front when someone yells "Go to the back of the line!"

I catch the eye of a very hostile looking girl in the skimpiest black dress.

"I'm looking for my sister," I reply.

The girl rolls her eyes at me. "Do you know how many people are here? There were more than two hundred people ahead of me and I've been on this line since nine."

I glance at my watch. It's nearly noon. "I think my sister got here around eight."

"Then she's probably in the second round of contestants that just went in like a minute ago," the girl replies. "But only contestants are allowed in."

"How do I get in?"

The girl shrugged. "You're gonna have to wait in the back or sneak in somehow." Suddenly she stood up straight and started fixing her hair. "Hey, get out of the way, the camera crew is coming again." She whips out a big sign and starts waving it in the air like crazy. The sign has the name of the show and a big heart around it. Everyone on the line is now screaming at the camera crew that's moving up from the back of the line, filming the crowd.

I sneak closer to the front. The security guards are busy talking to a bunch of people wearing headsets and the contestants are acting like wild animals on stampede. The crowd is going crazy. They surge forward, breaking the rope and causing several people to fall. The guards are yelling and trying to stop people from getting trampled. It's a mob scene. Now nobody is standing at the doors. I hear a guard calling for an ambulance. This is my chance. I move quickly to the door, open it, and slide in before anyone sees me.

Inside, there's another huge crowd of people. They're all waiting on a line leading to sign-up tables. A photographer is stationed at the other end. I try to walk around the line to see if I can find Hannah, but I'm stopped.

"You need to stay in the back, little girl," says a heavily made-up Asian woman with her head shaved on one side and long purple hair on the other.

"I'm looking for my sister..."

"Don't care who you're looking for, you need to stay behind me."

She's right in my face, her stale breath choking me. I back away and try to strain my neck to peer around the crowd. There's no way to see who's on this crazy line. I've no choice but to wait as the line inches forward. I study every person who heads to the photographer for their "Idol" shot. I don't see Hannah anywhere. I try calling her phone, but there's no answer. I finally make it to the first table.

"Fill out this application and take it to the next table to get your number." The surly-looking boy thrusts papers at me without even looking up.

"Excuse me, but can you tell me if a Hannah Lee has registered?"

The boy gives me the dirtiest look. "No."

I don't know how I'm supposed to find her. I try my sister's phone again. Now there's no signal. My phone sucks even when I'm not in a dead spot. I look over the application and scribble down everything as fast as I can. For talents, I just rush through and check everything and drop my paper at the next table. A slightly friendlier girl hands me a bunch of papers and a tag with the number 377 on it. I have my picture snapped and they point me toward the double doors in the back.

It opens into a large auditorium that is more than half full. I walk up and down the aisles looking for my sister, but I can't find her.

"Hey, you need to sit down in your section until you're called," someone with a clipboard yells at me.

Dejected, I turn back. There's no way I'm sitting next to purple bald lady. Instead I slink up a few rows to an open seat and sit down. It's now 1:30. The accident happens at 4:30. I have to find her.

I look down at the forms that the numbers girl gave me and hone in on the requirements. Dancing, singing, rapping. Wait, what did I check off? I wonder if I seriously am going to have to perform to find my sister. What was I thinking? I can't even sing.

I pull out my crappy phone and call Hannah's number

again, but the reception in the school is tragic. No bars, no signal. I curse my parents for being too cheap to pay for better service and being stuck with a cheap-ass no-signal carrier.

The people next to me are arguing loudly over who the better K-pop group is, EXO or Big Bang. They're getting really loud and obnoxious. I have to move away. I spot another open area a few rows up and sit down.

I'm trying to keep an eye on contest workers with the clipboards. Maybe someone will tell me where the first group went. Maybe I can sneak out.

"Hey." Someone nudges me. "You really nervous or something?"

Just then I realize that the girl sitting next to me is African American, and she's got a number. Only then does it dawn on me that not everyone in the room is Korean. Hell, most aren't even Asian. How did I not notice this before?

"Yeah," I reply. "I must be crazy to be here."

The girl laughs. She's got this really great smile and a musical laugh that makes me think she probably sings divinely.

"Don't worry, you're not alone in feeling that way," the girl says. "I'm Micah. This is my posse—Corinne, Sophia, and Pippa. We call ourselves Soul Sisters."

Corinne is sitting next to Micah and is the palest blond girl I have ever seen. Her eyebrows are so blond it almost looks like she has none. Sophia and Pippa are leaning on the seats in front of them. They both look Latina, Puerto Rican I think. I keep staring at the four of them like they're some kind of alien species. I'm having a hard time believing that they're a K-pop group.

"So you guys are into K-pop?"

Corinne reaches over Micah to grab my hands. "I may not look Korean, but I am Korean at heart," she said. She then repeats her words in near perfect Korean.

I can't help it. I bust out laughing. "Dude, your accent is better than mine!"

"Right? If you closed your eyes I could be a real Korean," she said.

"Almost. But how'd you learn?"

"Nonstop K-drama marathons!"

Everyone starts laughing but I'm nodding. "No, for real, that's how my sister's Korean got so good also."

"Are you singing a K-pop song?" I ask.

The girls all nod.

"It's too bad they won't let us audition as a group," Micah says. "We do a mean rendition of f(x)'s 'Four Walls.'"

The girls all strike a pose and begin to sing. Together, their Korean doesn't quite sound right, but I recognize when they hit the English chorus.

I clap because they really do sound great.

"So what about you?" Micah asks.

Now I feel awkward and young. These girls are cool and older. Would they still talk to a high school freshman?

"I'm Brooklyn Lee, and I'm fourteen."

I can feel myself scowling as I hear the "so young" comments until Micah tells the others to knock it off.

"She's fourteen, and got her ass to this audition by herself," Micah said. "I say she's pretty grown to me."

"Who's your favorite K-pop band or singer?"

I freeze at this question. How do I answer this? Do I admit that I'm not a fan? That I only came here to find my sister and save her from getting killed? God that sounds so crazy.

"2NE1," I say. They're the one band I don't mind my sister blasting on the speakers.

"Yo, that's my jam! CL is my girl," Micah said, naming the lead singer. "And you totally could be Minzy's little sister."

It takes me a moment to figure out who Minzy is. Usually I hate when people tell me how I remind them of some Asian who I look nothing like. I end up feeling resentful and offended. But this time, it doesn't bother me. Hannah has mentioned the resemblance to me many times before.

Hannah. My stomach lurches anxiously.

"Hey, do you know what happened to the previous group of contestants?" I ask Micah. "My sister was here earlier but I don't see her now."

"They've been taking groups of ten at a time out the front," Micah says.

I'm looking up front to the left of the stage where the doors are, and I'm wondering how I can get them to let me out.

Micah looks at me and shakes her head. "They don't let anyone out those doors before a group is called."

I'm nervous. It's now nearly two. I decide to wait for the next group to get called. I'm listening to the girls talk and I realize how cool it is that they like Korean music. They're really into it. They watch Korean dramas. They love my culture. It makes me proud in a way I have never felt before. Listening to them singing different lyrics from their favorite K-pop songs reminds me of what Hannah said to me when I told her I hated K-pop.

Don't deny your Korean heritage in your attempt to become All-American.

All this time I've hated it because I thought it was stupid and not as good as American music. But the truth is, I didn't respect my own culture. These girls make me realize how foolish I've been.

I can't wait to tell Hannah that I get it now. I need to tell her. Suddenly, I'm panicking and wondering if I'll ever see her.

Micah nudges me. A group of contestants are lining up near the front.

"Good luck with everything," Micah says. She reaches over and gives me a hug. She makes me tear up a bit.

I smile at the four girls and thank them. "You guys will be awesome!" I wave and head for the doors.

I wait at the end of the line until I reach a petite dark-haired girl speaking Korean into her headset. She then asks me for my number.

"I'm not scheduled until later but I'm supposed to find my older sister Hannah Lee," I say. "She was with an earlier group.

Is there any way I can find her? Her phone's not working and I know she must be worried about me."

I smile in what I think is a young manner, but only makes me feel sickly and weird, but I guess it works. She jots down my contestant number and opens the door.

"After you find her, please come back here for your audition," she says. "We must keep the order."

I nod and thank her. The time is now 3:00 and I'm tense and feeling off. I follow the group to a room where a few people are pacing anxiously. My sister's not there. I ask another contest member and she points at a large picture window in the front of the room that overlooks a small auditorium and that's when I see her. Hannah. She's just now crossing the stage toward the microphone.

My eyes tear up in relief. She looks so beautiful. I know what I want to tell her. I press myself against the window and listen as her voice comes over the loudspeakers in the room. She introduces herself and then launches into her song. The song I'd just been playing the night before.

Just like that, I remember crying in my room, listening to this song and thinking I'd lost my sister forever. Now I know I have a chance to change all that. This is not the dream. This is a second chance. A do-over.

The tears are falling so hard, I can't even see my sister on the stage, but I can hear her. I can hear her beautiful voice.

"Are you okay?"

I turn around to see a few people have crowded around

me in concern. I wipe at my eyes and try to tell them I'm okay, but I'm still choked up.

"Quick, someone get her water." They've got me by the arm and are moving me to a chair. I sit down in a daze as tissues are passed to me. I blow my nose and finally am able to clear my throat around the lump that was lodged in it.

"I'm all right," I say. "Thanks."

Then I realize that no one is singing. I bolt up and run to the window again. She's gone. There's some guy at the mic instead.

"My sister—where'd she go?" I ask the contest member.

"We just heard she got a callback," she replies with a smile. "She'll be in the callback room on the other side of the building."

I make for the door to the stage, but she stops me. "Sorry, you can't go that way, contestants only. You have to go the long way."

It takes me a lot longer than it should to find the callback room, and by the time I get there, fifteen minutes have passed. It's now 3:20. I barge into the room, anxious to see my sister, but she's not there. I'm panicking.

I stop a contest member and beg them for help.

"Hannah Lee? Number 127. Her callback is 5:30. She said she had to go to the store. She's got to be back by 5:15 or she forfeits."

I barely hear the rest of his words. I know where she's going. To that French bakery on Bleecker. I have to find her now. I have to save her.

Not having a smartphone means I have no way of looking up where the bakery is. All I know is that it's on Bleecker past Sixth Avenue. Outside, I don't know my way around so I have to keep asking for help. After some tourists stupidly send me running all around Washington Square Park, I'm finally pointed the right way by an old lady. It's now 3:45. I have less than an hour left. I try calling her phone again. Why won't she pick up?

I'm running down MacDougal to Bleecker. I feel like I've gone the long way again but I have to keep going. I cross Sixth Avenue with a horrible shudder. I keep moving as fast as I can, trying to run around all the crowds on the sidewalk and still keep an eye out for Hannah. I don't see her anywhere. I don't see anything that looks like a bakery. It's 4:00 now. I'm breathing hard and panicking. I've reached Christopher Street. There's no way it's this far. I must have missed it. I double back and almost miss it again. The store is so tiny, with a small pink awning over its door. I rush in and ask the clerk if they've seen an Asian girl that looked like me.

"Pistachio girl!" he says with a grin. "Yeah, she was here a few minutes ago. You just missed her."

I look at my watch. 4:20. "Oh God!"

This can't be happening. This is supposed to be a do-over. This is supposed to be a second chance. My chance to save her.

I run out and am caught behind the crowds of people on the narrow sidewalk. I'm so frantic I run into the road and get cursed at by the drivers. But I don't care. I have to reach my sister. I swerve in and out of traffic and barely pause for the red light. I don't care about anything but reaching Sixth Avenue. I'm still a full block away and my watch is reading 4:28. I'm sobbing and out of breath with a painful stitch in my side but I keep running. The light is red and I see the crowd of pedestrians at the corner waiting to cross. I can't see Hannah but I start screaming for her anyway.

"Hannah!"

The light is green and the crowd surges forward. I finally see her. But I'm still not at the corner.

"Hannah!"

She has her earbuds in and can't hear me. I see her crossing the street, and time slows down. I can't hear the noise around me. All I hear is the hoarseness of my own breath and my screams. I'm at the corner when I see the black Cadillac Escalade running the red light.

I'm screaming her name at the top of my lungs. I see her pause, her head turning slightly. And just like that time speeds up again, and I see it barreling into the stream of people ahead of me, scattering them, all except Hannah.

No! Please God, don't let me lose her again.

I need to reach her. I need to save her but I am a few seconds too late. Nothing changes. I watch as my sister is tossed in the air like a rag doll and comes crashing down on the windshield. I hear the glass shatter and then I slam my body into the driver's-side window, pounding my fists like a madman and screaming at her to stop. I see the woman drop the phone she was talking on as she finally jams on her brakes. I race around to my sister's side and I see that she's only inches from being rolled over by the front tires. At least I stopped her from being run over. But there's blood everywhere.

"Hannah," I'm crying so hard. "Please don't die. Please."

Her eyes flutter open.

"BK?" I hear her whisper.

"Hannah, I'm so sorry for always fighting with you. You're the best sister in the world and I love you. I'll always love you."

There's a slight smile on her face and I can feel her squeeze my fingers a little.

She tries to say something, but the effort is too much for her. Her eyes drift close and her hand goes limp. All I can do is scream her name over and over. When the medics finally come, they pull me off her, but I know it's too late.

It's all my fault. I had a chance to save her and I failed. This is too cruel. How could everything have conspired against me to make it impossible to save my sister? Why did I have to go through this day if nothing was going to change? Why did I have to live through this pain again?

I love you, little sister.

I catch my breath. I can still hear her. "I love you, Hannah."

I know.

AUTHOR PHOTO © ROBIN
SHOTOLA PHOTOGRAPHY

Ellen Oh is originally from NYC. She's cofounder, president, and CEO of WeNeedDiverseBooks, adjunct college instructor, and former entertainment lawyer with an insatiable curiosity for ancient Asian history. She also loves martial arts films, K-pop, K-dramas, cooking shows, and is a rabid fan of *The Last Airbender* and the *Legend of Korra* series. She is the author of the YA fantasy trilogy, *The Prophecy Series*, and the upcoming middle grade novel, *The Spirit Hunters,* to be published in fall 2017. Ellen lives in Bethesda, Maryland, with her husband and three daughters and has yet to satisfy her quest for a decent bagel. Visit ellenoh.com and follow her on Twitter @elloellenoh.

ANYONE OTHER THAN ME

A SHORT STORY INSPIRED BY DAVE MATTHEWS BAND'S "DANCING NANCIES"

By Tiffany Schmidt

As a student, and later as a teacher, "Dancing Nancies" was the last thing I listened to before heading out the door to start the first day of school each year. It's a song I always associate with new beginnings, opportunities for reinvention, reflection, and hope. But at the end of the day, I really wouldn't rather be anyone other than me, flaws, quirks, and all.

—TIFFANY SCHMIDT

THE GUY IN THE GREEN CAMP PINE HAVEN POLO SHIRT looked up from his clipboard. "What name do you go by?"

Mom's Explorer hadn't even bumped out of the parking lot, but I was already facing my first lie. Well, not *really* a lie, more of a *decision*. The last notes of a Dave Matthews Band song slipped out of the SUV's open window, Dave's raspy voice crooning questions about who else he could've been. I watched Mom wave, her rings flashing in the sunlight as she disappeared between pine trees and the camp's carved wooden sign.

I swallowed and turned toward the guy with the clipboard. It had the camp logo on the back—a cabin surrounded by clusters of pine trees. It looked a lot like the actual cabins and trees that surrounded us.

"Um." He extended the marker he'd been holding out this whole time. It was slightly sweaty from his grasp. His eyebrows had climbed up his freckled forehead, an expression that made confusion unfairly adorable. "Name tag?"

Had he said that more than once? Oh God. I'd been busy memorizing the back of Mom's car like there'd be a test on her license plate or the five stick-figure decals that represented our family. Six, if you counted the cat sticker my little brother, Franklin, insisted we get for Humphrey.

I tightened my fingers around the marker. "I'm supposed to get a purple one? That's my cabin?"

"Yup!" Relief melted into a smile on his face. And it was one of *those* smiles. The kind that transformed someone from cute to breathtaking. We're talking dimples that made me want to reach out and trace them. Not that I would. I'm housebroken, usually not socially inept, and I mastered 'keep your hands to yourself' a decade ago. He had gray-green eyes that sparkled like the surface of the lake visible beyond the trees. Top it off with ginger hair, like every Weasley brother I'd grown up crushing on, and I was pretty much uselessly staring.

"Purple," I said again, because I was clearly Pavlov and that word had gotten me that smile before.

"Right, purple," he said. "And you never did answer me: what do you like to be called?"

Oh, that. The question that had fuzzed my brain to begin with. The one that had me staring after Mom's tires like an abandoned puppy who'd changed her mind and would

rather be dragged along on Amanda's college visits than left
at sleepaway camp.

"Susannah? Sue? Suze? Suzie?" he prompted.

My parents didn't "do nicknames." *If we wanted you to
be called something shorter, that's what we would've picked.* The
only exceptions were my brother, Franklin, who called me
"Suze McSnooze" when I gushed about computer games, and
classmates at my homeschool co-op who called me by my
last name.

But in that pause I saw this was my chance—for once—to
write my own story.

"Suzie," I answered. Then, firmer, "Call me Suzie."

"Okay, Suzie." Dimples McMeltmybrain jotted it on his
clipboard. "Nice to meet you. After you've made your name
tag, you'll meet your group over there."

He pointed to a picnic table overflowing with a giggling
crowd of...strangers. My heartbeat accelerated and I had to
swallow past a lump in my throat. I looked back over my
shoulder, but Mom's car was long gone. I was stuck in Maine
for four weeks with girls I'd never met.

I hiccupped, and because my classroom was our dining
room and I'd spent hours facing a decorative mirror while
stumped by Spanish verb conjugations, I knew exactly how
pitiful I looked like when my lower lip trembled, my nostrils
flared, and my skin blotched.

The guy lowered his clipboard, revealing his own name
tag: *Mal*, and asked, "First time away from home?"

"Yeah." I huffed out a nervous laugh. "I was supposed to come with a friend, but—she canceled." Ava had been coming to this camp for years. Her family was friends with the owners' family. But she'd gotten a once-in-a-lifetime internship and understandably bailed. She owed me one and she knew it.

"No judgment here. I'd be just as freaked out if I went away."

I wanted to ask how that was possible, since he *worked* here. But ending the conversation *before* I cried seemed more important. "I'm okay. I'll get my name tag now."

"Good," Mal said. "Go meet some people; you'll forget about being homesick. You're going to love it here, Suzie. There's nothing like being outside in the summer—wait 'til you see all the stars. I'd never go indoors if they didn't make me." Tumbling stomach butterflies aside, I knew he was just doing his job. Then he blushed—like he'd said more than he should or gone off-script. And I wondered, just maybe, if whatever camper he checked in next wouldn't get *exactly* the same speech.

While I admired his enthusiasm, I wasn't sure I'd ever be "outdoorsy," and my throat clenched nervously as I glanced at the girls I was about to meet. "Thanks."

At the picnic table, I traded hellos and smiles, then survived the existential crisis of deciding how I would spell my new name—Suzy with a y? No. So then, *s* or *z* to go before my *ie*? While internally debating, I'd caught Mal's eye twice. From my end, this was easy. He was the only non-Dad-aged male at camp. But from his? I was one fifteen-year-old among a hundred girls. Why was he watching me? He probably *wasn't*. Except...he'd blushed. I hadn't imagined that.

Except, except, *I* was the one who was overwhelmed and wishfully thinking. Living in my head and writing a camp-romance-fantasy involving canoes for two, instead of living in the here and now where I had to extrovert. I wasn't shy... but I was shy with strangers. I usually hung back and let others approach me, took in a scene before deciding how to insert myself.

But I wasn't myself for the next month. I didn't have to be the girl who almost cried at check-in. I could be *Suzie*.

I *zie*'d my name tag, then dotted my *i* with an impulsive starburst. I didn't need to think about whether or not I was a heart-dotter. I was not.

"Purple posse, circle up." My counselor, Sheila, had a red stripe in her hair and wooden glasses. She couldn't be much older than my eighteen-year-old sister, Amanda. When she stood on a picnic bench and raised her hands, I joined the girls clustering around her and followed them down the path.

Susannah might've cursed Ava. Might've thought, slightly irrationally, that maybe a true friend would've turned down that cushy internship instead of abandoning her bestie at camp. But *Suzie* wasn't that petty. *She* could be anything I wanted. And I decided she wouldn't be shy or co-dependent. She would choose her own place in the crowd, be brave and assertive.

I scanned the girls filing into the cabin, claiming their duffle bags, and dragging them over to the bunks. My eyes settled on a girl with gorgeous dark skin and neat braids. She had an edgy confidence, was casually beautiful in a black tank top and cutoff shorts, when the rest of us were obviously dressed to impress. While everyone else was all frantic squeals, she was coolly opening her trunk and pulling out sheets.

Suzie is not *shy.* I took a deep breath and walked over. "Do you snore?"

"Like a drunken bear holding a chainsaw," she answered with a wry expression.

I let out a relieved breath—that was easier than I'd hoped. "Good, it'll be like sharing a room with my sister. Let's be bunkmates."

Her precise red lip stain stretched into a flawless grin and she tapped the name tag she'd stuck on her shorts—why hadn't I thought to put mine there? It was currently peeling off my boob and kept sticking to my hair. "I'm Kat. I hope you packed earplugs."

"Suzie. I'll take top bunk."

I was tugging sheets over my mattress's corners when Sheila asked us to circle up on the cabin floor. Once we were squished in—awkwardly close with girls we'd either just met or hadn't yet—she counted us, mouthing the numbers as she pointed. "Who are we missing?"

"The one with the crazy long hair," said the girl seated two spots down.

"Oh, I know who you mean," said the girl on my left. She leaned over and faux-whispered. "She looks like a home-schooled weirdo. Probably off panicking because she's actually going to have to socialize."

This set off a round of giggles. Even Sheila wasn't trying to hide a smile. "Girls, be nice."

I uncrossed my legs and pulled them to my chest. Thankfully I wasn't the only one not laughing—Kat looked bored—because I wasn't down for spending a month in a cabin full of girls who bonded via bullying.

It would be easy to stop this. Tell them I actually *was* homeschooled. Tell them I loved it. Tell them that, just like any students, homeschoolers came in a range from super-shy to super-social. I skewed somewhere toward the middle. Ava didn't have an introverted bone in her body.

But then I'd be *that* girl: the curious specimen of home-schooling who'd killed the first moment of group bonding. I'd spend the next four weeks answering questions and correcting misconceptions. It would become the first thing they'd learn about me, the one fact they'd never forget.

Instead I offered a weak smile to the long-haired girl who came out of the bathroom and took the last spot in the circle— oblivious to the giggles at her expense. For the first time I was *glad* Ava wasn't here. Because she would've spoken up, listed the benefits of being homeschooled: the flexibility, the co-op, the lack of wasted time, the way we got to pursue our own interests—how I was coding my own computer game, not stressing over state assessments.

It was all true—but it was all true for Susannah. And I'd left her back in Mom's car listening to Dave Matthews sing about "Dancing Nancies"—here was my chance to *be anyone other than me*, and I was certainly going to take it.

Sheila clapped her hands. "Let's go around the circle and tell a little about yourselves. Then we'll do a camp tour before the get-to-know-you rally."

I didn't pay much attention to the others' answers. I caught school newspaper, cheerleader, field hockey, ballet, drama—everyone seemed to define themselves by school activities. I was preoccupied with coming up with my response—Suzie's story. By the time the circle reached me, I'd cobbled it together based on the high school TV shows I watched—subtracting out the werewolves and vampires and murders. If they were going to base their opinion of homeschooling on stereotypes, it was only fair I do the same for public schools.

It was good Ava wasn't here, because there's no way we would've kept straight faces as I said, "I'm from north of Boston. I'm going into my junior year at WHS—" a vague set of initials that they could decipher however they wanted. "I do the usual stuff, fight with my sticky locker, avoid riding the bus. Sucky teachers, soccer team, homecoming court, skipping classes to spend time with my boyfriend—he's on the football team. I mean, my *ex*-boyfriend—we broke up." Current would've required photos I didn't have, and "ex" earned me sighs and a side-squeeze from Kat.

I looked around the circle. The girls were smiling—boldly, shyly, sympathetically—no one blinked at my lies. While I was still absorbing this fact, fighting a triumphant laugh, the girl next to me launched into her own intro, and the smiles switched to her.

Tour was a blur of cabins of various sizes and functions, canoes, archery range, climbing ropes. My mind was whirring with the lies I'd told and the ones I was still inventing and whispering to Kat and long-haired Lila, who was not only *not* homeschooled, she was also not at all concerned with others' opinions. A sweet and free-spirited girl, she carried her flip-flops and walked barefoot.

We ended at a fire pit where the camp directors, Mr. and Mrs. Alastair, welcomed us and introduced the meet-and-greet games. The first was simple—we formed groups based on our answers to different questions. It should have been brainless, but the first question was "How many kids in your family?" and the first person to reach *three* was my cabin mate who'd made the anti-homeschooling joke. Rather than join her, I turned and followed Kat to the group for two.

She grinned. "I've got an older sister—you?"

"Same."

"Coolness." Her smile felt like a shot of acceptance. It

wasn't quite a lie. I *did* have an older sister. And Franklin wouldn't care—wouldn't ever know—that I'd erased him to avoid being stuck with the cabin bully.

"They're doing college visits." I felt better slipping truth in my fictions. "Yale, Princeton, Duke, etc."

"Yikes. How does it feel to be the dumb one?" Kat's tone wasn't mean, but I tilted my head in confusion. My list would have similar caliber schools, only I didn't plan to leave Boston. She added, "You know, she's Ivy League–bound and you mentioned skipping class in your intro?"

"Oh, right. I—"

But Mr. Alastair called out another category, which saved me from answering.

It was easy enough to follow Kat around, so several rounds passed before we diverged. By that point we were laughing, inventing our own inside jokes as I reinvented myself.

Suzie:

- Chooses scary movies over action films (Forgive me, 007!)
- Baseball over football (No one tell my dad!)
- Gummy bears over chocolate (Oh my Godiva, not true at all!)

Only about Humphrey did I tell the truth. Because apparently I was willing to erase my brother and my personality, but not my cat.

It was a little unnerving how easily the lies slipped out.

Next were camp-wide intros—give yourself an alliterative nickname that tells two things about yourself. I tried to pay attention: *Laid-back, lit-mag Lila*, but it was hard not to be distracted by Mal escorting a pigtailed late-arriver who clung to his hand and made my heart melt. He left again and I focused on the circle: *Shopping, snorkeling Sarah. Kickboxing karaoke Kat.*

Just as I took a deep breath to begin my own intro, Mal approached again. This time with his arms full of ice pops and his eyes on where I'd stood to share my nickname. "Um," my voice trembled a bit before I pulled my shoulders back and stood taller, "I'm *Soccer sushi Suzie.*"

Except, the closest I came to seafood is Swedish Fish. Sushi just sounded more mature, more impressive. And maybe it *was* impressive, because I saw Mal smile and nod to himself as he walked away.

After games, Kat was telling me a story about a chemistry lab gone completely wrong and we were laughing with heads thrown back—when I got tingles down my spine. Mal was standing across the fire pit, stacking wood and watching *me.* I wanted to duck my head, hide the blush that raced up my cheeks, but Suzie, cosmopolitan girl I'd decided I now was, wouldn't. Instead I winked, and he dropped the log he was carrying.

As everyone headed back to their cabins, I loitered. Tying my shoe, then pausing to pick up an ice pop wrapper.

He glanced around the now empty campfire circle, then approached. "There's no sushi here." He pointed to the plastic crinkling between my fingers. "That's about as gourmet as it gets, but I hope you'll like camp anyway."

"Spy much?" I teased, wowed by the power of a wink and some amped confidence.

"I might've overheard a few things." He plucked the wrapper from my hand, trading it for a smile. "You should catch up with your cabin. Purple, right?"

I adopted a hip sway as I walked away, calling back, "You memorize all the campers?"

He held my gaze. "Nope."

❋ ❋ ❋

By day two of camp I'd learned the layout and gotten used to showering in flip-flops. I hated the slimy-stepped walk from the bathhouse to our cabin, but there were worse things. Like the rubbery eggs at breakfast and the first freezing seconds of swimming in the lake.

I'd also gotten used to watching for Mal. I caught glimpses of him running bread to the toaster at breakfast and helping Mr. Alastair carry canoes to the lake, but that wasn't satisfying. I sighed as he banged into the arts and crafts cabin, where the purple posse were making person-ality collages—but he grabbed a can of orange spray paint and banged back out.

"What's his story?" I asked Kat. This was her sixth summer here, and she was a walking *camplopedia.*

"Malcolm Alistair—the owners' son. Keeping track of him is the camp's version of *Where's Waldo.* Even if he wasn't such a slice of handsome cake, he'd still have groupies, but with those dimples, it's ridiculous." She cut out a picture of test tubes and added it to her collage of science equipment, equations, and musical notes. Kat was a bisexual, chem-whiz, trombone-playing daredevil. The first in the lake and to volunteer on the ropes course. I already wanted to keep her in my life after camp. She stole the bottle of glitter I was dumping over my pictures of clichéd high school crap. It was a joke of a collage that matched the lies I'd created on my first day. Each time I looked down, I had to bite back a laugh.

"So *that's* why he's the only guy here."

"Yup. He's not supposed to talk to us unless he has to for camp business."

"Really?" My voice squeaked.

"Yeah. He got in *huge* trouble last year when some girl snuck into the Alistairs' house. She was waiting in his room in her underwear. Maybe naked."

I felt my eyes go wide. Susannah wasn't totally naïve. I'd had boyfriends, had dated, had read all of Ava's romance novel collection, but sneaking into a guy's bedroom naked was beyond me—even in Suzie-mode. "Did he invite her?"

"Not at all! He was as shocked as his parents. She got sent

home and he spent the rest of the summer hidden away on kitchen duty where it's a hundred degrees."

"Oh." And *he'd never go inside if they didn't make him*—I wondered if Kat knew that, if he'd told other reluctant campers.

"They threatened to send him to some crotchety relative's if he was caught socializing again. He's been no-fun, no-talk eye-candy since."

"He talks to me."

Kat's expression was half dubious and half *spill-it-now*.

"I mean, he checked me in." And blushed. And talked to me after the campfire. And…I could recite everything he'd ever said to me, while he'd probably forgotten my name. Er, Suzie's.

"Oh." She snorted. "*Doing his job?* In front of half the camp. That's hardly salacious. Don't turn into a slobbering groupie on me, okay? You're too cool for that."

I straightened in my seat. I wanted to be "too cool" to worry about others' opinions. But if that were the case, I wouldn't be formulating my next lie. "Please, I'm *not* like Desperate, Naked Girl. Guys chase *me*, not the other way around."

She laughed and I turned to grab a magazine, because I didn't want approval for sounding like a bitch. I cut out another picture for my collage, both amused and unnerved that my whole cabin seemed to love the fake girl it depicted.

❀ ❀ ❀

The next day I won my game of "Where's Mal" when I encountered him on the path from the archery range to the infirmary. He nodded and would've kept walking, but I stepped in front of him, propped a hand on my hip, and scrambled for a flirty pickup line.

"So, Alistair, rumor is your parents own this place?" I cringed. Great job, Sherlock, you solved the mystery of matching last names.

Mal put down the handles of his wheelbarrow and took off a worn pair of work gloves. I swallowed. There was something about the bones and joints of guys' wrists that made my stomach butterflies giddy-up. Especially wrists like his. Toned. Tanned. Freckled. And, my personal Kryptonite: he was wearing a watch.

Mal pointed around. "It's true. I'm the prince of this pine kingdom."

"Do you live here year-round?"

"Yeah. Dad has a plow service in the winter and it's just me, my parents, and my little sisters. It's quiet before you all descend for the summer."

"Oh, poor you, spending the summer surrounded by a horde of adoring girls."

He grinned. "It's rough. Especially since you're off-limits."

I blinked and chewed my lip, trying to decide if "you're" was collective or personal. If it was collective, *whoa, there cowboy*, and maybe there was a reason that girl was in his room. If he meant *me*, then dammit, that still made me *off-limits*. "I'll let you go."

"I should." He looked over his shoulder at the empty path. "Where are you supposed to be?"

"The nurse. Archery injury."

"You okay?" His intense head-to-toe scan felt like being dipped in fizzy soda.

"I'm not hiding an arrow in my back or anything. It's stupid." I held out my hand. "Blisters. But one popped, so Sheila said I should get it cleaned and covered."

He exhaled—but I was holding my breath, because he'd reached for my palm and was cradling it. "Sometimes archery injuries are brutal. A girl last year ended up with the fletching embedded in her finger."

"Oh, cool." He shot me a confused look and my brain stopped obsessing over the way his calloused hand made mine tingle. "I mean, ouch?"

"Did I just—" He raised an eyebrow and his dimples emerged, "—leave you breathless?"

"That depends." I peered at him from beneath my eyelashes. A look I'd watched Ava perfect in selfies. "Did you want to?"

"God, yeah. But—" His face fell and he looked away, stepped away. Tucking his hands in the *back* pockets of his jeans to create even more space between us. He opened his mouth with what *had* to be an exit line or retraction.

So I cut him off. "Good to know—especially with all the other options hanging around."

"There are *no* options. Not unless I want to get sent to my great-uncle's house in the city." He pronounced "city" like it tasted bad and looked from me to the pine trees.

WWSS?—*What Would Suzie Say* to redeem herself from going breathless and his gentle rejection? I flipped my hair. "Well then, nature boy, I should probably leave you alone."

There, much better than my opening pickup line about his parents. But much more difficult too—because he was pretty much saying *he liked me*. He liked me, but...

"Probably." He shrugged. "Except...I want to know more about you. More than just what I overheard at campfire and memorized off that glitter bomb collage hanging in the arts and crafts cabin."

"You memorized that?"

"Slasher movies, palm trees, Skittles, boy bands, soccer, Red Sox, lots of makeup—though you don't seem to wear much." He leaned in and I ducked my chin, because he was right, I rarely wore any. "How am I doing so far?"

"A+ for memorization." My voice was tight, because none of that was *me*. "And that's way more than I know about you, so..." I took a step backward. Then another. "Your move."

Turning, I scampered into the nurse's cabin, joining a queue of kids with splinters and scraped knees. I wasn't going to be another crush-crazed camper chasing him. Both Susannah and Suzie were too cool for that.

That was the first night my pillowcase crinkled. I flipped it up to find a piece of torn construction paper from the arts and crafts cabin's scrap pile.

*I don't have time to make you a collage, so how about if I
just tell you about me?*

The next night was the label from an industrial sized can
of peaches.

*The strangest part of living here is the first few days after
camp ends. It becomes a ghost town and my sisters move
back from their cabins. Suddenly I'm not an only child/
employee and they're no longer campers and have chores.*

Day three was marker on the flap of a cardboard box.

*The lake freezes in winter. If you were here, I'd take you
ice skating and snowshoeing. There'd still be marshmallows—in cocoa, not s'mores. I wonder where you live—and
if you have harsh winters there. Maybe your palm trees
mean you're from Florida or California...*

Yesterday, it was a swim test checklist.

*You've probably heard the gossip, but last year there was a
camper who didn't get that I wasn't interested and crossed
a lot of boundaries. My dad still doesn't believe I didn't
encourage her. His trust is still pretty shaky, which sucks,
because until you...*

Tonight, an invoice for kitchen supplies.

The camp gets calls all the time asking what "kind" of camp it is. Everyone wants it to have some sort of specialty— theater, sports, band, etc. It makes me mad. Why can't we just be a camp-camp?

It's like at school—how by high school—it's too late to try something new. Everyone's so specialized in their sport, activity, or clubs that there's no room for novices. Is your school like this too?

CamperMal@me-mail.com

I wasn't sure how Mal got his notes under my pillow, but I loved them. Nothing was better than falling asleep with his words beneath my head and rolling through my mind. I hated not being able to reciprocate and smuggle notes back to him. I hated not being able to set the record straight about palm trees, school, and everything else. I hated the gut-twist of guilt when I realized he was betraying his dad's trust for *Suzie*, and wondered if he would for plain old Susannah.

On Saturday we were given our weekly hour of technology time. I sent a hasty "I'm still alive" email to my parents, then addressed a new message to the email scrawled on his last note.

Mal,

I've never experienced that aspect of school. See, I know there are lockers on my collage, but I'm actually homeschooled. I try new things all the time. Last year, Franklin—the younger brother I've denied having—got us all obsessed with Norse mythology. My sister and I tried Russian. She stuck with it; I went back to Spanish. And as a novice coder, I—

[delete]

Mal,

I'm the worst at ice skating. I broke my nose the only time I tried, but Franklin is a whiz on the ice. My dad doesn't have a snow plow to get us to school in bad weather (we have that down by Boston too), but since we don't *go* to school, it's not a problem. And Mom doesn't pause our lessons when the local schools close for snow days—but she lets us take them when the weather is glorious.

[delete]

I chewed my lip and watched the clock chew through my time. When Sheila called out: "Five-minute warning!" I swallowed and gave him the only truths that fit within the boundaries of my lies—thoughts about camp.

Mal,

I'm glad Pine Haven isn't specialized. Everything here is new to me. Okay, not everything. But my family isn't into hiking. I've kayaked on vacation, but never canoed. And while archery, disappointingly, didn't bring out my inner Katniss, I'm getting closer to actually hitting the target. I can see why you love it here. I'm so glad I'm at camp—and that I met you.

My fingers hovered over the keys—teeming with truths and revelations, apologies for not being worthy of the risks he was taking—but Sheila started a countdown. Threatening to power off our devices as soon as she reached *One*. I took a deep breath, added a brave *xox, Suzie,* then clicked *send* on a filtered version of myself.

❀ ❀ ❀

My flashlight thumped against my thigh as I walked to the bathroom, its glow small in the vastness of the night and towering pine trees. And stars. Like someone pierced holes in the velvet purple of the sky and was shining their own flashlight through them. I knew cities had light pollution, but I hadn't expected there to be such a difference from my sleepy suburb. I hadn't expected the air to smell like Christmas, or that I'd constantly be scrubbing sap off my skin because I couldn't stop leaning against the trees and inhaling.

I had an urge to linger and drink it in. The first week was over. In another week the first session ended. Two weeks after that I'd be leaving. Four weeks sounded impossibly long on the drive here, but as Suzie I'd thrived in the novelty and socialization. I could take or leave drama, canoeing, and archery. But I cherished my cabin mates, the hiking, the whispering after lights-out until Sheila's warnings crossed from good-natured to try-me—I wanted to stay suspended in this Christmas-sap-and-stars-s'mores bubble indefinitely.

I could hear the singing at the campfire, see the edges of its glow. It should've been cheesy. I should've been worried about the melted chocolate on my shorts, or the peeling sunburn on my shoulder. Mourning the sunglasses I'd lost in the lake when Kat and I flipped our canoe.

But above the campfire voices, I heard something else. A strum of guitar, a male voice singing "Dancing Nancies." There was only one person who it could be. And, yeah, he was part of the reason I wanted to stay too.

I turned off the flashlight and crept around the back of his house. Mal was sitting on the porch, guitar in his arms, eyes on the lake, mouth forming lyrics in a rasp that made my stomach butterflies pirouette.

"I'm impressed." I said from the porch steps.

He jumped and his fingers stumbled into a strum of

sour notes, but there was nothing sour about the shape of his mouth or the surprise in his eyes. His touch-me dimples emerged, then faded. "You're not supposed to be here."

"Want me to go?"

He looked around, then up at the stars, clenching his jaw before answering, "God help me, no. Not yet." He moved his guitar and I perched on the arm of his Adirondack chair.

"That's one of my favorite songs." It felt good to tell him something honest. I leaned in and rested my arm against his, feeling his hours of working outside in his sun-warmed skin. This moment was real.

"I know. I've been doing reconnaissance."

"How?"

He dimpled. "Not all of us only get an hour of connectivity a week."

My back and neck beaded with sweat. What information was on my Facebook page? My other social media profiles? How much had I revealed to the internet that contradicted what I'd said here? I should have spent my technology hour checking that—that my online persona didn't challenge Suzie's. "I should—I should get back."

"Hey—does it bother you? I didn't mean to cross boundaries."

That word again. "I'd rather you heard it from me," I confessed.

"Wouldn't it be nice if we had time to do that?" His

forehead was creased and I cursed myself for being flattered by his reconnaissance. He couldn't have found much if he wasn't using these precious seconds to confront me, right?

I forced my spine to relax and lean against him. "I like your letters."

"I can't wait until next Saturday and your next email."

I laughed, though my stomach tumbled at the thought of skating between lies and reality again. It was getting harder to keep this up. "Part of me can't wait until I *leave*, then I can email you every day."

"Yeah," he agreed. "But we won't be able to do this—"

I was hoping *this* was a kiss. It wasn't. He threaded his fingers through mine and goose bumps raced up my arms. Still good. Still very, very good.

"You're shivering." He unzipped his sweatshirt, but I shook my head.

"I can't—" and that thought was colder than the air. "I wish I *could* wear your sweatshirt, or hold your hand and stroll through camp." I rubbed my arms. "Have time to talk..." So I could tell him who I really was.

Mal squeezed my fingers. "Without all these consequences looming."

"I should go. Someone will miss me." I stood up and began backing off the porch, sliding a flirty-Suzie smile back over Susannah's somberness. "Besides, I bet you're already waiting in my bed."

It took him a moment to connect the dots, but then

the echo of his laughter kept me warm until I reached the campfire's glow.

✿ ✿ ✿

I can't believe the first session is over. Any chance you can convince your parents to let you stay the whole summer? Probably not, but a guy can dream...

Time passed in hikes and crafts, stolen moments and melt-me notes.

I hope you like popcorn. At tomorrow's movie-under-the-stars, I'm manning the popper. If you eat fast or "accidentally" spill yours—we can talk while I refill your cup.

Camp was as postcard-perfect as the sunsets over the lake.

Mal,
Only one week left. I don't want to go home...

On Sunday morning, I bumped into Mal on my way back to the cabin for sunblock. We were alone, and I was delighted, but his dimples didn't come out and play. His eyes stayed dark and guarded.

"Hey," I said cautiously. "Everything okay?"

He shrugged. "Just some little sibling drama."

Relief hit like a cool breeze, because the line of his jaw and the intensity in his gaze had felt personal, but I could totally empathize with this. "I know that feeling. No one gets under my skin like Franklin."

His eyes blazed—skewering mine before his triumph faded to pain. I swallowed, my fingers flexing like I could claw the reckless truth out of the air. *He knew.* "I mean—"

"So it's true...or *not* true. Everything."

"I—I—*How*?"

"Ava called last night. Did you forget we were family friends? She wanted to know how 'Susannah' was doing. Franklin was over playing with Benji yesterday, it made her miss—*you*?"

Even as panic and regret made my cheeks and stomach burn, my heart clenched with how much I missed her too. I would've traded anything to be avoiding *this* and sitting on her bed watching YouTube videos.

"Was anything true? I feel like I've been writing letters to a stranger."

"No!" I searched our conversations and grasped onto the first thing I could think of. "I do play soccer."

"So you were honest about your sport, but not even your siblings? And the rest? Your high school? All lies?"

I winced. "Mostly."

He shook his head. "Why? Was this a game for you?"

"No!" Except that's exactly how it had felt in the beginning and maybe he read that on my face because he cringed.

"What then? Some sort of camp hazing? Last year's dare landed Lydia in my bedroom, half-dressed. This year, what was it? See if you could get me to fall for some act?" He looked down, grabbing the back his neck and growling his frustration. "Congratulations—you won. I hope the rest of the girls are impressed."

"No! Nothing like that! I haven't said a thing—well, except to Kat." Two days ago she'd heard my pillow crinkle and I'd confessed everything.

He shut his eyes. "Do you know how much trouble I'll be in? I put my neck out there for you."

"I know."

"I thought you were worth it." He turned to go, eyes bright with betrayal and disgust.

Everything in me recoiled from his emotions. I'd spent my whole time here *avoiding* that expression, seeking praise and affirmation—but this is where it ended anyway, with revulsion. "Let me explain." I grabbed his hand and bit down on my lip. I would not cry. I wouldn't.

He pulled away. "I've got to go."

"Later. Please?" Maybe it would've been better to collect what was left of my dignity and leave, but being too proud to be honest had gotten me into this mess. "Mal, *please.*"

He shook his head.

I turned to leave, then paused and looked back one last time. Not coyly through my lashes. No flirtatious wink. This was pure vulnerability—the look of the homesick girl he'd

met during camp check-in, not the stranger I'd been playact-
ing since.

His expression softened and he held my gaze for a long
moment before walking away.

❧ ❧ ❧

"Do you think you're the first camper to lie about stupid things?"
Kat unrolled more toilet paper and handed it to me with a
no-nonsense expression. She'd been sent to find me and now
we were curled up on her bunk while I sobbed and filled her in.

"I'm Katie at home. Do I strike you as a *Katie*?" She didn't
wait for my answer. "Here I get to be Kat. No big deal."

"I'm Susannah." I sniffed.

She crinkled her nose. "No, you're Suzie. But you're Suzie
who's homeschooled and hates scary movies. I don't care.
You don't *have* to be anyone but you, but if you want to
pretend—go for it."

Maybe she didn't care—maybe the rest of my cabin mates
wouldn't care what lies I told. But Mal did.

❧ ❧ ❧

"This is me." I held up the collage I'd spent hours making
after I begged out of the afternoon hike by telling the
truth: I had the beginnings of a migraine. Luckily, the
crafts cabin was dim.

Even luckier—when I'd stopped by the cabin afterward, my pillow crinkled.

Talent show. 8 p.m. Back porch.

I'd counted down every second. And now I was standing on Mal's porch, my fingers still covered with Modpodge and glitter. They trembled as I held the paper out. "I'm a middle child. I'm homeschooled—and I love it. I'm into politics, and soccer, and gaming, and watching cat videos on YouTube. Ava's my best friend. I live near Boston. I'm allergic to shell-fish. My favorite foods are anything chocolate and carrots dipped in peanut butter."

He took the paper, studying the wrappers, letters, and photos I'd glued on every inch. "I'm a girl who made stupid decisions three weeks ago. Who wanted to know what it'd be like to be someone else. Who thought 'Suzie' was way cooler than she was. And who has fallen helplessly for the guy in front of her."

Suzie was officially dead. I didn't need—or want—her anymore.

But that didn't make the seconds pass faster as we stood silently in a soundtrack of crickets and the distant talent show applause. I studied my chipped toenail polish, his bare feet. The boards of his deck. Counted to thirty. I was sucking in a breath to apologize again and leave him alone, when he groaned.

"You didn't have to be cooler. I *like* the girl who was homesick before her mom left." He shook the paper. "I like *this* girl. I like you. By all means, reinvent yourself; that's what camp's for... But you don't need to lie about who you are." He took a deep breath before lifting his chin and gluing his eyes to mine. "Not when you're this spectacular."

His expression was full of understanding and forgiveness I hadn't dared to expect. "Really?"

"Really."

His dimples emerged. As I grinned back, the sky exploded with a ferocious summer rain. I giggled at Mal's surprised squeak as drops landed on his forehead, slid down his nose, splashed on his hands as he hastily tucked my collage beneath his shirt.

I threw my head back. Twirled and spun on legs that felt foamy with giddiness. I caught raindrops on my tongue, on my cheeks. They washed off salt from my earlier tears, leaving me clean and light and ready to meet his eyes and his hand. Meet him step for step as he closed the gap between us, laughing every bit as hard as me.

Our mouths met too. For the first time, but the sparks were both new and familiar, explosive and soothing. He tasted of rainwater. Of campfires—like the ones that were currently all tinder and matches in my stomach.

Mal pulled away first. He tugged a dripping lock of my hair. "How are we going to explain this?"

His words were loud with laughter and I leaned in to swallow them—

"Start thinking, because I would very much like an explanation."

The deep voice made me shriek and jump backward—the rain and wet clothing suddenly freezing without Mal's warm body pressed to mine. Downright glacial once I turned to match the person with the voice.

"Inside. Now. Both of you," demanded Mr. Alastair.

For weeks, I'd wondered about the inside of his house. About the growing-up pictures of a freckle-faced boy. But dripping on his front hall rug, I was too preoccupied by the lecture to look around.

"—inexcusable. You both knew better! This *sneaking around*—"

"Hang on a sec, Dad." Mal didn't wait to see his father's face turn redder. He dripped down the hall and dripped back carrying a sweatshirt, which he handed me before turning to his father. "Okay, continue."

Even if my teeth weren't chattering, I wouldn't have refused—this was our only chance to have a shared-sweatshirt moment. I inhaled his scent as I slipped it over my head.

"I forbid you two to even *look* at each other on camp grounds. Malcolm, you know your consequences; head upstairs and start packing. Suzie, you'll be calling your parents in the morning. Right now I'm escorting you to your counselor."

❀ ❀ ❀

The gossip burned through camp. *Suzie + Mal* became a tragically romantic story and I was more popular, more sought out then I'd ever dreamed. Lots of suggestions that I "talk about it" and sympathetic offerings of perfectly toasted marshmallows.

But all I wanted was to be left alone.

Once Mal's scent faded from his sweatshirt, I left it on the front porch of his house. I'd slipped an apology note in the pocket, but had no idea if he received it. There were certainly no more notes flowing in the reverse direction—my pillow was crinkle-less each night.

And my days, all five that remained of my time at camp, were Mal-free. I'm not sure if he was stuck in the back of the kitchen, locked in his room, or banished to Siberia. I spent the time setting the record straight with my campmates, undoing all my lies.

And then time ran out.

I'd grown to like the girls in my cabin. I doubted I'd keep in touch with any but Kat, but I'd online friend the rest and offer up birthday greetings and such.

Kat, however, I clung to, and she clung to me. Repeating our plans to meet up in Boston when she got home from her last month at camp. "You've got to see the cannoli place I was telling you about. And I want to try the game you're coding."

"Done and done."

"Speaking of done—" her red lips pulled down in frown. "He's not here."

"What?" I stopped scanning the crowds of parents arriving, girls leaving, camp personnel carrying bags.

"I saw Mal get in his mom's car this morning. It's not back."

"Oh." I licked my dry lips. I shouldn't have been surprised. But still. "I didn't know... Thanks."

She hugged me. "Hang in there. I'll email you Saturday."

"Susannah! Over here!" Mom called from behind me.

Kat and I suffocated each other in one last hug. I said, "Be kind to whoever takes my bunk." She stuck out her tongue.

I shouldered my duffel bag, turning around to face Mom. For now she was too happy to see me to get into drama, but I knew we had a hundred miles to discuss the consequences she'd threatened on that horrible camp-office call home.

Mom engulfed me in her arms. "C'mon, my wayward camper. Let's get this show on the road."

I stared out the window as we bumped down the drive. I wanted to memorize the trees, the lake, my last glimpse of Mal's back porch.

"Want to stop for lunch? One of the other moms told me about the cutest café in town." Mom was chirruping and I just wanted to keep my head pressed against the cool glass.

"Whatever." Which made me roll my eyes at myself for being so stereotypically sulky.

I wished I'd kept his sweatshirt, because at least then I'd have a memento. And I could've pulled the hood up to shade my eyes, because they were starting to water—the sun glare, I told myself.

One last glimpse. That was all I'd needed.

Mom hummed along with a song, the same Dave

Matthews one that had been playing when she dropped me off. The same one Mal had been picking out on his guitar. I skipped to the next track.

Mom frowned. "I thought you loved that song."

"I used to."

She squeezed my knee as she maneuvered into a parking space. "The café's right over there. Go snag seats. I'm going to pop in this candle store."

"Candles?"

"I'll be five minutes—ten—you won't even miss me." Mom winked.

I eye-rolled in response and shuffled though the café's blue door. Wind chimes above it made everyone sitting at the mismatched tables turn. They were wearing bland welcoming smiles. At least I assumed everyone was smiling—I saw two smiles, then stuck on the third and dismissed everyone else in the restaurant.

Because smile number three was dimpled. Was Mal's.

He stood up. "You made it."

"I—what?"

"I might've called your mom yesterday. Might've spent all week talking to mine, begging her to see that I was serious about you."

"You called my mom?" I sat my shaky legs down in the chair he'd pulled out. "You're serious about me?"

He nodded. "Turns out I'm going to need a ride to Boston. Know anyone headed that way?"

"Your great-uncle? Lives in *Boston*?" All squeaky questions, slow to process.

"Which, your mom and Ava—who has been working your mom from her side too—inform me is only a quick train ride from your house."

I nodded.

"So your mom is graciously letting me borrow part of your back seat—with the understanding that I'm surrendering myself to her interrogation for the length of the drive."

"You're coming with us?" This fact was finally starting to penetrate, leaving me breathless and grinning. "I'll make sure she gives *you* time to interrogate me. Because I'm sure you've got questions."

"I might," he answered.

I leaned in until my smile rested on his and reached up to finally, finally give into my urge to trace his dimples.

AUTHOR PHOTO ©
REBECCA J. ROMERO

Tiffany Schmidt is the author of the YA novels *Send Me a Sign*, *Bright Before Sunrise*, *Hold Me Like a Breath*, and *Break Me Like a Promise*. When she's not writing about superstitions, life-changing nights, or organ-trafficking crime families, she can be found chasing her impish sons and puggles around their backyard, baking, running, or watching Netflix with her saintly husband. While the rest of her family is ridiculously musical, Tiffany can't even clap to a beat and is frequently encouraged to "just lip-synch" during long car rides. Visit TiffanySchmidt.com and follow her Twitter and Instagram @TiffanySchmidt.

THE
RIDE

A SHORT STORY INSPIRED BY
JIMMY EAT WORLD'S "THE MIDDLE"

By Suzanne Young

Going away to college was one of the scariest choices I made as a young adult. I was starting over, and part of that meant leaving everything I'd ever known behind. Everyone. "The Middle" by Jimmy Eat World seemed to sum up my excitement, my fear, and ultimately—my perspective. I held on for the ride and it changed my life.

For my grandmother Josephine Parzych. Every story is for you.

—SUZANNE YOUNG

'M STILL A LITTLE HIGH WHEN I PULL A TUBE OF LIPSTICK from the plastic bag. I'd randomly bought it at Walgreens, along with a stack of Slim Jims and a Hershey bar. I don't even wear lipstick. I pop off the cap, and laugh when I see the color is a bloody shade of red. I pose in front of the mirror in Melissa's living room, and try it on.

"You'll never come back," she calls to me. I look over my shoulder at her, only my upper lip ringed, and see Melissa shake a cigarette from her pack. "Once you leave town, I'll never see you again."

"That's not true," I say. "Plus my gram lives here, so I'll obviously come back." I smile winningly at her because after six years of friendship, she shouldn't worry about this kind of crap.

Melissa and I met in middle school, the only two people who refused to wear swimsuits on pool days. Luckily, the teacher couldn't fail us because of it, but we did have to spend time in detention. And nothing bonds a couple of trouble-makers faster than unjustified punishment time.

I finish putting on the lipstick and stare at my reflection for a moment, unrecognizable, before grabbing a tissue and swiping it over my mouth. Melissa laughs and says I should have listened to her. She was right. I look weird in makeup.

The lipstick isn't really the issue though, although I guess it symbolizes our problem. I'm willing to take a chance, try something different. Melissa is content exactly where she is.

"Sure," she says, taking a drag of her cigarette, and talking through the smoke. "You'll visit, but you'll never live here again."

When I got accepted into college, I thought that Melissa would be coming with me. I thought we'd be going to parties and sneaking in late to class together. I hadn't considered that she wouldn't have applied there, let alone not applied *anywhere*. It wasn't until I signed my loan paperwork that she told me she wasn't going. She was staying here, in this tiny converted apartment above her mother's garage.

The air conditioner hums loudly in the window, not quite achieving enough coolness to justify its noise. I sit in the worn armchair, the one covered in cat hair, and face Melissa.

"Why would you say that?" I ask. "Besides, where would

I go during breaks or after I graduate? College doesn't let you stay indefinitely."

She shrugs one shoulder and lets her eyes wander to the muted TV. "You don't belong here. You never did." She looks at me and smiles. "And I know you know that."

She's being serious, reflective, and I can't deny she's hurting my feelings. Shouldn't she want me to stay? I feel like she pushing me out the door.

"Look," she adds. "I'm not saying it's bad, or whatever. But it's like the other day when you thanked the lady at Dillard's so hard that she thought you were being sarcastic and threatened to kick your ass."

"True story."

"Or your dumb exes—going away will be the best thing for you and them." She's not wrong about my exes either. They are dumb, and sure, there's been a bit of relationship trauma in my past. A little back-and-forth. I've gotten my heart broken, broken a few myself. But I'm certainly not worried about how any of this affects them.

Melissa's cat, Louie, saunters into the room, looks at her, and then lunges onto the back of my chair to camp out behind my head. I don't dare reach to pet him; I still have scratches from last time.

"I'm not sure what to say here," I tell her, my stomach knotting up. "I want to go to college. But I'm still coming home. This *is* my home." I want to defend myself, but I can't deny there is a small tug of freedom—the fact that I'm leaving when it seems like no one else ever has. But it's scary as hell to walk away.

Melissa's smile fades and she smashes out her cigarette in the crowded ashtray. "Okay, Leigh," she says. "Whatever. So what time are you leaving tomorrow?" She turns her dark eyes toward me. She's shutting me out emotionally.

"About eight a.m.," I say. "I've got to finish packing tonight."

"Is Gram driving you?" she asks.

"Yep. She's already packed the cooler with sandwiches for the drive. In case I get hungry." We laugh because my grandmother assumes everybody is always hungry.

I didn't really want Gram to drive me, but with my comforter, clothes, and mini-fridge, it wasn't like I could take it on the train. And I would have used my own car, but I sold it so I'd have some savings when I got to college. I'll have to work, but at least this way, it won't have to be full-time. And it's not like you use a car much when you live at the dorms. Everything's in walking distance.

Besides, I can always take the train home on the weekends if I want.

Melissa and I draw out our last moments, taking about nothing important, avoiding the dreaded goodbye. When I get up to leave a half hour later, she doesn't stand. She lights another cigarette.

"Call me after you meet your roommate," she says. "Hope she doesn't suck."

I smile, not even trying to start worrying about that yet.

"I'll be home soon," I say. My throat feels tight, my eyes itch. I watch Melissa clench her jaw, and then she nods and says goodbye.

❈ ❈ ❈

It takes three tries for me to get the trunk closed on my grand-mother's car in the morning; I've definitely overpacked. I sip on a hot chocolate (I hate the taste of coffee), as we drive off. I woke up on the wrong side of the bed—Melissa's words bothering me more than I wanted to admit. Because if I'm not coming back, where's home? I have no idea where I fit in anymore.

I feel like shit.

"I don't know how to program this damn thing," my grandmother says, touching all the buttons at once on her navigation system. I laugh, and enter the address of the dorm, but we both groan when it says it'll be three and a half hours until arrival.

We settle in for a long drive. Gram blasts the air-conditioning, and soon I have to turn it down because the tip of my nose is freezing off. And I keep thinking about what Melissa said.

"Are you worried that I won't come home?" I ask my grandmother, looking sideways at her.

Gram crinkles her nose, like she doesn't understand the question, and glances at me before turning back to the road. "Well, I hope you'll come and visit me."

Although she says it sweetly, Gram-like, it sinks my heart. "So you don't think I'll come back here to live?" I ask, a catch in my throat.

"Why are you asking this now? You're already on your way."

"Melissa said something last night. And I just...I just want to know what you think."

Gram is quiet for a long while, so long that I think she might not answer. I adjust the air-conditioning again.

"You're just starting your life," she says quietly. "And if you have the chance to start something new, then you should. You already know what's waiting here. So maybe it's time you see what else there is."

My eyes well up. "I don't understand," I say. "Why does it feel like everyone's trying to get rid of me? Are all of you mad that I'm leaving—like I've betrayed you or something?"

Gram's gaze snaps to mine. "Of course not. The people who love you...we know you, Leigh." She turns back to the road. "Your heart is wild and restless. If you were to stay here always...you'd be miserable. Some people are just wanderers."

I'm washed in guilt, like I've abandoned her already. I get what she's saying, and I do feel restless. I do want to explore. But loyalty should have been engrained; it seems to be in others. Why don't I feel the same way?

"I just want to be like everyone else," I say, sniffling. "I feel like I'm in the wrong life or something."

Gram presses her lips together, and reaches out her hand

to mine. Her rings press against my palm. "You just haven't found your life yet," she says. "Your ride just started."

I hold my grandmother's hand for a while, and then I reach in back and pull a sandwich out of the cooler. I'm not even hungry, but I have this sudden and complete need to make her happy. Show her that I appreciate the time she put into making me a sandwich.

Because for a moment, it feels like I might never see her again.

✲ ✲ ✲

I'm a transfer student, and it comes with some perks. I get to move into the dorms with suites—no floor-shared bathrooms. Each set of four rooms has its own bathroom, its own living room. But I barely glanced at the online "Student Life" section beyond that. I basically just enrolled, carried along by my own curiosity rather than on a well-thought-out path. So now I have no idea what to do next.

Gram parks her car, and I stare up at the large dorm building, intimidated. It's at least twelve floors. I've barely been out of Central New York.

I'm too nervous to talk as I get out of the car and walk around to pop the hood. Gram wants to help, but I won't let her carry anything other than my comforter in plastic wrap. I'm looping bags and backpacks over my arms, sure I won't actually be able to carry this much, but wanting to make it to the seventh floor with the least amount of trips possible. I'm about to slam down the truck on the rest of my things, when two guys appear at the other end of the car.

"Hey," one of them calls to me. "Need a hand?"

I immediately look at my gram and she smiles, and tells him that we'd appreciate the help. He smiles at her, as if he loves his grandmother too, and he and his friend round the car to where my entire life is packed into a trunk.

The guy is cute, and I think it's adorable that his red hat is on backward, something about it effortlessly casual and charming. His friend is big and burly with a long blond beard and hair. He has a flannel shirt tied around his waist and he's wearing sandals. I like then both immediately.

"Vincent," the guy in the red hat says to me. He reaches in and grabs a box with clothes while his friend, who introduced himself as Charlie, picks up my small refrigerator with a grunt.

Between the four of us, we manage to get all of my things in one try. I start into the building, my grandmother grinning to herself like she's in on some joke. I look at Vincent.

"Is this your dorm?" I ask.

He shakes his head. "Nope. I'm a freshman. They place us close to the class buildings. Transfer?" he asks me.

"Yeah. Junior."

"Older woman," Charlie jokes, and all of us laugh, even if it's mostly out of embarrassment. Of course, nothing is as awkward as the elevator ride up to the seventh floor.

Gram stays facing the buttons, pretending she's not even here. She'll definitely bring it up to me later—she's full of opinions. But for now, she's letting me do my thing. And my thing is leaning against the wall, pretending I belong on this college campus.

The elevator smells a bit like BO, and I think it might actually be Charlie. Then again, he's carrying my refrigerator. And he probably spent too many hours playing hacky-sack in the field.

Without meaning to, I glance over at Vincent and catch him staring at me. We both smile awkwardly and turn away. The elevator dings, and Gram is the first one out.

I try to look confident as I walk toward my suite door, only to realize it's on the other side of the hall. There's the faint scent of weed in the air, whether someone's smoking it here or brought the smell in with them, I'm not sure. Gram doesn't seem to notice.

I fumble with the door lock.

"Take your time," Charlie says, hiking up the fridge as it starts to slide down. "Not like this is heavy or anything."

"Sorry," I say, but Vincent waves him off.

"Ignore him," he says. "He's joking. But mostly he's just mad because he hates exercise."

"Obviously," Charlie replies. "I don't get to look this good by chance."

I finally unlock the door, and the four of us enter the suite. My room is the first one on the left, and I poke in my head, sort of relieved that my roommate's not here yet. It gives me a second to adjust.

Vincent and Charlie set down my things, and Gram immediately gets to work making my bed. Before I even take a moment to look around my room for the first time, I walk the guys to the door and thank them.

"I really appreciate it," I say. "Honestly, this was really nice of you."

Vincent shrugs. "We just happened to be passing by," he says.

"He thought you were cute," Charlie says, grins at him, and then leaves. My face catches fire and I can barely hold my shit together when I look at Vincent again.

"So I'll see you around," I say.

"Definitely." He holds up his hand in a wave, but then pauses in the doorway. "And hey," he starts like he's just thought of something. "There's a party later if you...if you're not busy. It's at 96 Broadway. Guess they do it every year. They call it the Opening Ceremony."

I laugh. "Maybe," I say. "Not sure..." I trail off because the answer doesn't really matter. It was cool that he asked me. We say goodbye, and when I close the door, I let the flutters of flirtation vibrate through me.

I walk back into my dorm room and see that Gram has already started unpacking my clothes. "You don't have to do that," I say, going over to take my jacket from her hands. When I do, I turn toward the closet and get my first look at the dorm room. It's pretty spacious—at least, bigger than I imagined.

Two beds, two dressers, two desks. One wall is made up entirely of windows, and it looks over a bright patch of green lawn. There are a few people playing Frisbee out there right now.

"Those boys seemed nice," Gram says nonchalantly. "Are you going to that party later?"

"Ew," I say, jokingly. "You can't eavesdrop."

"Yeah, well," she says, grabbing a few books and setting them on my desk. "Your mother liked younger men, too."

"Gram!" I say, cracking up. My gram is actually hilarious, sometimes scandalous, and always awesome.

We finish putting away my things, my roommate still nowhere in sight, and when we finish, it's past lunchtime. She asks if I'm hungry, but I'm actually not. I'm starting to worry, dread her leaving. Maybe this was a mistake. I mean, what the hell am I doing here?

"Hey," Gram says, furrowing her brow. "What's wrong?" She sits on the edge of my roommate's mattress. "You should be excited."

"I don't feel excited," I say. "I'm not that smart. I'm not really adventurous." I rub my palm over my face, overwhelmed by everything. "I should go home with you," I say, sounding more like a kid than a college student.

"Honey, you're strong enough to do this," she says. "But more importantly, you deserve this."

"What? To be alone?"

She laughs. "No. To be free. And yeah, you're alone. But what better way to figure out what you want."

"And Melissa? She hates me right now. So does everyone—they think I'm stuck up for leaving."

"Melissa will understand," Gram says. "And who cares what the rest of them think? Leigh…you haven't had it easy, I know. Your dad didn't take care of his responsibilities, and your mother—she's a little lost. But you've always taken care of yourself. You don't need anyone else. And you sure as hell don't need their approval."

I have a flinch of pain thinking about my parents. My father left about the same time I was learning to walk. He never called, never paid a dime of child support—not even when our heat got turned off. Hell, he never even sent a birthday card. A therapist would have told me that his leaving wasn't my fault. But blame doesn't matter to me—my dad is a ghost. I've learned to deal with it.

And my mom…she's around, trying to get her life in order. She even started taking classes at the community college. She had me when she was too young, she remarried twice, and now she's finally getting around to figuring herself out. I was lucky—I happened to have the best grandparents in the world. I've lived with them for as long as I can remember. I've been loved greatly. So my pain at abandonment never lasts long. Because I'll never lose my grandparents. I'll always have my gram on my side.

"You really think I should stay?" I ask my grandmother, sniffling back the start of tears.

She nods, her brown eyes welling up. "Yeah," she says. "I

do. And I'll miss you. But see where this ride takes you. You can always come home if you need to," she adds.

I stand up and go over to hug her, memorizing the smell of her detergent, the feel of her arms around me. When it's time for her to go, I walk her out of the building and pause at her car.

"I love you, Gram," I say.

She gets in her car and slips on her sunglasses. Before she closes her door, she looks up at me, the baddest granny anyone ever met. "I love you, too. Call me after the party. I want to hear all about it."

I smile. "Drive safe."

She closes her door, and I wait until she's gone before heading back into the building. My shoulders slump—I've never felt more alone.

I pause in the lobby, and see a crowd of students near the mailboxes. I hadn't thought to check mine, so I take out my key and head over to find box 18236. When I do, there's a loud clank and then a laugh.

I look over and see it a pretty red-headed girl rubbing the heel of her palm. She looks over at me, embarrassed. "Sorry," she says, motioning toward her mailbox. "My key got stuck and now the damn thing won't open."

"Oh." I lean in like I'm the mailbox expert, and after a few minutes, I manage to get her key out—bent.

"Shit," she says holding it up for us to examine. "Well, that sucks." She exhales, and I turn to close my mailbox. "I'm Shelly," she says.

"Leigh."

"Cool," she says. "Thanks for your help. What floor are you on?"

"Seventh," I say.

She gasps. "Me, too! Please tell me you're my roommate. 716?"

My lifted heart quickly falls. "No," I say. "I'm across the hall."

Shelly scrunches up her nose adorably. "Well, at least we're on the same floor, right?"

I nod, and we start toward the elevator, the silence between us comfortable and easy. The sort of stranger bonding you can get when waiting in a long line at the post office.

"Weird question," Shelly says, spinning to face me. "Would... would you cut my hair?" She gathers up the ends of her long hair. "I hate it. It's a knotty mess. I want something cute."

"Uh...sure, I guess. But I can't claim to know what I'm doing."

She shrugs. "Neither do I. But I figure you'll have a better angle to cut the back. So will you?"

"Yeah, okay."

We go to Shelly's room, which happens to be the first door I had gone to when I arrived. Her other suitemates haven't gotten here yet, so we have the place to ourselves. When we get in, her room is an absolute disaster, clothes and boxes everywhere. But she hung a poster on the wall—one of an aging soap star. She tells me she's had it since seventh grade.

She rolls out the desk chair to the center of the room, and grabs a pair of small scissors. They're hardly hairdresser-worthy, but I take them from her hand anyway.

"How do you want me to cut it?" I ask, grabbing a wide-tooth comb from her dresser.

"Whatever you think looks good." She walks over and clicks on her stereo, skipping through her playlist, until she grins and hits play.

"The Middle" by Jimmy Eat World starts, and she turns it up. "I love this song," she says, bopping her head from side to side playfully, her red curls bouncing. "It reminds me not to take myself too seriously."

"You're letting a stranger with no prior stylist experience cut your hair, so I'd say you're doing pretty well at that."

She laughs again and sits in front of me. My heart swells, and I decide I love the easiness of this. She's so free of judgment, of rules. This moment is honest and open—and back home, you don't form relationships this easy. They take time. Take tests to prove yourself. I'm at once exhilarated and scared of this new world.

I rake the comb through Shelly's red curls, measuring them to her shoulder blades. The music plays in the background, the world coming to life around me. My loneliness abates slightly when I make the first snip.

Shelly looks down at the red lock on the floor. "Hah!" she says. "I can't believe I'm doing this."

"Me neither," I murmur.

We both laugh, and I continue to cut. I think about Melissa, and there is a second of guilt—like I'm betraying her by making a new friend. Am I? Or is this the engrained loyalty that I thought I didn't have?

"I thought my best friend Melissa was going to come to college with me," I admit to Shelly. "It's kind of weird being here without her." I snip another lock and it falls on the lap of Shelly's jeans.

She smiles, looking a bit nostalgic. "I was Melissa last year," she says. "My best friend moved to England—fucking England." She laughs. "She asked me to come with, but I'm not rich. And I didn't want to go. My sister graduated from here; this is where I belong. But I still gave Claire a ton of shit about leaving. We're cool now, though." Shelly turns to look back over her shoulder at me, her wide-set eyes a sparkling shade of green. "She's going to stay with me during break. You'll have to meet her. She even has a little accent now."

"Sounds fun," I say, meaning it. This insight into Shelly's life…it makes me feel a little better. It reminds me that Melissa and I are forever, and that she has a right to be mad. But we'll get through it. We've always gotten through it.

"Oh, shit," I say, taking a step back. "This is totally uneven." I take the ends of Shelly's hair and stretch them. There's at least a two-inch difference between the sides.

Shelly shrugs. "Go shorter then," she says.

"You sure?" I ask. I feel kind of bad about ruining her hair.

"Why not?" she responds. It's so simple. I'm not sure I've

ever had a fresh slate before—I always expect strings. The
song finishes playing, setting us in a moment of quiet. Like
reality waiting for me to decide how I'll live.

"Okay, Sinead. Let's do this," I say, making her laugh. I
continue to cut as Shelly and I discuss our majors, our friends,
and our ex-boyfriends. We have a lot in common, more so
than most of my friends back home. It makes me wonder if
this is what's it like when you leave high school. There, our
friends are circumstantial for the most part, determined by
neighborhood and class schedules. But then the world opens
up. My world is opening up.

"I met two guys earlier," I say. "They seemed nice."

"How nice?"

"Well, they carried my fridge," I say.

"Oo...I like them already."

I smile, crouching down to snip the last hanging threads
of hair. Shelly's hair is mostly even now, just below her chin.
She stands and shakes it out, and I have to say that it looks
damn cute. She walks over the mirror and turns her head from
side to side, examining the cut from all angles. She spins.

"I love it!" she says. "I feel like a new person." She exhales
and then drops down on her zebra-print bedspread. I grab
a paper towel and clean up the mess we left, even though I
don't have to. When I'm done I sit on the bed across from her.

"So what else did the boys say?" she asks, leaning back on
her arms. "Wait—what are their names?"

"Victor and Charlie. They're freshman." To this she

scrunches her nose, but lets me continue my story of how they helped me and Gram carry stuff to my room. I tell her about Victor's invite to the Opening Ceremony, and Shelly gasps.

"I've totally heard of that," she says. "My sister said it's the best way to meet people. We have to go."

"Really?" I'm still unsure, a little intimidated.

"Yeah," she says. "Let's see what this school is all about. Make some friends."

Her smile is infectious, and it gives me a bump in confidence. "All right," I agree. "Plus you'll get to show off your hair."

She runs her fingers through it. "I'll have boys carrying my furniture by the end of the week."

Shelly and I continue to talk, cracking each other up, amazed at the coincidences in our upbringings. It's like we've know each other forever, and the uncertainness I had starts to clear itself up. Not all of it, of course. But I can't help but think that Gram was right. I am free here. Free to live. Free to change. And yes—it's terrifying. But it's also exciting and full of possibilities.

So I let go and enjoy the ride.

AUTHOR PHOTO
BY DAWN GOEI

Suzanne Young is the *New York Times* bestselling author of The Program series. Originally from Utica, New York, Suzanne moved to Arizona to pursue her dream of not freezing to death. She is a novelist and an English teacher, but not always in that order. Suzanne is the author of several bestselling books, including *The Program*, *The Treatment*, *The Remedy*, *The Epidemic*, *Hotel for the Lost*, and *All in Pieces*. Visit authorsuzanneyoung.com and follow her on Twitter @suzanne_young.

DOOMED?

A SHORT STORY INSPIRED BY MARCY PLAYGROUND'S "ALL THE LIGHTS WENT OUT"

By K. M. Walton

This song is in my "Top Five Favorite Songs of All Time" list. The quiet start and massive, rocking crescendo give me chills without fail. It's one of those haunting songs that refuses to get old.

—K. M. WALTON

SCARLETT

My arms and legs shot straight out in my normal morning stretch, and that's when I felt the sand.

I was not in my bed.

Instinctively, I rubbed my eyes. Bad idea. Sand scratched my corneas. "Owww!"

I blinked and sat up. And blinked and blinked. Tears ran down my cheeks. I pulled up the bottom of my T-shirt and used it to dust off my face. The wind whipped my hair, stinging my cheeks.

"Hey, beautiful," someone shouted over the howling. I snapped my head to the left, sand flying, and it all came back to me. It wasn't morning. It was dusk. Billy and I ran across the street to check out the waves, laid down to cloud watch, and I must've fallen asleep. It was so easy to do here. I licked my lips and tasted coconut.

I'd kissed Billy.

Billy.

He was blurry in my teary eyes but now I could see him—lying on his back with his forearms crossed underneath his head. His muscled chest slowly rose and fell with steady, even breaths.

Blue T-shirt, long surf shorts, bare feet.

Sun-drenched brown hair, amber eyes, full lips.

Yeah, Billy. He'd been my next-door neighbor and best friend since we were six. We were seniors now.

I looked away and ran my finger over my mouth.

The ocean raged, all waves and white foam. I was glad we were up by the dunes.

Another massive gust took my breath. I tossed my head back to feel its full force. "Wow," I shouted. "Is this normal? This is way more intense than they said it would be."

"Nothing's normal now," he said, looking away, and I didn't know if he was talking about the weather or about us. "It'll never be the same."

All of a sudden my stomach dropped. Dread, warm and thick, spread through my veins, my bones. My brain. Kissing him was a mistake. Right? Was that what he meant? He regretted it? It felt like kissing my brother, except I didn't have a brother, so how would I know?

Shit.

I was not weird, or dumb, or annoying. Okay, maybe I was sort of annoying. I did ask a lot of questions. I'd admit that. But I wasn't weird. My family ate dinner together every night, I loved my older sister Francine, and I had Billy—but I'd always had Billy. It had always been us. We were a team.

He had patiently taught me how to surf. I had taught him how to do a cartwheel. Turned out I was better at both, and he was completely fine with that. We'd stayed up all night watching Donavon Frankenreiter concerts, quizzed each other before every test we'd ever taken, puked on the beach from stealing and drinking his dad's whiskey. Basically, we'd been glued to each other for the past eleven years.

That was the problem, though. *What about me? Just me?* I wasn't sure I wanted to be an "us" before I found myself. I shook my head. *Us?* We kissed once. *Get over yourself, Scarlett.*

What if I still needed more time here?

Billy draped his arm across my legs and said, "Think we blew that fuse in heaven yet?"

I turned away. Him and that stupid, stupid dream. That's how the whole kissing thing started. He nervously bumbled through the story for, like, the ten millionth time: in the dream I run into his house during a hurricane and head straight into his arms. He pulls back to see my face and tells me, "I love you, Scarlett. I've always loved you. If you give me a chance, our love could blow a fuse in heaven." And then we make out in his little fantasy.

He called it a dream. I called it a fantasy.

Then (and this really happened—no dream), maybe it was the intense gentleness of his stare or the salty wind coming off the ocean, or maybe it was even because I was curious, but, *I* kissed *him*. I shit you not.

I had never—as in e v e r—initiated a kiss. I'd been kissed, yes, but I'd never made the kiss happen. Without hesitation I leaned over and pressed my lips to his. He kissed me back, warm and soft.

The thing was, after the kiss I could tell he was solidly convinced I was ready to move on. In addition to using the word "destiny," he told me that he'd never love anyone like the way he loved me. That if we stayed together we actually *could* blow a fuse in heaven. Again, I shit you not.

I was not sure what his heaven contained, but mine did not contain fuses. I mean, what kind of heaven had fuses? Would heaven even need fuses? The whole thing was crazy.

My sister Francine had a saying: you can love someone and you can be *in* love with someone—massive difference.

A clap of thunder boomed overhead. Heaven definitely still had power. That was a sign, right? Fuses were not blown. My gaze dropped to Billy's face. Right then, right that very second, I wished Billy, his soft lips and impossible fantasy, dream, or whatever you wanted to call it, could be lifted *into* the heavens.

We kissed, yes. I know. I remember every single second of it because *I* kissed *him*. But one kiss doesn't mean I'm in love. It just doesn't.

I need more time.

I'm pretty sure I've ruined everything.

BILLY

There was a storm coming, a big one. Scarlett's long, brown hair billowed out behind her as we ran off the beach. Barefoot, holding hands. A sudden gust of wind stole my breath, or maybe it was the way she looked at me. I'd never be sure.

"Faster, Billy!" she shouted and squeezed my hand, pulling me as we ran.

Our houses loomed ahead, across the street from the beach. They sat side by side—mine white with tan shutters, hers tan with white shutters—with only ten feet between them.

"My house?" I asked.

Without turning around, she nodded and continued leading. We ran up my front steps and bent ourselves in half, panting just as the skies opened up. A fresh crack of thunder made us jump.

Scarlett stood up straight and crossed her arms. "Y-you're lucky I'm faster than you, pokey-pants. You'd still be out there."

I lifted my brows. "Pokey-pants? Wow, that's a throwback. What are we, eight again?" I shook my head. "And I let you lead, just so we're clear, Scarley-warley." My pace was slow on purpose. I didn't want to leave the beach. I would've stayed there forever, buried us deep in the sand to preserve what happened, what I said to her. What she leaned over and did to me.

That kiss. Holy shit, that kiss.

No one had ever kissed me like that.

Looked like my recurring dream held some power after all. If I'd known talking dreams would make her kiss me, I would've made one up when we were in sixth grade. No, maybe even earlier. I've loved Scarlett Marcy since the day we met.

She huffed. "Scarley-warley? I hated when you called me that when we were little kids." Her eyes darted, refusing to lock onto mine, which made one thing very clear: Scarlett regretted kissing me.

My insides sank. To the porch floorboards. "Hot chocolate?" I asked in an effort to appear totally normal. I had said too much down there. Blowing a fuse in heaven? Really? She was my destiny? Oh my God. I wanted to throw myself into the eye of the storm. To hide my shame-covered face, I bent down and brushed the wet, sticky sand from my feet.

Scarlett did the same. "Do you have whipped cream?"

I gave her a side-eye. She knew I had whipped cream. I always had whipped cream. Hot chocolate was part of our friendship, something we made almost every day. But she questioned everything.

Especially me.

Scarlett ignored me and walked into my house. "Are you coming or not, pokey-pants?"

Even though we lived in New Smyrna Beach, Florida, hot chocolate was a sacred experience with my family. My mom grew up in Pennsylvania so she knew all about warm drinks and winter. Actually, winter was how we ended up down here. She hated it and convinced my dad that moving to Florida the summer before I started first grade would be perfect. We moved next door to the Marcys—I met Scarlett about ten seconds after I got out of the car.

Scarlett and I went around the kitchen in silence, each grabbing our usual ingredients. I always got the cold stuff— the milk, half and half, and whipped cream. She gathered the unsweetened cocoa powder, cinnamon, coconut palm sugar, vanilla, and salt, placing it all next to the sink.

She rummaged through the utensil drawer. "Where's the whisk?"

I walked up behind her and tapped her on the shoulder with it. "It was in the dishwasher. It's clean."

Scarlett whirled around and we were practically nose to nose. She lifted her big brown eyes to mine and we stared. Hard. So frigging hard. My heart battled against its cage. *She is so beautiful.*

"Billy?" she whispered.

I swallowed before answering. "Yeah?"

"How do you know—" She stopped, huffed, and shook her head. "I mean, no. Not that." Scarlett turned on her heel, giving me her back. "Forget it."

A crashing boom of thunder filled the kitchen. I walked away, legs shaking. "Let's make this hot chocolate fast, in case we lose power."

"Hand me the milk and cream, okay?" she said.

I grabbed both containers and put them in front of her. "How do I know what?"

Scarlett stared at the empty cooking pot for a few seconds. "H-how do you know exactly how much sugar to put in?"

Clearly she was making up something stupid instead of finishing what she really wanted to ask me, and knowing she was both embarrassed and outrageously stubborn, I decided to ignore it, play along. Like a total wuss.

"Seriously, Scarlett? You *know* this is my mom's recipe and you also know she taught me how to make it. You were here, standing where you are right now, but on a chair. You could make this hot chocolate blindfolded. You know how much sugar to put in. So do I."

She disregarded me, completely, and measured out a cup and a half of milk and poured it into the pot.

I reached across her, grabbed the half and half, measured a half-cup and dumped it in with the milk. "Do you want to whisk in the rest of the stuff?"

Scarlett shrugged and started tossing in the other ingredients, whisking as she went.

I walked to the cabinet and grabbed two mugs. I squeezed their handles till my knuckles went white. Some force of nature consumed me, filled me up with insecurity, with words. With a question. I used every ounce of restraint I could muster, placed the mugs on the counter, and asked, "Why did you kiss me if you didn't want to?"

Okay, maybe I wasn't a total pushover after all. Maybe my balls were swelling in my boxers. Maybe I shouldn't have asked her that question.

She was crying.

Scarlett Marcy never cried.

SCARLETT

I was crying.

I didn't cry. I used to cry when I was younger, at the normal kid stuff like smashed knees and sunburned shoulders, but I didn't cry anymore.

Maybe I *was* weird.

I turned away from Billy and quickly used each shoulder to wipe my cheeks dry. He didn't hover or ask me a bunch of "What's wrong? Are you okay?" questions. I knew he wouldn't. It wasn't his style. He knew to pull back and let me work through it.

My attention returned to whisking the hot chocolate. Milk and cream could scald so easily if you didn't pay close attention. I knew because I'd done it and it ruined the flavor, made everything taste burnt. Even the sweet whipped cream had no power to save scalded hot chocolate.

I guess I'd been gripping it pretty tightly because my fingers were hurting. When I loosened up, I lost control and dropped it. The whisk clattered around inside the pot all by itself for a few seconds before coming to a stop.

"Dammit," I muttered under my breath. I dried my

sweaty palms on my shorts and began whisking again. I kept my gaze down, staring at the frothy chocolate mixture. "I kissed you because I wanted to, that's why." I scrunched my nose. *Why did I blurt that out?* Did I *want* to or was I just being spontaneous? Did I really want to?

Shit, maybe I'm crazy, too.

He nodded slowly and then gathered the ingredients, going from cabinet to fridge, putting everything back. He closed the refrigerator door and said softly, "You need to move on, Scarlett. Just let go."

I held a mug over the sink, tilted the pot and poured the hot chocolate. "Here." Billy took it from me and his fingers softly brushed mine. The other mug shook as I poured one for myself. Somehow I managed to not splash any steaming liquid on my skin.

Billy held up the red can of whipped cream. "Ready?"

I nodded. He squirted a heaping, swirled mound of perfection until I said, "Stop." He knew when to stop. Of course he knew. I didn't have to tell him but I did anyway. I always did.

He handed me a spoon and I stirred once, twice, and then took a small sip. Without warning Billy gently wiped the tip of my nose, and I flinched. "You had some whipped cream..." His voice trailed and his cheeks went red. "Sorry. I didn't mean to scare you."

I put down my mug and thoroughly wiped my face with both hands, just in case. "You didn't scare me." His house shook with the biggest explosion of thunder yet. "Sh-shit." My eyes went wide. "*That* scared me!"

"You know what scares me?"

"Banana spiders, duh."

His lips tightened and he drew in a big breath through his nose. "Besides those creatures of the devil."

"Isn't this a fun role reversal, you asking me a question?" I slurped up some whipped cream and studied his face. He seemed so serious, maybe sad even. He *did* think the kiss was a big deal. I am an idiot. Of course he did. He told me he loved me. He looked me right in the eye and said it. "So what scares you? Regrets? The dark? What?"

"You."

BILLY

Scarlett's face. God, I wished I was able to take a picture of her face. Mouth hung open, eyebrows lifted towards the sky. Her mug slid forward, spilling the dark brown liquid onto the counter. "You're gonna lose your whipped cream," I said.

She put down the mug and without a word walked out of the kitchen and out the front door. I abandoned my hot chocolate and darted to catch her. "Scarlett! Wait!"

She stopped on the top step and turned around. Torrential rain poured down in sheets behind her. The wind blasted and she had to hold onto the banister. I had never felt a gust so powerful. "Me?" she shouted. "*I* scare you? Since when?"

Maybe everything was wrong. Maybe this was more than a bad storm.

"You know what? Forget it, Billy!"

"Come back inside. Please. Our mugs are still full." I held out my hand.

She crossed her arms and barreled past me. I followed her back inside. Scarlett plopped into a kitchen chair and looked out the window. "Guess what?" she asked.

I placed our mugs down onto the table and took a seat across from her. "What?"

"You scare me, too."

"Great. So we're afraid of each other. Sounds like we're doomed."

She laughed, deep and solid. And perfect. "Maybe. Maybe we are doomed."

I took a sip. Even lukewarm the stuff was delicious. I nodded and then quickly shook my head. "No, wait. That can't be true. Can it? I mean, doomed? That sounds horrible."

"You know how if you don't pay attention to the hot chocolate during the whisking? Like, if you lose focus for even five seconds, it can scald the milk? And then everything tastes awful?"

I swallowed a new sip and narrowed my eyes. "Uh huh." Where was she going with this?

She spooned what was left of her whipped cream into her mouth and licked her lips. Heat. I felt heat.

She tugged on her bottom lip with her teeth and

dropped her eyes. "I feel like I lost focus here. On us. I think I scalded *us*."

I didn't understand. "But everything tasted amazing."

Scarlett grinned and rolled her eyes. "I wasn't talking about the kiss, Billy. Jeez."

So she agreed with me. The kiss was...delicious.

She slowly spun her mug a few times, thoughts painted her face. Even though I knew every freckle, every inch of her, I still wondered what it meant that she was rubbing her lip now. She was nervous, that was obvious. But there was something else. Something different. Something exciting almost, some kind of undercurrent. Maybe. Maybe I was misinterpreting this whole thing and she hated everything about that kiss. Maybe she wasn't ready after all.

Scarlett cleared her throat. "Remember the car accident?"

I tilted my head and gave her a confused stare. I *had* misinterpreted. And she was kidding wasn't she? Did I remember? I was there. We both were.

"Sorry. Right. Dumb question. *Really* dumb question." She put her hands on her lap and kept talking. "The accident just—"

Scarlett snapped her mouth shut and dropped her chin. I didn't press her. Actually I didn't have to, especially not when it came to the accident.

That accident changed everything.

She took a huge breath, and then with puffy cheeks, slowly let it all out. "Yeah, soooooo, after my dad's viewing, the funeral guy came in and said, 'Take all the time you need.'

I remember thinking that if I could have as long as I wanted, then I wanted forever because the thought of never seeing his face again made my heart hurt. Like, it actually ached, which probably wasn't possible, but it felt so real. And I remember my mom saying to Francine, 'We're gonna be okay. We still have love. Right? Your father was the love of my life. What a gift. What an absolute gift.' Do you think—"

A boom of thunder cut Scarlett off and we both startled.

I looked out the window. "Holy…"

"What?" she shouted. "What?"

"The ocean. Look." I pointed. "It's coming across the street. Holy crap."

She stood up and went to the front door. "This is bad, Billy."

I took my place beside her and grabbed her hand. "I know."

"Am I the love of your life? Do you really love me? Like you said on the beach?"

I tightened my grasp. "Do you *really* have to ask that?"

She shrugged.

"That's like asking me if I believe the sun will rise or if the tide will come in or, or, or, like, God, I don't know, asking me if I like hot chocolate. How can you doubt it? It has always been you, Scarlett. Always." She was all that I ever needed. Ever.

"I know."

SCARLETT

If I knew, then what the hell was I so afraid of? What exactly? Kissing him didn't make me disappear. I *was* still there. Just me.

Billy Whitford loved me. I guess he had always loved me. Love for me wasn't so simple. Love had ways of tricking me, pulling the rug out, punching me in the gut.

Not Billy. My sweet Billy.

He was real and there and he loved me.

"Let's go finish our hot chocolate. I'll warm it up for us." He led me back into the kitchen. I was too jumpy to sit down so I stood next to him as he heated the mugs in the microwave. He held out the can of whipped cream. "More?"

I nodded. I didn't care that I was having too much, because there was no reason to stop now. I let him fill the mug with white. He handed me a fresh spoon and I dug in. "Isn't it so good?" I asked.

"Perfect."

We stood shoulder to shoulder, sipping and staring out the kitchen window above the sink. He had a single palm tree in his front yard. It had been through many storms, and I had never seen it bend like that. "Do you think it'll break?"

"Never."

"Do you think I ruined everything?"

Billy placed his mug on the counter, took mine and sat it next to his. He stood himself in front of me with no space between us. "No." Everything was touching except our mouths. "*I* want to kiss *you* this time, Scarlett. May I kiss you?" He rested his hands on my hips.

"Y-yes," I mumbled. I didn't care if things were ruined. What did that matter anymore?

The heat from his body melted us together, a blazing mass of want. "May I kiss you here?" He lightly kissed my cheek. "How about here?" His lips brushed mine as he turned and pecked my other cheek. We locked eyes and the room exploded with thunder. Neither of us was fazed this time. Maybe the explosion came *from* us.

He tilted his head and warm, tender kisses went from ear to collarbone. I arched my back to press all of me into him. He ran his hand up my side and rested his fiery palm on my neck. Pulling back to look in my eyes, he said, "Now, Scarlett. I need to kiss you now."

The scent of chocolate and coconut was overwhelming. Soothing. Effective.

I searched his eyes and saw everything. There were no more questions.

"Yes?" he pleaded.

"Yes."

"I love you, Scarlett." Billy leaned in and touched his lips to mine.

Another thunderous crash shook the world. All the lights went out, plunging us into darkness.

I laughed and hugged him tight.

We stood in his dark kitchen and devoured each other.

Every inch. Every single inch, until our knees buckled, until our eyes were heavy, until the end.

Eventually, he led me to the front porch. Waves broke against the top step. The thickly clouded sky was gunmetal gray.

Billy looked out and took my hand. "Even after our car accident, your dad and I never doubted you'd find your way. We knew you'd move on." He turned to face me. "Remember our first day here? And how all we wanted was to go back? Remember how much we fought being here?"

Why did I ever doubt loving Billy?

I nodded. "God, did we want to be alive again or what?" I rested my head on his shoulder. "Crazy thing is I'm going to miss this place. It's almost like home, isn't it?"

"Almost."

The ocean was now up onto the porch. It was as warm as melted butter on my feet. I wiggled my toes. "That fuse in heaven? I think we finally blew it. I'm not afraid anymore."

He smiled. "I can tell." Suddenly, Billy's wings opened wide. I didn't gasp or pull back. Everything clicked into place. Everything.

I thought I'd seen his wings once, twice maybe. I was never sure. It was hard to tell here. But they *were* real. And they were beautiful—downy, light-gray feathers.

Billy squeezed my hand. "You ready to move on now? Your dad is waiting for us."

I leaned over and kissed his cheek. "I *am* ready, but can I say goodbye to my mom and Francine?"

"Sure."

I closed my eyes and put myself back down there, back in my real house.

Back in the place I was last alive.

There I was, just like that, standing in the corner of my kitchen, unnoticed. I guess the dead were undetectable. Francine and my mom were having dinner. The windows were covered in night. God, I missed night.

Francine's hearty laugh filled the room. Then my mom joined in. I rested my head against the wall and listened. They *were* going to be okay. My stomach dropped as I blew them a kiss. "I love you, Mom. I love you, Francine."

The room went silent.

Francine turned around and looked right through me. "Did you hear something, Mom?"

Mom's eyes went wide. "Maybe."

"Dad? Scarlett?" Francine whispered to the empty corner where I stood.

"Oh, F-Frannie," my mom whimpered.

"I swear I feel like one of them is here right now, Mom. Do you feel it? Tell me you can feel it," Francine said, never taking her eyes off of where I stood.

Mom reached for Francine's hand across the table, and my sister's gaze snapped to her. "I think it's Scarlett, Mom. I don't know why but I do."

Their tears started in unison as they nodded. I didn't want to freak them out any more. They'd been through enough.

The accident. Losing me and dad and Billy in one horrible instant. "I'm all right. I love you guys. Goodbye," I mouthed.

I blew them another kiss, closed my eyes, and heavy tears rolled down. I was back on Billy's porch. The storm was gone, just gone. Golden sunlight streamed from all directions and the ocean was where it should be—across the street.

Billy pulled me in for a hug. He knew going back among the living was harder than dying. He knew because he'd done it too. "Are you okay?"

I nuzzled into his chest and tried to release the weight of sadness still clinging to my skin. With each breath I felt lighter and lighter until it vanished.

He lifted my chin and kissed my forehead.

"I think you were right," I said, grinning, "We *are* doomed to love each other."

"I hope so."

ALL THE LIGHTS WENT OUT

© *1999 MARCY PLAYGROUND*

She came in from stormy weather
And asked her friend to be there with her
When she slid down Cupid's bow
Oh lookin' fine that day

I had a dream that we were lovers

I had a joke and she would smile when I'd say
We could blow
Blow a fuse in heaven
Yeah, yeah, yeah, yeah

Well today
All the lights went out in heaven
Yeah today
All the lights went out in heaven

And I knew that she was all
All that I needed
Yeah, yeah,

Cause today
All the lights went out in heaven
Yeah today
All the lights went out in heaven

And I knew that we were doomed
Doomed to love each other

AUTHOR PHOTO © SERGE
NIKOLICH PHOTOGRAPHY

K. M. Walton loves when art—especially reading and music—makes her deeply feel something. So, it's no surprise her contemporary YA novels *Cracked, Empty,* and *Ultimatum* have been known to make readers feel. Hatred is the one feeling that baffles her, and she's so passionate about acceptance that she gives school presentations titled: "The Power of Human Kindness." As a former educator, she also coauthored *Teaching Numeracy: 9 Critical Habits to Ignite Mathematical Thinking* for mathematics teachers in grades K–8. K. M. lives in Pennsylvania with her husband, two sons, and cat. Visit kmwalton .com and follow her on Twitter @kmwalton1.

PLAYLIST

1 **"THE SUBURBS"**
BY ARCADE FIRE
Inspired David Arnold's
short story "Suburbiana (or,
the Return of Super Frog)"

2 **"MISS ATOMIC BOMB"**
BY THE KILLERS
Inspired Anthony
Breznican's short story
"Miss Atomic Bomb"

3 **"COLD BEVERAGE"**
BY G. LOVE
Inspired G. Love's personal
essay "'Cold Beverage': The
Song I Wrote That Changed
My Life"

4 **"HOTEL CALIFORNIA"**
BY THE EAGLES
Inspired Ellen Hopkins's
short story "Tiffany Twisted"

5 **"PLANTING TREES"**
**BY JAMES HOWE AND
MARK DAVIS**
Inspired James Howe's
personal essay "How
Miracles Begin"

6 **"SOMEWHERE (THERE'S
A PLACE FOR US)"**
**MUSIC BY LEONARD
BERNSTEIN; LYRICS BY
STEPHEN SONDHEIM**
Inspired Beth Kephart's
personal essay "The
Opposite of Ordinary"

7 **"WONDERWALL"**
BY OASIS
Inspired Elisa Ludwig's
short story "About You
Now"

8 **"BALLAD OF A THIN
MAN"**
BY BOB DYLAN
Inspired Jonathan Maberry's
personal essay "You Know
Something's Happening
Here (But You Don't Know
What It Is)"

9 **"OCTOBER SONG"**
BY AMY WINEHOUSE
Inspired Donn Thompson
Morelli, a.k.a. DONN T's,
short story "Time to Soar"

10 **"SOMEWHERE ONLY
WE KNOW"**
BY KEANE
Inspired by E. C. Myers's
short story "City Girl"

11 **"IT HURTS"**
BY 2NE1
Inspired Ellen Oh's short
story "Second Chances"

12 **"DANCING NANCIES"**
BY DAVE MATTHEWS
BAND
Inspired Tiffany Schmidt's
short story "Anyone Other
Than Me"

13 **"THE MIDDLE"**
BY JIMMY EAT WORLD
Inspired Suzanne Young's
short story "The Ride"

14 **"ALL THE LIGHTS
WENT OUT"**
BY MARCY PLAYGROUND
Inspired K. M. Walton's
short story "Doomed?"

ACKNOWLEDGMENTS

FROM K. M. WALTON

Thank you to David Arnold, Anthony Breznican, G. Love, Ellen Hopkins, James Howe, Beth Kephart, Elisa Ludwig, Jonathan Maberry, Donn T, Eugene Myers, Ellen Oh, Tiffany Schmidt, Suzanne Young, and Ameriie for enthusiastically agreeing to participate in this anthology. Thank you for your stellar contributions and hard work. Working with such a fine group of talented people has been an honor.

Thank you to John Wozniak, lead singer of Marcy Playground, for making this fan an even bigger fan.

Thank you to my agent, Jim McCarthy, for loving the idea for this anthology, helping me cultivate it and bring it to life, and then selling it!

Thank you to the amazing Sourcebooks team for *everyth* Annette Pollert-Morgan, Alex Yeadon, Cassie Gutman, Rahn, Sarah Kasman, Kate Prosswimmer, and Stefani